Free Your True Self 2

The Power of the Soul

Free Your True Self 1

Releasing Your Unconscious Defence Patterns

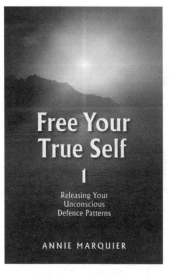

Your behavior in this lifetime is conditioned by at least one of the five major mechanisms of the unconscious that block you from realizing your true potential. Your view of the world and how you relate to other people and situations will be dictated by one or several of these underlying character structures, each one bearing very precise dynamics.

Using the tools in this book you will easily be able to recognize your own and others inner structures. The unconscious is not mysterious anymore. You will quite simply 'learn what makes you tick' and in doing so understand what makes other people 'tick' too! Once you understand this you are able to make changes that will help you to realize your full potential in this lifetime.

This book is based on Annie Marquier's 30 years experience of teaching and guiding people to discover their inner selves along with her deep knowledge of contemporary psychology and the Ageless Wisdom. This book goes beyond philosophy; offering as it does concrete observations of daily human behavior and the underlying structure of humanity in the light of our evolutionary process. It is quite simply a life changing book and one that anyone working on their inner self will find an invaluable tool. It also brings wonderful insights and tools to all counselling and psychotherapy professionals.

Annie Marquier's extensive training and experience in the various aspects of human development, as well as her scientific approach, have led her to acquire considerable and original knowledge of the mechanics of human consciousness. Her qualities as a communicator and writer allow her to share this knowledge in a clear and efficient manner both in her workshop presentations and lectures as well as in her writings.

ISBN 1-84409-061-2

Available from your local bookstore
or order directly from ***www.findhornpress.com***

Free Your True Self 2

The Power of the Soul

ANNIE MARQUIER

FINDHORN
Press

First published in English by Findhorn Press in 2005
First published in French by Editions du Gondor in 1998

ISBN 1-84409-054-X

British Library Cataloguing-in-Publication Data.
A catalogue record for this book is available
from the British Library.

Translated from the French by Alain Groven
Edited by Shari Mueller
Cover design by Damian Keenan
Interior design by Pam Bochel.

Printed and bound in the USA

Published by
Findhorn Press
305a The Park, Findhorn
Forres IV36 3TE
Scotland, UK
tel 01309 690582/fax 690036
info@findhornpress.com
www.findhornpress.com

To my Teachers,

With profound gratitude
and respect.

Acknowledgements

First, I would like to thank all the people to whom I owe the privilege of sharing some of their inner journey in the context of my workshops, and who have allowed me to witness the magnificent process of their soul's awakening.

I also want to thank those who have taken the time to review the manuscript and make detailed comments, especially Thierry Pasquier for his extensive editing, as well as Stéphane Richard.

My thanks also to those who made the final corrections, Francine Laliberté, Éric Chevalier, Nathalie Jolicoeur and Réjeanne Nault.

I also want to express my very special gratitude to Julie Nantel for her invaluable support throughout the writing of this book, and for the enormous amount of energy, which she put into the presentation, and in-depth review of this work.

Finally, a heartfelt thank you to my daughter Véronique for her technical support in the final formatting and the cover page, and especially for the constant inspiration, which she instils into my daily life.

Contents

PART THREE
THE TRANSFORMATION PROCESS
ON OUR WAY TO FREEDOM

Foreword

The white birch said to me: I am limited in my form, but not in my spirit. If you look at me closely, you will see God among my limbs, within my trunk, and then in my leaves. But your vision is blurred by what you see. What you see is like static that prevents you from truly seeing. As long as you haven't let go of your attachment to your individual specialness, as long as you haven't thrown your whole being away to be swallowed by the stars, as long as you think you can still exist, what you see is just a reflection of your own lack of consciousness.

To exist—there lies the great illusion. You do not exist, I do not exist, none of us exist. Only this consciousness of non-existence can allow us to really see. But then once we get to that point, there is no one left to see, for between he who sees and that which is seen, there is no longer any distance; existence becomes simultaneous, common, and there is nothing left to see, nothing left to be experienced. What is left is ultimate freedom, the freedom to be and not to exist.

Why should you want to live in separateness, at a distance from everything? To take upon yourself what belongs to the Universe? The Universe will not allow it. If you try to do that, you will lose yourself and spend your time in vain attempts to find yourself again. This will mean suffering, despair and death.

And you will thus die many deaths, until the moment when, having given up everything, which mattered, to you, including your own sense of identity, you will rediscover... what I truly am as a white birch... within yourself.

Introduction

The Quest

For thousands of years, human beings have sought to know themselves and others, and to master their environment in order to have more control over their existence. The great spiritual and philosophical traditions, and the more recent trends in psychological and scientific research, are trying to respond to this quest. With every discovery, answers are being suggested, examined, tested in the light of experience, rejected, improved upon, or broadened as the case may be. While we are still a long way from ultimate truths, humanity is progressing step-by-step towards a more and more elaborate understanding, or mastery, of both the material world—through physical science—and the inner world…the domain of the human psyche.

This quest is what motivates every facet of mankind's constant activity. To be sure, this activity has to do with survival, but it goes beyond that. We think, we struggle, we destroy, we build, we hurt and we heal, we take and we give, we love and hate, we dream, sing, laugh and cry. Through all this, we are constantly seeking. We are looking for a way to live, for happiness, for an ideal way to dwell in this world. But these words evoke very different realities depending on whom you talk to, and the means of achieving them are even more varied.

In fact, this ceaseless activity is just an expression of a deeper aspiration which, if examined in a clearer perspective in terms of its ultimate goals and the means to achieve them, would point the way to such potential fulfilment that life itself would take on a whole other meaning, from an individual as well as a collective viewpoint.

This inner calling can take many different forms, from the simple urge to ensure one's physical survival—through the ordinary attitude of seeking pleasure and self-gratification—to the most involved spiritual quest. Faced with the complexity of modern life and the failure to create genuine well-being through a materialistic approach, more and more people are turning their attention inward. They want answers to the fundamental questions that any human being must face, sooner or later, in one form or another: Who am I? Who are the people around me? Where do we come from? Where are we going? What are we doing on this planet? What is essential? What is life's purpose?

The answers to these questions vary, depending on your philosophical standpoint; but these differences ultimately stem from the fact that they are incomplete. In reality, they become consistent if examined in a broad enough perspective.

Some Presently Available Answers

For thousands of years, mankind has been exposed to valuable spiritual teachings. Yet these teachings sometimes seem contradictory.[1] Some tell us that we are the outcome of a long spiritual evolution, yet such statements are often obscured or distorted through a limited interpretation of the original teachings. New Age schools of thought state that we are divine, but our day-to-day behaviour does not really confirm this. Others seem to say that this world is nothing but illusion, and that we must seek to escape from it as quickly as possible; but why are we here? On the other hand, conventional "morality" or traditional religions would have us strive to become better people by making us feel more or less guilty for not yet being angels; but how is one to achieve this exalted state?

Our materialistic philosophy[2] leads us to believe that we are all just flesh and bones and that when the body goes, we go. Not a very encouraging prospect, and for a growing number of people nowadays, it just doesn't sound right.

Conventional psychology, stuck as it is between these two trends (spiritual vs. materialistic), is searching for answers and, for the time being at least, provides only limited explanations and methods to work on human consciousness, such as, methods that focus more on attempting to adapt to the normal world, rather than to attain a deep level of Self realization. How can we reconcile all this?

For this quest, this desire to know is always there. Mankind hungers for freedom, wisdom and happiness, but does not know how to go about satisfying this need. We are like a starving person who, while standing in the middle of an apple orchard with fruit laden trees all around, desperately seeks nourishment by clawing at the bark of the trees. The hunger is real, the apples are there, available at will, but what is lacking has to do with consciousness and perspective. We believe that by finding better methods of gouging the trunk, we will eventually get to the apples. We just don't realize that what is needed is to change our perspective, let go of old habits, forsake the false sense of security we get from our contact with the trunk and the soil, stop being afraid and dare to climb the tree, for that is where the real nourishment we need can be found. And then maybe, once we are up in the tree, a magnificent bird will carry us away on its powerful wings to where we can discover spaces even more vast and beautiful than this one apple tree. Anything can happen when we stop being afraid and are able to let go.

How Can We Do This?

This is easier said than done. How do we let go? How do we get rid of fears and conditionings developed over millennia, in order to recover our freedom? And how did we get into this situation in the first place? How can there be so much beauty within us along with so much suffering?

Ineffectiveness of Spiritual Pep-Talk

All spiritual teachings, even the simplest moral teachings including those termed "New Age", will tell us: Be open, truthful, simple and joyful, stop being afraid, love, let go, be free, "live in light". We know all that and we are certainly willing. But to make it so, it takes more than simply knowing and wanting it. For many of us, that is no longer the issue. The problem is finding out how we can manage to live like this, in a real and natural way. If, while driving a car, we skid out of control and find our self in the ditch because the brakes failed, we don't need some teacher or some book telling us that in order to travel safely and pleasantly we should use the brakes to slow down. We know that already, and we tried, but the mechanism didn't follow our intention. We've been told that we should love, that we should let go, that we should be this way or that. We know, and the will is there, but the (mental-emotional) mechanism just doesn't seem to be in alignment with it. We know the theory. We now need some practical knowledge that will allow us to understand how everything works, so that we can truly control our vehicle, fix it if need be, maintain it, and use it to its maximum potential. Only when we have increased our level of mastery over our mental, emotional and physical vehicle, will it be possible for us to practice these teachings.

Otherwise, these teachings and these pep-talks, these "dos and don'ts", just end up making us feel guilty for not being saints, for having lost control and found our self in the ditch; or we judge our self as being inept, incompetent drivers, we blame our self and we fall into depression. We can also blame the road for not being straight, the ditch for being there, or the oncoming driver for not having left us enough room to pass, etc. None of this will make the situation any better. On the contrary, all this does is create more problems, and the issue remains unresolved. We can also deny that we are in the ditch and philosophise on the art of driving, thus having a long intellectual conversation with whomever happens to have brought an instruction manual, which will keep our minds occupied and help us forget the reality of our present sticky situation, at least for a while. The sad reality is that we are stuck by the side of the road, with hardly any hope of getting out of our predicament. In the end, in all of these scenarios, we remain as slaves to a (mental/emotional) mechanism which we have not yet mastered and which is all too often a source of frustration, suffering and limitation, rather than a means toward a joyful and interesting journey.

Those spiritual and philosophical principles, which are excellent in themselves, are definitely useful as a door to inner inquiry. They have been around since the beginning of the world, and have come back in the limelight through New Age literature. This is great in terms of awakening a very wide spectrum of people to a higher set of values. However, as inspiring as these beautiful statements may be at first, they can soon prove to be inadequate in the context of our day-to-day struggles. A music teacher, who talks about the beauty of his chosen art form and about the joy of playing great musical pieces, without giving his students any practical means of learning how to play, is just creating frustration. Trying to translate such pep talks into action seems so easy that surely our failure to do so must have something to do with a lack of good will on our part.

No matter how marvellous these spiritual teachings may be, the practical means of putting them into practice often remain vague and far too general in scope. They can then be recycled quite easily to create a sort of spiritual stupor. We dream of a world of love and light, we talk about it, we philosophise, but our day-to-day life continues to bring its string of frustrations, suffering, illness, and violence. We are uplifted by all the beautiful talk, while continuing to criticize our neighbour, hate our mother-in-law, blame our spouse, abuse our power over our children or our employees, live under stress, complain of our lack of energy, feel victimized by an unfair system, etc., and thus end up frustrated and basically unhappy, if indeed we are at all willing to face the truth about our life.

Or, we can make desperate attempts to use our willpower to rid our self of these negative behaviours. We can thus manage to spend a few days or weeks in peace, especially if we can do this outside of the context of our daily life. And then, all of a sudden, all this negativity jumps out at us once again at the moment when we least expect it. For when they are not really integrated, these beautiful teachings can often lead us to suppress an important part of our self, if the latter does not happen to coincide with the proposed ideals. In our enthusiastic and blind response to the wonder of our human potential, to the relevance of what is being presented to us and its resonance with our soul's innermost desire, we want to be able to achieve this state immediately. We forget that mastery over one's ego takes a lot of work, time, knowledge, and practice. It is as if we left a concert where we were deeply moved by the talent and sensitivity of the pianist, and decided right then and there to play the piano. This is fine, as long as we realize that long, and often arduous, hours of practice are required in order to master such an instrument.

When it comes to mastering a musical instrument, it is easy to steer clear of illusions: false notes and lack of mastery are painfully obvious. It is much more challenging to avoid deluding our self when it comes to learning to gain mastery over our self, much easier to believe we are filled with light when our shadows have yet to be worked on. We attend workshops and practice certain disciplines, read books, stock up on a lot of philosophical knowledge, and occasionally have some beautiful inner experiences. Yet the false notes are obvious: they take the form of failed relationships, inability to live in peace, physical and moral fatigue, daily frustrations, dissatisfactions, depressions, inability to love and to feel loved, etc. It is then easy to adopt a victim's attitude (if happiness is out of our reach, it's because of other people or because of circumstances), or to get discouraged and think that these practices or these teachings are useless and that it is impossible to reach total fulfilment in this world. Yet life can be so beautiful, and these teachings can be genuinely experienced, as long as we get to know and master our instrument…our own inner dynamics.

If we want to be realistic, it is important to recognize the fact that a genuine change in consciousness, which naturally leads to a better quality of life, requires precise and rigorous inner work. If it were easy, everyone would have reached a state of bliss a long time ago.

In order to get a clearer picture, we need to be extremely vigilant, to dare to face the truth about our self, to pay attention to the workings of our own minds in order to get to know them, and to accept the fact that this is a step by step process.

For a Better Understanding

Many people are now ready to reach beyond spiritual generalities; the openness is there. What we need to know now is: Why is it so difficult to live according to these principles, even if they reflect our most ardent aspirations? Why is it so difficult to hang onto our creativity and energy, when this is what we really want? Why is it so difficult to stop being afraid, even when we know how good it would be to live this way? Why is it so difficult to love, when this is what we desire most of all? Why is all this so?

In the context of this book, we will go beyond the basic principles of a "good spiritual life". We will look for more specific answers, which can lead to a deeper understanding of our self. This knowledge will allow us to find practical ways to bring on the kind of transformation we would like to experience naturally in our daily existence; therefore, we will explore **the inner workings of consciousness, which underscore human behaviour,** in order to gain mastery over them. We will be better equipped to live by those beautiful teachings, in a natural and spontaneous manner, without having to force or repress anything. It will be an inner spontaneous experience. We will then be able to radiate the peace, joy and freedom we have found within our self.

One might relate to this as a mere utopian fantasy. But in the Middle Ages, it was utopian fantasy to imagine that a mass of several tons such as a modern airliner could be kept airborne. Yet today we see this as completely natural. It was just a matter of knowledge and mastery, which mankind was able to acquire through research, experimentation and intelligent observation over time. If we put the same amount of effort in getting to know and master the workings of consciousness as we have invested in getting to know the laws of the physical world, we will most certainly attain a quality of life, both on the inner and outer plane of existence, that may seem out of our reach at this point.

When we describe the workings of certain dynamics of the mind, we will strive to use a similar method to that of genuine scientific research, which recognizes initial hypotheses as models to be used rather than as ultimate reality. The working method we plan to adopt is based on observation, uses testing as a function of concrete experience, and opens up new avenues of thought and research, while avoiding the presumption of giving absolute and final answers.

This presentation will focus on two aspects. One, which is based on theory, will introduce concepts that are essential in order to better understand the workings of the mind (much like a course in mechanics). The other, more practical in nature (much like driving practice and vehicle maintenance), will focus on everyday human behaviour. All this is presented not as a final approach but as an opportunity to try to gain a better understanding of oneself and of life, and as a window on some interesting possibilities for more in-depth research into human nature.

In the first part of this book, we will take stock of the situation, and look at the inner dynamics that govern most human beings at this time. We will get to know their roots and their guiding principles. This will lead to a better understanding of our habitual behaviors, and will eventually enable us to begin to transform them. We will also gain a better understanding of what goes on in our relationships with others and in the world.

In the first volume of *Free Your True Self-Releasing Your Unconscious Defense Patterns* (published by Findhorn Press), I offered an overview of these mechanisms in the form of five major characteristic structures of our unconscious in its present capacity. For the benefit of the reader who may not have read Volume One, I will give a very brief summary of these structures at the end of Chapter 5. This will allow the reader to see this information in the light of the broader perspective taken in this Volume.

In the second part of this book, we will proceed towards discovering another set of dynamics, a higher one this time, that is just as present in each human being yet is still largely unused. I will describe their mechanisms and their practical outcomes when they are activated in our everyday existence. This will lead us to a detailed definition and study of two fundamental dynamics of human consciousness: the dynamic of personality, with its practical outcomes, and the dynamic springing from our inner being, with its implications in daily life. Knowledge of these two dynamics and of their source opens the door to self-mastery and provides a solid basis for effective inner work, no matter what method is used.

In the third part of this book, once we are equipped with this knowledge, we will be in a position to examine some essential aspects of the inner transformation process which can take us from the point of functioning on the basis of personality to a point where a higher level of consciousness prevails. This process of transformation has its laws. I will attempt to define these laws in order to shed some practical light on the path of inner seeking; this will facilitate the application of any chosen method of inner work and enhance its effectiveness. Indeed today there is a profusion of inner developmental approaches, some of them ancient, some more contemporary, which address different parts of our make-up. Beyond these methods, once we have recognized the merit of seeking a deeper understanding of our psychological structure, and are aware of the basic principles of transformation, our consciousness development work will be greatly facilitated and accelerated. The content of this book thus offers useful information to any seeking person, no matter what approach he or she may use.

The data presented throughout this book stem from observations made in the course of many years of consciousness-oriented research and work. I will also call upon certain principles of holistic psychology, which I have experienced and found to be relevant. In addition, we will proceed on the basis of a very broad context, which will include either direct intuition or certain underlying esoteric facts stemming from the teachings of the Ageless Wisdom, which have been substantiated through practical experience and observation. We will attempt to reach a better understanding of the mechanisms of consciousness, not just on the basis of theories, but rather on the basis of an in-depth study of practical observations which are directly related to everyday life. We will thus go beyond wishful and hopeful thinking and become more aware of the work that needs to be done. Then we can do the work if we feel thus inclined.

---

[1] God has been described as either transcendent or immanent. There are "non-dualistic" approaches such as Vedanta, Zen and Tibetan Buddhism, or Taoism. There are also so-called "dualistic" paths such as bhakti yoga, Sufism, Christian mysticism, the Theosophical approach, etc. These approaches, which are actually just models of reality, can easily be reconciled if a broad enough model can be found which could include them all without taking away any of their truth. Having reached a more advanced state of mental development, mankind is now capable of directly grasping more specific concepts relating to human functioning. We shall see how this deeper understanding can help us to harmonize these apparent contradictions and bring all these teachings together. For these teachings all convey a message, which is essentially similar and springs from the same great truth that is beyond the limits of any specific religious heritage. Furthermore, what is most important is that this perspective makes it easier to practice these teachings.

[2] According to Webster's Dictionary: Materialism: The philosophical theory that regards matter and its motions as constituting the universe, and all phenomena, including those of the mind, as due to material agencies. The Larousse French Dictionary adds: "Materialism as a philosophical trend goes back to Antiquity. [...] It was renewed as a result of the invention of mathematical physics and the teachings of several philosophers in recent centuries. It denies the existence of the soul, of God and of the hereafter. It describes thought, as indeed everything else, as a strictly material phenomenon.

PART ONE

Human Evolution
From the Past to the Present

✦

The Quest for Freedom

chapter 1

What is a Human Being?
A MODEL REPRESENTATION

In any process of scientific research, in order to be able to study phenomena and evolve through constantly ascending levels of mastery, it is necessary to use a model as a starting point. This model must be experienced, and must provide a satisfying description of observable reality. Once used and tested in a concrete way, this model can then lead to further observations which will allow us to improve upon it and to broaden its scope, so that it becomes an even more accurate reflection of reality. This is a natural process in any form of research, in any field of inquiry. We will apply this principle to the study of consciousness-related phenomena such as those presented here.

A Model of What Constitutes a Human Being

Let us begin with a simple model such as the one that will be presented in an upcoming book, *The Power of Free Will*.[1] This model is widely known, and it is easy to work with. When we refer to the history of mankind according to esoteric science, it becomes self-evident. It is also consistent with the most recent discoveries in the field of holistic and transpersonal psychology, as well as with my own practical observations of thousands of people. I will state this model briefly, in a perspective that is consistent with the purpose of this book.

According to this model, we recognize that the very essence of mankind is made up of a "higher consciousness", which bears various names depending on tradition and culture: the higher Self, the Solar Angel, the spiritual Self, the Angel of Presence, the inner Christ, the Ego (with a capital E), the Spirit, the indwelling divinity, Atman, etc. Here we will refer to this essence of all human beings as the Self or soul. It is the direct expression of a very high level of consciousness, a level of consciousness that can be referred to as "divine" as a way to express, among other things, the fact that it has all the finest and greatest qualities imaginable. Words are inadequate to describe this essence, as its reality is far beyond the reach of mental consciousness, from where words spring. And yet, as soon as people go through any kind of inner development, they can feel the existence of this reality and eventually experience it directly and clearly. Our view here will be that any human being is essentially this Self, this soul.[2]

The Self exists at a higher vibrational level than that of the three worlds (physical, emotional and mental), and it needs an instrument to manifest its will at these three lower levels. This instrument is what we know as the human form, which consists of a physical-etheric body,[3] an emotional system and a mental system. We shall call this instrument the personality, or ego. These two terms will be used interchangeably, in the course of this book, as representing the same thing.

Thus, from our perspective, a human being is intrinsically a soul possessing an instrument (the ego), which will allow it to express itself in the three worlds. We could compare the Self to a violinist who needs a violin (the personality) to express in perceptible form the beauty of the music he carries within himself.

At the level of the Self, we can assume that man is perfect. The goal of the process of evolution—the goal of our very existence on this earth—is not to achieve a level of perfection which is already there, but rather to build an instrument (personality, ego) that is totally supple and responsive to the energy and the will of the soul, so that we can manifest its perfection directly and concretely in this world. When the goal is eventually reached, our three bodies (physical, emotional and mental) will be a direct expression of perfection, beauty, intelligence, love, and power, in fact, of all the "divine" qualities of the Self. When that happens, we will be able to create a world of peace, beauty and love for our self and for all mankind (the "kingdom of God"), here on Earth.

As for the instrument, it is still under construction as far as we are concerned at this time. The goal of what is generally called the process of "evolution" has not yet been reached; for this reason, even if each human being is in essence perfect on the level of the Self, this perfection is not being substantially manifested here on earth…far from it. Where we should experience the peace of the Self, there is war; instead of love, there is fear and hatred; instead of joy, there is sorrow; instead of awareness, there is ignorance; beauty is hidden by disharmony; respect is thrown away for the sake of manipulation; happiness disappears under a sea of suffering; and where there should be freedom and mastery, we find nothing but limitations and powerlessness.

If we go back to our metaphor of the musician and his instrument as described in Volume 1, the Self is a brilliant, marvellously inspired and extraordinarily talented violinist. The ego is a violin that is still under construction: the body is not completely finished, the tuning pegs are not quite right. No matter how brilliant the violinist may be, there is no way for him to make beautiful music. No matter how perfect our Self may be, it cannot as yet manifest all of its beauty, its richness and its power in this world.

The present structure of each human being, particularly the structure of the personality (the present state of the violin) is the outcome of a complex process called involution-evolution.[4]

We are presently right in the middle of the unfoldment of this process. The violin is not yet finished; our personality is not yet fully tuned. The fact that our behaviour does not always radiate wisdom, love, equanimity and intelligence does not mean that we are incapable or bad. It just means that at the level of the personality, we are still under construction, unfinished. No more blame and guilt because we are not yet saints; no one is to blame. We just need to become aware of this reality, to stop blaming the violin for not working very well at this point, to stop expecting it to sound as good as other people's, to take responsibility for our own instrument and continue to build it and perfect it so that it produces more and more beautiful sounds, expressing the artistic genius that we all are in essence.

Problems Stemming from This Unfinished Personality:
The Horse and Carriage Analogy

In order to have a general idea of the way we function and of the source of our difficulties, let us briefly go over a traditional oriental analogy that illustrates the structure of our consciousness.[5] This analogy compares a human being to a combination of elements, which include a carriage, pulled by a horse, with a coachman who controls the horse, and the Master who sits in the carriage behind the coachman. This combination of elements is proceeding along a path.

The carriage represents our physical body, the horse is the emotional body, the coachman is the mental body, and the Master is the Self or soul. The path symbolizes the great journey of the Self so that it can experience the world of matter and gain mastery over it through a well-coordinated personality.

In order to proceed effectively along the path, you need a carriage that is in good shape: a healthy physical body, including a brain and a nervous system in top working condition.

You also need a good horse. The stronger the horse, the quicker we will proceed along the path and the more possibilities we will encounter in terms of discovery and experience. This means that it is good to have a powerful emotional system. However a vigorous horse must be controlled, otherwise it may get carried away and start galloping here and there in a way that is totally inappropriate. When this happens, we usually end up in the ditch with an often seriously damaged carriage (our physical body). This is what happens when we allow our life to be controlled solely by our emotions. The horse is necessary, however, to move the carriage effectively. The condition of our physical body depends to a large extent on the number of times we allowed it to get carried away and to lead us into the ditch, thus damaging the carriage, or the number of times the coachman (our mind) was unable to control the horse. We know that the condition of our physical body largely depends on our emotional state.

In principle, the coachman ought to be able to control the horse in an intelligent manner, and to use all this power with wisdom. The role of the horse (the emotions) is thus to provide the energy needed to get things going in the material world; the role of the coachman (the mental body) is to control this energy with wisdom. But the coachman has no knowledge of the path. In this regard, he must tune into the directions coming from the Self (the Master sitting in the carriage) and faithfully abide by them. In order for the trip to be interesting and smooth, the Master, who alone has an accurate perception of reality at any given moment, must direct the whole combination of elements.

Thus, in order for the mental part of a human being to wholly fulfil its purpose, it must on the one hand develop its capacity to be in direct and conscious contact with the soul so as to clearly tune into its directions, and on the other hand develop a thorough understanding of its emotional nature so as to remain in control when the latter gets carried away and thus to channel its energy wisely. It must also know how to maintain the carriage effectively and intelligently. When this ideal and balanced mode of functioning is reached, we have a personality (a physical, emotional and mental combination of elements) that is wholly subservient to the Master. The Self can then fully manifest all of its qualities in the physical world. But of course, we have a way to go yet before that happens.

The Two Sides of the Mind

In order to understand our present situation, we have to take a closer look at how the coachman operates. The latter is in fact a two-sided character. Indeed, according to esoteric teachings, which we have verified through countless practical observations, the mental body can be perceived as being made up of two parts:

- The first, which we will call the lower mind, intrinsically belongs to the personality. For the time being it is intimately linked with our emotional mechanisms. This part of the mind has no knowledge and operates much like a machine, based on automatic responses derived from past experiences. It is very active in our present collective consciousness, too active in fact. We will call this lower physical, emotional and mental combination the ego, or personality.

- The second part, which we will call the higher mind,[6] is in direct contact with the Self; it provides a link between the soul and the personality. Through its connection with the Self, this part of the mind has access to knowledge. When the mind is active at this level, and the other part is silent and receptive, all is well: the energy of the Self circulates freely and the personality is guided so as to bring its most positive manifestations into the world. Life becomes deeply satisfying.

The analogy of the carriage is useful in that it allows us to grasp how important the mind is for the human system to function properly. The quality of our life depends on what part of the mind is in control. If the lower mind is in charge, we find our self constrained by the mechanisms of our personality, and we shall observe the many limitations this entails. If the higher mind is in charge, we are then in contact with the Self, and this will have entirely different tangible consequences. This aspect will therefore be the focal point of our work, for what goes on at the level of the emotional and physical bodies, and thus the entire personality, essentially depends on the activity of the mind. To be sure, the physical and the emotional bodies each function according to their own laws. The role of the mind is precisely to learn how to control these mechanisms effectively and smoothly, in synch with the will of the Self.

Any experience of inner transformation is in fact geared towards transferring the control of the personality from the lower mind to the higher mind, through a process whereby the point of identification of one's consciousness shifts from the personality, via the lower mind, to the realm of the soul, via the higher mind. The experience of inner transformation can therefore be defined as a transfer of the point of identification of one's consciousness from the ego all the way to the Self.

We shall see, that when our consciousness is identified with our ego via the lower mind, the consequences are an inadequate perception of reality, along with ignorance, subjection to automatic reactions stemming from the past, and a difficult and limiting experience of life for our self as well as others. When our consciousness is identified with the Self via the higher mind, our understanding is accurate at any given moment; we have a joyful experience of the world, along with a feeling of mastery and freedom. Our behaviour and the quality of our experience of life directly stem from where our consciousness is.

Relocating the Point of Identification of Consciousness

The work of changing the point of identification of our consciousness is central to the process of transformation. To understand our present difficulties in our attempt to live in a permanent state of peace and harmony, we must understand both the process of identification with our ego, which our consciousness had to go through in order to foster its (the ego's) construction, and the process of unidentification, which must be undergone in order to recover our freedom. To illustrate this process, we could go back to the metaphor of the musician.

We are in the same situation as a violinist who, for the longest time, has had to work on building his instrument, his attention being entirely focused on this work. This focus was appropriate in the context of the past millennia. In any case, since the violin was not up to scratch, the musician was not able to play real music during this time, or else the music he played was necessarily very limited (in all this time, humanity was not able to manifest the greatness and the power of the soul). We now find our self at the point where the violinist aspires to something more than just perfecting his instrument. However, with all this energy and time focused on construction, he has become almost exclusively a technician. He has forgotten his goal, which was to play music, as well as the talent he has for this calling. This is the source of his present state of dissatisfaction. He now wants to be able to play, as he feels that his instrument is ready. In order for this to happen, he must retrain himself to focus his attention not on the violin but on the practice of music. This means a major shift in values and attitude—a relocation of the point of identification of consciousness. It would be a mistake to throw away the violin because it made us forget that we were actually musicians (as is the case with people who engage in a spiritual quest as a way to escape the world, thus withholding the richness of their music from this worldly plane). Another error would be to remain solely concerned with perfecting the violin, through force of habit, or to derive a false sense of security, and to refuse to acknowledge the fact that we are musicians first and foremost (as is the case with people who keep focusing on materialistic concerns, identifying with their personality, while denying the reality of the soul).

It was in the natural order of things that consciousness should identify with ego in order to build it up. During this construction period, in the absence of the wisdom of the Self, the ego developed an operational mechanism in the form of the lower mind. The latter can function independently of the will of the soul. For millennia, humans have thus aligned their lives according to the dictates of this part of the mind. Even though this entailed a great deal of suffering, it was appropriate, for a while at least.

As far as many people are concerned these days, the personality is no longer in need of reinforcement. Within their consciousness burns an ardent desire for liberation from the fetters of their lower mechanisms. The time has come when our identification with the inner workings of ego is no longer perceived as appropriate, but has become a source of suffering and limitation; what was helpful at a certain point in our evolution has now become a liability.

Consciousness identification swings from the ego to the Self to varying degrees, according to each person's level of evolution. This is the reason we find humanity involved in such conflicting behaviours and such an apparent contradiction between our potential for generating separation, destruction and suffering, on the one hand, and our potential for generating beauty, creativity, wisdom and pure love. Two different dynamics are at work depending on the point of identification of our consciousness.

The Apparent Contradictions and the Ultimate Goal of the Process of Evolution

As we have already mentioned, seekers are often puzzled when faced with the apparent contradictions between different spiritual traditions. In fact there are no contradictions, just a lack of perspective. The perspective, which we are supporting here already, allows us to bring together two often controversial viewpoints.

The first maintains that this world is nothing but illusion and that the best thing to do is to try to extricate our self from it through detachment, liberation from worldly desires, and forsaking one's identity on the ego level, in order to quickly attain a state of grace that no longer has anything to do with whatever is going on in the world. There is no need to "evolve", since we are already perfect: liberation can thus be achieved instantly.

The second viewpoint maintains that our purpose in this world is to evolve, and that we will eventually reach perfection if we work rigorously and consistently on our self over an extended period of time. In fact these two approaches are two different ways of saying the same thing.

True, we are perfect at the level of the soul, and on this plane there is no longer any sense of identity, in the separative sense in which the term is ordinarily used. It is also true that the goal is to become once again this divine aspect, which is our true identity, and to liberate our self from the prison of our personality.

But why are we prisoners of this personality? Did we fall into this trap as a result of some error on our part or on the part of nature? Should we attempt to shed this personality as quickly as possible by rejecting and despising everything that is part of this worldly plane of existence? Or should we abide by another, more familiar tradition, according to which we have fallen because we have sinned, because we are inherently stupid and bad? What does it mean "to sin"?

While it is true that we should disengage our self from our attachment to this world, this should not be taken in the sense of trying to escape this relationship, but rather in the sense of attempting to gain mastery over it. This is where a good deal of confusion originates.

Both approaches have their advantages and pitfalls. The first has the advantage of promoting unidentification with the desires of our personality and from the whole mechanism of our ego, as a result of an overall attempt to annihilate these aspects of our make-up. This makes it easier, to some extent, to further the process of unidentification of consciousness with ego. The pitfall to be avoided here is the tendency to slide into a pseudo-spiritual retreat, which actually blocks any genuine progress towards mastery. To forsake this world in order to experience some sort of pseudo-nirvana is to transgress the law of love. Indeed to love is to rediscover one's unity with the whole universe, including this lowly world and all its creatures, rather than to isolate oneself and leave them all to their sorry lot. The confusion stems from the separative influence of ego, which has diverted this approach to its own advantage, so as to avoid doing any real work and to continue focusing on individual survival. The trap has to do with this ego appropriation rather than with the approach itself.

The second approach has the advantage of promoting the work of relaxing the personality so that it can eventually be totally receptive to the energy of the soul and thus make it possible to manifest divinity directly through matter. With the emphasis on personality, the pitfall to be avoided is one where we remain caught up in the identification of consciousness with the ego, from which we are trying to liberate our self.

The two approaches merge when we understand the process of evolution from a more global viewpoint. Personality identification was not an error; it was necessary during thousands of years in order to make it possible to build a physical, emotional and mental instrument for God to become manifest in this world, and for the union of spirit and matter to occur.

The instrument is now sufficiently built up. What is needed now is to disengage our consciousness from its fixation on matter, i.e. from separativeness and identity at the ego level, in order to place the instrument under the control of the Self. "Denial" of ego is therefore not a bad thing, as a learning process; it just has to be done in the proper perspective.

We could illustrate this by comparing the process to a journey. We leave our country to go to a foreign place and learn to cultivate certain fruits that can only be found there, as we would like to grow these back in our home country. We get to that place where, as it turns out, life is no picnic. We start working with the peasants in the hope of gaining needed expertise. We work so hard for so long that we come to forget our home country, and the goal that brought us here in the first place. We end up cultivating fruit simply because that is what everyone else is doing and because, as far as we know, "that's life!" Yet we feel more and more dissatisfied and it seems to us that something is missing deep inside. In fact we have forgotten that the purpose of our journey is twofold: it was not just to learn how to cultivate certain types of fruit, but also, once that learning process was completed, it was to bring this knowledge (mastery of the three worlds) back home.

The first approach says: "Stop worrying about these fruits, and try to head back home as quickly as possible; this is not your country, you belong somewhere else!" And we try to leave without completing the learning process for which we had come. If we return home without the necessary knowledge, we will eventually have to go back there to complete our training (acquiring mastery of the three worlds). The second approach says: "Learn to cultivate these fruits; this is the purpose of your journey." But this fails to remind us that we are also supposed to bring this knowledge back to our home country and that we were not meant to stay there permanently. All the more so since the materialistic urge that drew us to this place is not about to let us leave now that we are hooked—this force would lose all of its manpower. And so we remain stuck in that place, endlessly toiling in the fields, wondering what on earth is life all about? The fact is we have stumbled into the trap, and forgotten that we should head back home.

Many people nowadays are ready to shift their operational focus to the soul, but the old mechanisms remain active in our consciousness and we continue to experience both modes of functioning depending on circumstances. We then come to a crossroads where a choice has to be made: either we continue to let our consciousness identify with the workings of our ego—and put up with rather dire consequences, which will be further described in the next chapter—or we shift our focus towards the reality of the soul through conscious inner work, so as to reconnect with our true nature, with the deeper meaning of our life, with joy and freedom (i.e., we finally return home, bringing the fruits of mastery as an offering to our soul).

What can we do so that our personality can eventually be considered fully functional and receptive to the will of our soul? Following are some general points, which will be covered in the course of this book:

- Get familiar with the workings of one's instrument, of its components, with the way it functions at this point in time; become fully aware of these unconscious mechanisms (self knowledge in terms of the conscious and unconscious mechanisms of our personality); acknowledge the fact that one is not the instrument, but that one is responsible for its construction; and through this awareness, begin to stop identifying with the instrument (the ego).

- Take stock of the needed improvements and repairs to one's present structure in order to make this instrument more capable of manifesting the qualities of the Self (healing, freedom from past hang-ups).

- Get acquainted with the higher elements that need to be developed so as to activate the full potential of the instrument (developing one's higher mind, intelligence, heart, and all the qualities of the Self).

- Strengthen one's direct connection to the Self; identify one's consciousness more and more with the soul.

And get ready for a great inner adventure; one that is demanding, no doubt, yet so deeply enriched with newly recovered freedom.

In the first part of this book, we will take a close look at the mechanisms of our personality, as well as their source. *In other words, we will examine the condition of the "violin", the way it performs, its limitations, and the type of "music" it can generate in its present condition.*

To this end, in the following chapter, we will first of all take a look at what goes on in a concrete sense in our everyday life when our personality is driven by our lower mind.

-- --- --- --- --- --- --- --- ---

[1] Provisional title. To be published in 2006 by Findhorn Press.

[2] These two terms, Self and soul, will be used indifferently throughout this book as representing the same reality. In addition, I use the term "soul" without any religious connotation: in this context it will mean "essence", as when we talk about "the soul of all things".

[3] The etheric body is also called the vital body in certain teachings. It is the energetic replica of the physical body, which, if it were not for the etheric body, would be nothing but a blob of matter without energy, without consciousness and without life. This is the body that acupuncture is concerned with, to name but one example.

[4] I will describe this process at greater length in Chapter 3.

[5] This analogy was used in my previous book. (Op. cit., page 11)

[6] Calling each of these parts "lower" or "higher" does not mean that one part is better than the other. Both parts have their role in our inner dynamics. These adjectives simply stem from the fact that the vibrational rate of the higher mind (also called the abstract mind in some traditions) is higher than that of the lower mind (also called the concrete, or automatic mind). The various functions of these two parts will be described in greater detail in Chapters 4 and 6.

chapter 2

Human Behaviours Associated with Ego Consciousness

Human beings can sometimes behave in magnificent, intelligent, creative and beneficial ways, and sometimes in very destructive ways, for themselves as well as others. Why is that? As we look for answers to this question, it becomes clear that our behaviours and reactions to life's circumstances are not a matter of chance. Human beings are neither good nor bad: they simply find themselves in certain states of consciousness, which automatically lead to certain types of behaviour.

This wide variety of reactions stems from the fact that our personality can act in very different ways depending on what part of us is in control, just as an automobile will travel smoothly along the road, or cause accidents, depending on the driver's competence. Depending on who is in charge, the Self (via the higher mind) or the ego (via the lower mind), we get two types of behaviour, two ways of relating to reality, two very different ways of responding to circumstances.

In the course of this chapter, we will simply observe what goes on in real terms, in our everyday life, when our consciousness is trapped in the structures of our ego, and out of touch with our Self. This is where most of mankind is at present. This is what makes the world what it is, and what we would eventually like to improve upon.[1]

As we noted in the first chapter, any behaviour is often the outcome of mixing the will of the ego and that of the Self. We sometimes sense very clearly whether our experience has to do with our lower mechanisms being activated, or whether this experience is related to the Self. At other times, it is not so easy to tell the difference. Patanjali, a great philosopher and teacher in India's ancient times, compares the difficulty we have in discriminating between our ego impulses and the promptings of our soul to the difficulty a swan has in separating milk from water that was mixed together before its eyes.

Should we recognize our self in some of the behaviours we are about to describe, or recognize others, it will be important not to blame our self or those around us. We will realize of course that these behaviours are a source of suffering, and for this reason we may be interested in changing them. This description is an opportunity to become clearly aware of the situation, without judgement, simply in order to be better equipped to make progress. As much as possible, we will make these observations with the same detached attitude as we would have when opening the hood of a car following a series of breakdowns. We will take stock of the engine's condition, and the eventual repairs or changes that need to be made, with patience and caring for our machine, and even with a touch of humour, always mindful that we are not the machine. On the other hand, we are responsible for this machine, and it is in our best interest to make sure that it works properly if we want our life's journey to be a satisfying one.

The Cycle of Dissatisfaction or The First Great Ego Illusion

Behind each choice, each gesture that we make, there is a quest for a sense of accomplishment, of fulfilment, or at least for satisfaction. This covers many very different things, depending on each individual's level of consciousness. This quest, when it is experienced on an ego level, keeps us in an almost constant state of tension and dissatisfaction. Indeed it could be aptly represented as a cycle, such as the following:

Let us suppose that, at some point in time, we may be going through unfavourable life circumstances. We are not getting what we want (see Diagram 1, point 1). We feel that we could be happier if only things, or people, were different. So we act, we strive to change what is not going well for us. We look outside for conditions or people who will make us happy (point 2). With a lot of work and searching, we manage to generate circumstances and meet people who appear to bring us satisfaction (point 3). And yet, no matter what the circumstances and the level of success thus obtained, our "satisfaction" as defined in this state of consciousness, or rather unconsciousness, is short lived (points 4 to 8). Eventually we become dissatisfied once again, we go back to the starting point, and start all over again.

Diagram 1
The Cycle of Dissatisfaction
Brought on by the Mechanics of our Personality

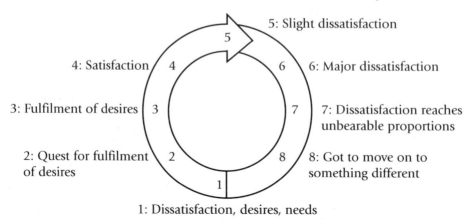

4: Satisfaction

5: Slight dissatisfaction

6: Major dissatisfaction

3: Fulfilment of desires

7: Dissatisfaction reaches unbearable proportions

2: Quest for fulfilment of desires

8: Got to move on to something different

1: Dissatisfaction, desires, needs

When our consciousness is caught up in ego, this is the cycle that characterizes the way we function:

- At worst, we remain stagnant at points 1 and 2, living in a constant state of unfulfilled expectations, frustrated hopes and dissatisfaction.

- At best, we go round and round from point 1 to point 8 and back again, with brief moments of satisfaction now and then. This is the highest measure of success we can hope to experience on the ego level.

Let us describe two classic concrete examples to illustrate the dynamics involved here:

◆ The Cycle of Material Dissatisfaction

Let us imagine that we are in a precarious material situation. We hang onto the illusion that, if we only had financial security, we would be happy. So we work for years in order to gain this false security (point 1). If we fail to achieve this, we spend our life mired in this feeling of dissatisfaction, thinking how happy we would have been if only we had gained this financial security. In this case, we remain caught at points 1 and 2, in a state of permanent dissatisfaction, expectation, hope and illusion. Or we do obtain it (point 3), which is what happens most of the time, even if it takes a while. This is what our materialistic society glorifies as "success" (house, car, travels, vacation homes, all kinds of appliances, etc.). We are content (point 4), but not for long. Indeed we soon realize that something is still missing in our life. That sense of fulfilment and peace that we were looking for is still out of reach (points 5, 6 and 7). This accumulation of material wealth, that we had dreamed of for so long, is not generating the happiness we expected, either because we are stressed out and afraid of losing it, or because other aspects of our life which we may have neglected (relationships, health, creativity, freedom, etc.) are now creating other subjects of dissatisfaction. So in order to deal with this new source of dissatisfaction, we start looking yet again for something outside of our self that might appear as the key to happiness (point 8 and back to point 1). We decide to travel, to build a respectable social status, to take some courses or to dive headlong into this or that endeavour in the hope that, in the end, we will soon be happy because we will finally have what we always wanted. And the cycle starts all over again.

> To presume to satisfy one's desires through possessions
> is tantamount to assuming that we can stifle a fire with straw.
> —**Chinese proverb**

◆ The Cycle of Dissatisfaction in a Couple Relationship

The dynamics of dissatisfaction are also vividly illustrated in what happens in couple relationships. We feel lonely (1); we think that if we could only find that ideal partner (based on our criteria, of course), we would really be happy. So we start looking (2), and one day we finally meet someone who seems to fit (3). We are walking on air...for a while (4). Then some clouds begin to darken our blue skies (5). Several scenarios can unfold at that point. For example, in the simplest and most frequent cases, the Prince or the Princess becomes less and less charming as time goes by (6), to the point where we wonder how we could ever have been attracted to this person (7). We then put up with an unsatisfactory relationship (we end up back at point 1 for good), or we end up separating (8) and we go back to the starting point of the cycle, alone and dissatisfied. And without thinking about the dynamics involved in our behaviour, we automatically fall back into the seeking mode, looking for someone with whom we will finally, hopefully, find true happiness. We thus get back into the cycle and go through all the points, from 1 to 8, only to end up back at point 1 yet again.

In this example, we can also follow another very common scenario which goes back to the same dynamics: through all this searching (2), we eventually find someone (3) and it seems to us that this person is really a rare gem, and we are just as happy as can be (4). This person becomes more and more precious to us, and we become attached, dependent and demanding (5), jealous, possessive, worried and anxious (6 and 7). Our behaviour then grows more and more stifling for the other person, who eventually decides to leave. And we find our self alone again, at point 1. We think we're just not lucky in love, and that it's all his/her fault if things went wrong; we'll try to do better next time, though we're not sure how we'll go about it. So we're back on the hunt for that rare gem, and this time we won't let him/her get away: we'll make sure we bind that person to us for good! Of course the same dynamics will come into play, so that we end up alone once more and start again, holding firmly to our illusion that someone will be able to make us happy. Or, the other person may take advantage of this dependent relationship and stay, and we then put up with an alienating, often painful situation (we stay stuck at points 1 and 2). We are all quite familiar with any one of these scenarios.

These dynamics are not inescapable. It is possible to create outstanding relationships, or any other life situation that is genuinely satisfying. **This is not a matter of circumstances, but of consciousness.** This cycle of dissatisfaction is inescapable if we are stuck at the ego level. It is a law of the human psyche, like the law of gravity in the physical world. For example, however much we hope to be able to jump from the fourth floor of a building without injuring our self, the law of gravity will kick in and bring us back to reality. If we could but realize this simple fact, we would end up looking in another direction for happiness and fulfilment, instead of constantly turning our backs on it and complaining about how life is tough and how you just can't trust anyone. (Instead of insisting on jumping from the fourth floor every morning and complain about our bruises for the rest of the day, we will perhaps look for a stairway.)

This dynamic is what keeps us bound in the illusion that something outside of our self (circumstances or people) will eventually make us happy. It leads to brief interludes of fulfilment, followed inevitably by long periods of waiting, hoping, and feeling dissatisfied. It creates a permanent state of tension and stress. Indeed, since happiness depends on external circumstances or on the people around us, we become dependent on them, though we may be unaware of that dependency. If circumstances are favourable, i.e. if everything is going exactly the way we want, we are content; otherwise, we feel unfulfilled.

As we are buffeted this way and that by external circumstances and by the people around us, we have two choices, either of which are unsatisfactory: a) feeling victimized by bad people who are "not OK", or by unfavourable circumstances which we feel we can do nothing about; or b) trying to manipulate or control external circumstances as well as the people around us so that they will fulfil our expectations and desires. We sometimes succeed in this after years of arduous effort (but the sense of fulfilment we get is necessarily short-lived), and sometimes we fall completely off the mark. In any case, sooner or later people and circumstances change and we are once again dissatisfied. So then we complain that happiness is a rare thing and that life is a bitch.

This dynamic involving the search for external sources of fulfilment is not just applicable to these simple yet classic examples. To the extent that our consciousness is stuck at the level of our personality, this will determine all of our choices, preferences, actions, as well as our major and minor decisions. It is indeed the driving force of our life. We thus spend our time and energy trying to generate circumstances and relationships, which will fulfil our desires and expectations. This is the only way we were taught to find a little happiness, once in a while. This is a somewhat inefficient way to go about finding fulfilment, as it requires a lot of effort for very low investment returns.

Although these examples are applicable from a long-term perspective, the mechanism can be very similar in short-term instances. How about all the working people who look forward to the weekend, hoping for a pleasant outing perhaps, in order to finally feel good ("Thank God it's Friday!")? Then the long-awaited moment arrives and, though we may be having a good time, in the end it all goes up in smoke. And then we find our self chasing after something else the following weekend. Not to mention all those people who spend months, or even years, planning a holiday, a trip, or their retirement! As if at least then they might finally have a good time. Holidays, trips, and all that sort of thing, may be enjoyable experiences, yet rarely do they match our expectations. And if we truly do find some fulfilment there, we face a depressing re-entry back home and then we just can't wait for the next opportunity to escape. Thus we spend our life hoping that tomorrow, or sometime later, things will get better. But "tomorrow never comes", as we remain focused on tomorrow. This is how the richness of the present moment forever eludes us, as we are forever unable to experience it. We either live in a past that is no more, or in an imaginary future. In fact this can hardly be called living: this is nothing more than basic survival. Since this is the case with just about everybody we know, we think, "Such is life". Small wonder that we find life somewhat unfulfilling.

Yet this quest for "satisfaction"—which on a more fundamental level is a reflection of our quest for fulfilment—is genuine and real. But in the absence of the Life energy springing from the Self, we just cannot find what we are looking for; no matter what we may gain, it will never be enough. For the simple fact is that our ego, as long as it remains disconnected from the Self, is by its very structure an **empty mechanism** that can never afford us any sense of fulfilment or profound satisfaction.

The illusion that propels us to look for happiness in external circumstances is deeply rooted in the collective consciousness. Most of us do not even question whether there might be another way to live: we are so used to living this way that we are not even aware that there might be an alternative. We swim in this sea of limitations like fish in water, without noticing the dynamics that motivate our actions. This is one of the first illusions of ego, and we can disengage our self from it by recognizing the fact that **deep and lasting happiness that is above the constantly changing circumstances of life can never spring from anything external.**

Yet though we may know this in theory, it takes more than knowledge to set us free from the limitations of this mechanism. Though we may know from hearsay or reading certain books that happiness lies within, we nevertheless continue to be bound by this cycle of dissatisfaction and we wonder why. In order to answer this question, and begin to find ways of disengaging our self from the mechanisms of our ego, let us take a closer look at the various dynamics of consciousness.

In order to get a more complete idea of the situation and define as clearly as possible the problem we face with regard to our ego, we shall now describe some of the most common characteristics of the way human beings function when mired in the quicksand of personality consciousness.

Nine Other Ego Dynamics That Make People Unhappy, Powerless and Subject to Manipulation

Before we go into the details of these characteristics, let us note some of the fundamental aspects of these ego mechanisms:

- They **keep us forever bound to the cycle of dissatisfaction.**

- No matter what we do to gain happiness, **it is never enough.**

- They lead to **automatic behaviour patterns** that in most cases are inappropriate, generating very little happiness and a great deal of suffering for our self and the people around us.

- They keep us bound in dynamics that make us highly **subject to manipulation.**

- They make us dependent on circumstances and other people, **and thus rob us of our freedom.**

1. Fear and Insecurity

Fear is a major ego mechanism. It is the root of many other personality aspects that will be described in this section. It is a very familiar feeling. We know that it can make us act, or stop us from acting, in totally inappropriate ways. Ever present in some latent form or other, it poisons our life, limits our ability to clearly perceive reality, separates us from others, and compels us to make lousy or destructive choices both for our self and for those around us. Many spiritual or moral teachings suggest that we transform this fear into love. OK, we say, but how do we go about it? Very often, despite our best intentions, we remain overpowered and dominated by fear; or what is worse, we are not even aware of our fear. In our collective conditioning, it simply is not a feeling we are used to recognizing in our self. Our activities are then all the more conditioned by it.

◆ The source of this mechanism

Fear is inherent in the way we function as long as our consciousness is solely identified with our ego, for it springs from the ego's very structure. Indeed, during the entire period of development of the personality, the lower mind, being out of touch with the Self, was equipped with a basic protection mechanism so that survival could be ensured. Fear is an integral part of this mechanism. As long as the connection with the Self remains too weak to ensure any kind of genuine security, the old mechanism will remain active.

Yet one might think that fear could be a valuable safeguard, and in some cases a lifesaver. This has indeed been the case when the ego was attending to its own development. Fear is an automatic device which does not require consciousness in itself, and which will always partially remain even when our ego is eventually totally transformed. But then that mechanism will function in a way that is totally appropriate for any given situation, without exceeding its purpose as it does when our life is ruled by ego. When the Self is in charge of the personality, we will see how its intelligence is able to ensure perfect safety, in a way that is far superior to the very limited security afforded by this rather coarse mechanism. But in the meantime, as long as our life is played out at the ego level, we cannot help but remain prisoners of fear.

◆ The projection of fear, the source of insecurity

This underlying fear, which shapes each of our lives to a great extent, must externalise itself one way or another. Consequently, we will tend to project it on just about anything. Some of us are afraid of loss (relationships, material possessions, social status, image, approval and love from others, etc.); others are afraid of being in need; some are afraid of solitude or, conversely, of being with people; fear of life; fear of death; fear of ridicule; fear of being unloved or unrecognised; fear of oneself or of others; fear of failure or of success; fear of being moved or unmoved; fear of being conned (one of the great fears of the ego which undermines our power of self-manifestation, our creativity and our readiness to cooperate); fear of being afraid—all kinds of fears that keep each of us hung up by constant feelings of insecurity, stress, mistrust, separativeness, whether on a physical or a psychological level. **Anything can be used by our ego to justify its basic experience of insecurity. Fear and insecurity do not come from external circumstances; they spring from the point of identification of our consciousness.** If that point is our ego, there will always be stress and insecurity, for one reason or another.

> Constant fear and insecurity are the lot of every human being as long as our consciousness identifies with ego.

Along with this illusion of constant danger comes the illusion that something external will some day give us a sense of security—money, material or affective possessions, working conditions, certain specific circumstances (points 1 and 2 of the cycle of dissatisfaction). This illusion is a tough one to shake. Even when we are aware of it, there is always this little voice in us that says, "Yeah, but if I had fifty million dollars in the bank, now that would give me a great sense of security," or "If I had an ideal partner, or this or that kind of occupation, or if I were recognized for my talents, that would be nice." Yet no matter what we eventually obtain, our ego will soon come back with a new set of good reasons to live in a state of anxiety. We fail to realize that our ego is only projecting its own reality, in this case fear, onto our life circumstances, no matter what they may be. The sense of fear is an inherent part of our ego. **Any security derived from external circumstances is an illusion** in which we remain bound by our ego.

The fact that security is an illusion does not mean that we do not suffer or that our suffering is an illusion. Anxiety and stress, whether conscious or latent, are genuine experiences of suffering. But the only way out of this suffering is to shake the bonds of ego rather than try to change external circumstances.

In our relatively privileged Western world, many people can be quite unaware of their fears. The underlying stress is nevertheless constantly there, ready to reveal itself at the least provocation. For example, if we were to hear on the radio that within two days there would be no more food supplies available in stores, we would see otherwise very nice, gentle and respectable people suddenly behave like wild animals.

◆ Fear ruins relationships

When it is projected upon others and on our relationships, fear will destroy any possibility of having open and fulfilling relationships, any potential for genuine support and sharing. Indeed, we then either live in a state of mistrust, defensiveness and self-protection—where others constitute a threat to us—or we live in a state of emotional dependency and we are afraid of losing what we hold dear, or of being hurt. For one reason or another, relationships that are experienced at this level are a constant source of stress and insecurity.

◆ The illusion of fear and insecurity makes people subject to manipulation

In our society, it is easy to manipulate people through fear, a fact that is commonly exploited by the media and the powers that be. People are led to believe that they are powerless, that they should be on their guard, and that they should therefore place their power in the hands of external authorities. Fear is an excellent manipulation device for those who want to exert power over people who are caught in unconscious mechanisms. Our consumer society is also constantly manipulating people by selling security in all kinds of forms.

It might be interesting to play along with our ego and ask the following question, "What would I need in my life to feel really secure?" The answer to this question will show us where we are hung up as a result of ego illusion.

2. Separativeness

A second characteristic mode of functioning for an untransformed ego is the experience of separativeness. We feel set apart, separate, alienated, superior or inferior, or just plain different. We do not feel any connection, any affinity with people we do not "know", or who are not a part of our past. We keep our distance, and we certainly do not want to get close. If there is no way to avoid getting close, we will do it with a lot of wariness and fear, be it conscious or unconscious. This attitude generates a lot of inner solitude, and by that very fact, a lot of suffering, for we are basically meant to relate to others.

On the one hand, this separative reaction is a consequence of the fear mechanism (any other person is de facto considered as a potential threat), and on the other hand, it is a remnant of the dynamics involved in the process of involution.[2] In order to define itself, the ego had to differentiate itself and build an illusion of separativeness. Based on this mode of functioning, we feel comfortable with others to the extent that they are exactly like us: that they think, feel, and live in like fashion. The rest is "foreign", and thus should be avoided from the outset, or dominated, or even destroyed. This mechanism is where fanaticism springs from—a false unity based on separation. This was necessary for the process of involution to be completed; we must now reverse the process. We will continue to experience its after-effects as long as we have not disengaged our self from the mechanism of an ego-dominated personality.

◆ The illusion of separation makes people subject to manipulation

By preventing human beings from relating to each other, from openly cooperating with one another in a wholesome manner, from giving and receiving support, this mechanism leaves individuals feeling totally alone, totally dependent on their own resources, and thus highly vulnerable. Here again, the powers that be use these dynamics very skilfully to make people wary of each other. With the masses thus weakened, the decision-makers can concentrate all the power within their own hands. Another tactic is to create fanatic ideals, which separate groups from one another, and make it easy to manipulate these groups through their sense of separativeness. Let us not forget the famous Machiavellian principle: Divide and conquer.[3]

3. Lack of Energy

Another limitation inflicted upon us by our ego when it is in charge of our life is that it cuts us off from our true source of energy, that of the Self. We are only half alive. We may feel a burst of energy when the mechanisms of our ego are reactivated but when that happens, this energy can be very destructive for our self and for those around us, and our reserves of this kind of energy are limited. Sooner or later, we end up feeling exhausted, and happiness eludes us in any case.

This limited energy reserve is felt at all levels. At the physical level: constant fatigue, illness, weakness, burnout; at the emotional level: insensitivity or hypersensitivity, fragility, depression, sadness; at the mental level: no creative energy, routine, habits. We usually come up with all kinds of explanations for this energy depletion—weather, workload, other people who wear us down—it is always because of someone or something.

The explanation we often cling to is that we are getting old, as if time were an unavoidable factor leading to physical, emotional and mental degeneration. It is indeed, but only when our consciousness is ego bound.

> Degeneration is not caused by time but by the crystallization of ego structures

And you do not necessarily have to be old to lack energy. Many young people and relatively young adults feel lost in a society that gives maximum reinforcement to personality-based behaviours, and find that they are quickly tired and incapable of sustained effort. They lack the enthusiasm to create, to build, and to extend themselves. As long as our consciousness is ego bound, we can expect low levels of vitality—whether we are young or old—and we will inevitably degenerate over time.

◆ Lack of energy makes people subject to manipulation

Obviously, when a person is weakened physically, emotionally or mentally, he or she will be an easy prey to all the manipulators of this world.

4. The Need for Stuffing or the Illusion of Satisfaction through Stuffing

When our consciousness is caught up in the mechanisms of ego, it is impossible to experience fulfilment. Instead we get this sense of inner emptiness which can never be filled. This emptiness is a painful experience, for any human being knows, deep down, what fulfilment and beauty feel like, and will seek this experience through whatever seemingly appropriate avenue.

When our consciousness is trapped in ego, the only solution is to look outside for this experience, through stuffing. **Yet no mechanism can ever give us a profound and permanent sense of fulfilment.** No matter what we do, it is never enough, and we have to constantly start all over again. It feels like a bottomless pit, and it is.

In practical terms, how does this quest for stuffing manifest itself? Each individual has his or her own ways of going about this, though they are not very original. In fact, anything can be used as filler.

There are roughly two types of stuffing: the passive type is perhaps the most popular and the most debilitating. You don't do anything, or just about, and you fill yourself physically (food, sex, drugs, alcohol, tobacco, etc.) or psychologically (TV, shopping, music, outings, recreational activities and consumerism in all its forms). Yet no amount of filler is ever enough to provide any real sense of satisfaction. This explains why people watch TV ad nauseam, go shopping and fill themselves with anything they can get a hold of, without ever having enough to feel content. They always want more.

The second type is active: you are constantly doing things. This is often the case with work and all kinds of activities, which at first glance may seem very laudable, like sports or volunteer work. This type of stuffing tends to be less destructive, for it can be combined with a genuine intention to act originating from the Self. It is nevertheless ineffective in terms of genuine fulfilment, if the energy of the Self is not sufficiently present to fuel the activity in question. In this case, the individual ends up exhausted due to an excessive amount of compulsive, uninspired activities. **It is never enough.** The individual is never really satisfied, and is always thinking of what to do next, as he/she is caught in a race in search of that deep and full experience of satisfaction which never comes, except perhaps during brief moments, only to quickly vanish soon afterwards.

At this point, it is important to emphasize that the problem is not the activities themselves, but the motivation, the source fuelling these activities. It is perfectly OK, indeed desirable, to enjoy a good meal, listen to music, go shopping, do some work, engage in some kind of sport. Our Self wants us to do this so that it has an opportunity to experience and to manifest its will in this world. The trap does not lie in the activity itself, but in what motivates this activity. When our ego takes charge of our life, under the direction of our lower mind and its memories, any activity can be recycled and turned into stuffing (and that includes spiritual seeking). When we are caught up on the personality level, any experience of fulfilment completely eludes us. This quest for stuffing is so pervasive that most people are not even aware of it. The following is a very simple example, among thousands, that we can witness any given day:

We are on a spectacular beach. The sea is gorgeous, the sand is warm and fine, and seagulls are soaring gracefully over turquoise blue water. This is nature in all its splendour. There is practically no one around. A young man arrives quietly, drops his towel and heads for the edge of the water, while wearing a set of headphones and holding a Walkman in his right hand. He goes into the water and starts to swim, holding the Walkman over his head so as not to get it wet. The beauty of the sea, the gentle warmth of the water, the cries of gulls, the wind's caress, all of this is still not enough. He's got to have more, in this case music; in another situation it will be something else.

Music, one of mankind's most beautiful creations, can be reclaimed and turned into stuffing by our ego, just like anything else. And if not music, then let us at least have noise. Ego is terrified of silence, for it must then face its own emptiness.

◆ Stuffing is an illusion that makes people subject to manipulation

We can easily see how this insatiable need to fill the emptiness inside with anything we can get our hands on is a boon for the materialistic forces at work in our society. These are manifested through the great global production cartels, whose purpose is to sell anything at any cost. With well-designed manipulative marketing, they activate this inner mechanism, which keeps people bound to the illusion that by consuming more—by increasing the amount of stuff in our life—we will end up being happy. They thus manage to entice just about anyone to buy all kinds of things in great quantities. These manipulative forces are well aware of the mechanisms of the lower mind, and they know how to exploit them for maximum profit.

Does this mean that we should eliminate any kind of advertising in order to protect the poor, vulnerable individuals that we are? Let us emphasize that we are vulnerable and subject to manipulation only to the extent that we identify with our ego mechanisms. If we want to stop being manipulated, all we need to do is disengage our self from these mechanisms and change our level of consciousness. This is our responsibility and our choice to make. If we do the necessary work in order to let go and to free our self from the bonds of ego, we can become a free being, be in touch with our true needs, and no one can ever again manipulate us. If we have an open line to the intelligence of the Self, we can truly benefit from the kind of information that honest advertising can afford us, while the more dubious kind of advertising will leave us unaffected. Advertising which is intended as information on certain products is highly desirable. We live in a world where things are rapidly changing, and it is essential that we have access to appropriate means of information. When these are used at a higher level of consciousness, advertising and marketing will be subservient to people's needs, providing useful information. This is not always the case, these days—far from it in fact—but it is up to each of us to develop our own discernment.

Let us note that **the fear of being conned is no protection** from manipulative techniques—quite the opposite in fact. Like any type of fear, it disconnects us from our Self, from its intelligence and its sensitivity. It cuts us off from any kind of receptivity to information. In this sense, it weakens our powers of discernment and common sense and in the end we get taken in by the more sophisticated techniques of manipulation. Simple and honest information will not get through the shield of this fear, and we will not be able to freely benefit from this information. Thus we lose our power as long as we allow our consciousness to be caught in our lower mechanisms.

◆ Stuffing applied to relationships

This sense of inner emptiness that we feel when our consciousness is ego bound has a direct influence on the quality of our relationships. In its constant effort to fill this emptiness, ego is always looking to take as much as possible while giving as little as possible. This is what is commonly called selfishness, which has many facets, from the obvious to the subtle. This can translate into specific behaviours related to dependency and expectations, or it can simply affect the way that energy is exchanged between two people.[4] During emotional interactions, one's ego can feed on the other's energy while giving as little as possible in return. It is constantly calculating to check whether what was received was more than what was given. When the answer is yes, there is a temporary sense of satisfaction, but the feeling is short-lived as other circumstances will soon trigger the ego's survival mechanism and it will once again need that sense of getting more than it is giving.

This mechanism also feeds the fear of being conned. Indeed our ego, which perceives others as being mirrors of itself, will constantly be on the lookout for people trying to take advantage, steal our money, our relationships, our energy, our status, etc. All the ego sees is self-serving manipulation. Even when it witnesses acts of great generosity or selflessness, it will perceive everything in terms of manipulation.

5. The Quest for Comfort (laziness, resistance to challenges)

The quest for ease and comfort is worth noting since it is such a widespread attitude in our culture. We dream of a problem-free existence where everything would come to us spontaneously, as if by magic, where we wouldn't have to lift a finger to have all our wishes come true. Now that would make us really happy. Such is the illusion to which we are bound by our personality. Yet the way these dynamics work, there can never be enough comfort and ease of living to make us feel really good; we always want more.

This passivity and resistance to effort on the part of the ego has often been described in various spiritual disciplines as being an attitude springing from the law of inertia. This law, or "tamas", as it is called in Eastern thought, is traditionally seen as one of the major impediments to human evolution and to our ability to experience our true nature, with all its power and freedom.

> The ripe fruit falls on its own,
> But it does not fall into one's mouth.
> —*Chinese proverb*

The following story aptly illustrates this aspect:

Mr. Leblanc[5] had not always been completely honest. His dream was to have a life of ease where he could get anything he wanted at the least possible cost. He was intelligent yet lazy by nature, not really a bad sort, and had been able to exploit many people on his way to achieving his aims. At the time of his death, he dreaded his meeting with Saint

Peter. As he came before the saint, he expected a serious scolding. To his utter astonishment, he found an angel directing him simply to his new quarters. His surprise was even greater as he found himself being taken to a splendid castle and told that he could stay as long as he liked, with even a servant at his beck and call to cater to his every need. Mr. Leblanc started with a tour of this magnificent residence, and then settled in the most luxurious room. At supper time, an exquisite meal was served, and, after a stroll in the gardens, he went to bed feeling delighted, as he felt sure that God had forgiven all his shortcomings and that he was now in Heaven. The next morning, he slept in and his servant appeared only when called, to bring him breakfast in bed, which was rather pleasant. Mr. Leblanc thus spent this day and the following in leisure, feeling very happy with this situation. Then one day he felt like doing something. Since he enjoyed gardening, he went to see the gardener and offered to help him plant a beautiful flowerbed. The gardener categorically refused; Mr. Leblanc was not allowed to help. This rule surprised him, but since he also liked to cook he headed for the kitchen to offer help in this area. He met with the same response as he had from the gardener. Thus he tried to get involved in various occupations but each time found that he was forbidden to do anything, even his own housekeeping. In the end he was fed up and called his servant, with whom he shared his frustrations, saying that these restrictions were totally ridiculous and that it was actually becoming unbearable for him to remain idle in this manner. He was getting really angry and he told his servant that living here was turning into a kind of hell. Whereupon the servant answered, "But Sir, where do you think you are?"

Finding an easy path to happiness is another ego illusion. The same goes for comfort, which is just one aspect of this illusion of ease.

◆ The illusion of ease and comfort makes people subject to manipulation

Ease

Once again this illusion is thoroughly exploited. We want to feel good yet at the same time our ego is reluctant to make the necessary effort (since it seeks to avoid giving, especially its energy). So our consumer society offers easy solutions, miracle recipes, ways and means that will produce quick and effortless results. We are presented with a whole array of recipes, techniques and tools that will do the work for us and are supposed to deliver a lot of enjoyment at low cost.

A classic example among many: witness the number of miracle diets that are supposed to make you lose weight quickly and effortlessly. To the ego, that is all that matters: quickly (to be rid of the problem and not to have to face it, as if it did not have anything to do with us) and effortlessly. Similarly, we dream of a job where we would have nothing to do and the money would just miraculously flow, of totally satisfying relationships where we would not have to give anything, of always being in top shape while living any old way, of being happy without having to lift a finger to create this happiness. Today's youth is weaned on these models of ease, and it is not surprising to find so many young people trying to devise schemes that will provide maximum enjoyment at the least possible cost, rather than extend themselves so as to attain self-realization.

Comfort

Major marketing companies also use this unconscious mechanism to saturate the public with messages that promote the illusion that comfort means happiness.

This doesn't mean that we should avoid comfort and make life unduly difficult for our self. Here again, what matters is why we seek to make our life easier. The issue is not comfort in itself, but rather its ultimate purpose as well as the underlying motivation behind this quest. It is quite appropriate to seek a certain level of comfort, not as an ultimate goal with the hope that happiness will spring therefrom, but as a way to allow us to create, to get involved and to contribute in a more effective manner. Comfort is then simply a springboard that will allow us to fully manifest our talents and our capacity to serve our world. On the other hand, living in discomfort under the guise of spirituality is also subject to ego recovery, where one nurtures a sense of superiority over others who are unwittingly caught up in worldly affairs.

For a doctor, for instance, who must often travel by car to visit patients, a comfortable automobile will be of great help and will allow him to be more readily available to provide medical care. Travelling on a bicycle in this case, or in an old and unreliable vehicle, would certainly not be a desirable option. This quest for comfort and for ways of making life easier is totally appropriate, from this perspective, as it stems from a desire to gain mastery over the physical world in order to be able to create and to fully express the will of the Self. Yet somewhere along the way, we lose sight of this goal, and the means are seen as the ultimate objective, which binds us to an illusion that robs us of our power and freedom.

One could even state that one of the aspects of the way the Self manifests its will on this earth will be the achievement of a pleasant and comfortable way of life for everyone. But this comfort, which will be simple and just, will spring from the soul's capacity for mastery rather than from the quest for ego gratification, which can never be attained in any case since, on the ego level, one can never have enough to be satisfied. This will happen especially when the most materially endowed segment of humanity will cease to live on the basis of lower consciousness mechanisms, monopolizing material resources in order to gratify an insatiable ego while the rest of humanity is deprived of the most basic necessities.

◆ Avoidance of Effort, Resistance to Challenges

This is a natural consequence of the quest for ease and comfort. In this case, the illusion to which we are bound by our ego could be stated as follows: if we could only manage to have a problem-free existence, then we would be happy. We then try to avoid problems at all cost, and whenever they do in fact arise—for such is life—the only thing we can do is resist. There are many ways to resist the challenges of life, depending on the structures we have unconsciously built and solidified in the past: avoidance, victimization, attempts to maintain control at all cost, etc. One way or another, the ego's loathing for effort translates into resistance towards any difficulty and anything that does not provide immediate gratification.

Now let us remember the well-known psychological law of energy: **Anything we resist will persist.** The very fact that our ego's basic tendency is to keep us bound to an attitude of resistance all but guarantees that our problems will never end. We are thus caught in a vicious circle: the more difficulties we encounter, the more we resist, and the more we resist, the more these difficulties persist. We think that life is difficult while it is just our state of consciousness that prevents us from quickly resolving these difficulties. As we will see, when we describe the workings of higher consciousness, there are other potential dynamics that are entirely different and far more satisfying.

We live in a social culture that is largely based on the illusion of ease and avoidance of effort. Yet what keeps us alive is precisely our effort to extend our self in any given field. Only in this way can we give our self the opportunity to discover and develop our unused potential. Only through conscious and deliberate effort can we overcome the limitations of ego. The illusion of ease fostered in our collective consciousness short-circuits the life-giving creative force springing from the Self. This is how we lose the power and freedom that are part of our birthright as human beings.

6. The Need for Approval and Love (performance, submission, seduction)

Just as was the case with fulfilment, the empty mechanisms of ego can never give us a true sense of existence or a sense of our intrinsic value. When our ego is in charge of our life, we have a tendency to look outside of our self for something that will make us feel alive and give us a sense of personal value, since we are unable to get this feeling from within. We are thus caught up in a quest for approval, a quest for love, under the illusion that if we get enough of this approval and love, then we will feel good.

Depending on the personality structures we built in the past, whose fundamental mechanisms we will examine further along in this book, this need for approval can translate into spectacular performance displays (wanting to be the best at all cost) or into more subdued aspects (manipulation, submission, seduction). As far as performance is concerned, our ego can move us to extend our self beyond our comfort zone and attempt spectacular exploits, not for the sake of self-transformation and increased flexibility (the ego's intent cannot help but be at odds with this), but rather for the sake of proving to our self and to others that we are good, or perhaps even the best.

This mechanism can lead to a great deal of violence, as the ego will go to extremes in order to satisfy its need for recognition. Our society glorifies competition, which might be beneficial if it allowed each of us to extend our self while drawing inspiration from others; but in most cases, the goal is to surpass others. Competition is then reclaimed by our ego for the sake of performance, dominance and gratification, which unfortunately can only be short lived. We will then have to perform and seduce even more, to the point of exhaustion. In this game, we will quickly burn away our energy and disappointments will accumulate over time.

This quest for approval can take on more subdued, more passive variations, which translate into submission or seemingly harmless seduction. The substance of our ego's attitude here is, "I'll do anything just as long as you love me and I can thus feel that I exist and that I have some value." We know, of course, how much this attitude can generate repressed anger and frustration, which, sooner or later, will have to explode.

This dynamic is the root of a great deal of suffering. Indeed, on the one hand we live in a state of stress and fear of not succeeding, of not being perfect, of not getting love or approval; and on the other hand, even if we do succeed, we will never get enough congratulations, enough success, enough love or enough recognition to feel good. Even if we have been congratulated dozens of times in the course of a day, all it takes is one person expressing a minor criticism to ruin our day. As we go after successive forms of approval, whether through spectacular performance or through seductive submission, we burn our self out and completely lose any sense of who we really are. **We will always need more.** The sense of accomplishment that springs from within, regardless of peer judgement or circumstances, is constantly beyond our reach and we remain worried and unsatisfied.

The same goes for the search for love. Since a mechanism cannot experience love, we will never get enough of it to experience the feeling of being loved, at the personality level. Whether through performance, seduction or submission, we will do anything to be loved by others. Yet no matter how much they try to demonstrate their love, the experience of being loved will elude us as long as our consciousness is caught up in ego. As soon as we identify with the Self, the experience of love becomes a presence within us, one that is totally independent of others or of circumstances.

◆ The Illusion of Image

Focusing on appearance to fill the absence of a sense of being

In this instance, one's ego exaggerates the importance of one's image, whether it be psychological (we act out roles for the sake of appearance and pleasing others), or physical. In our society, fashion, for example, which has the potential of being a genuine expression of art, is almost totally based on the quest for identity through image. The system of excessive consumerism in which we live has reclaimed this quest in order to lead people to consume even more. We buy a car not because it is useful and appropriate in terms of our real needs, but because of the image it projects in the eyes of others. This gives us a sense of being somebody while nurturing a false identity. We don't realize how little it matters to other people, who are themselves engrossed in the task of polishing up their own image

◆ The search for approval and the emphasis placed on one's image make people subject to manipulation

Living under the illusion that our well-being depends on the way other people judge us and on the love they are willing to bestow upon us, we will do anything to maintain a good appearance and to attract love. Those around us will obviously be sorely tempted to manipulate this mechanism. We are thus bound to their will and prisoners of any manipulative entity we may encounter.

7. Powerlessness (irresponsibility, victimhood)

Victimhood is a widespread attitude in today's world. It stems from a very strong feeling of powerlessness, which can translate into a number of different manifestations.

When we are trapped in this ego mechanism, we live in a permanent state of dissatisfaction and anger, which may or may not be outwardly expressed. There is an endless stream of complaints, and nothing is going right. We blame and criticize: people are mean, incompetent, selfish, ungrateful, bad, dishonest, not OK one way or another. There is also a strong sense of injustice: "Why me? Life is good for the other guy, but not for me. Life is tough, no fun, poor me, I am hurting (sigh); but one fine day, given half a chance, I'll get even."

All of this generates mountains of negativity, which may or may not be repressed: anger towards this unfair world, aggressiveness, violence, resistance, anxiety, fatigue, sadness, inability to communicate, ill will, guilt, irresponsibility (it's always someone else's fault), sabotage, fanaticism, fears (especially the fear of being conned), etc.

The effects are devastating in every respect: all aspects of our life are affected, including our relationships, our energy level, our creativity, our self-esteem, and our health. Experiences such as inner peace, the joy of living, freedom, fulfilment and love, become impossible.

When we study our basic unconscious mechanisms, we will see how this mechanism originates in very specific past personal and collective experiences, and how it is possible to disengage our self from it.

The illusion of powerlessness makes people subject to manipulation

It is very easy to manipulate someone who suffers from victimitis by activating his or her anger towards this cruel and unfair world, and towards all those who are not OK. One can easily galvanize large crowds through the use of this mechanism.

8. The Hunger for Possessions

This dynamic also stems from the ego-generated sense of emptiness, but it goes further than simple stuffing. When we remain in an ego driven state, we need to possess and we are attached to our possessions, whether these are material or emotional in nature. We want to "have". And as we saw with all the other ego mechanisms, we will never possess enough to feel good; it always takes a little more. How many acts of violence, how many tragedies, and how much suffering has been generated by this need for possession, both in material and emotional terms? All of human history is filled with painful events stemming from this mechanism.

Our world is dominated more and more by the passion for possessions, focusing on acquisitiveness, material power and aggressiveness, when the only chance for its salvation would be to concentrate on the mode of being, founded on love, spiritual accomplishment, and the joy of sharing significant and fruitful activities. If mankind does not wake up to the seriousness of the consequences of this choice, we are heading for an unprecedented psychological and ecological disaster.[6]

◆ The need to possess makes people subject to manipulation

The need to possess is deeply rooted in the collective unconscious. It is one of the major ego mechanisms, and it is very easy to manipulate anyone who is caught up in this mechanism, which fosters fear and is used by materialistic forces, just like the need for stuffing, to lead people to excess consumerism.

Because I stand to lose what I have, I cannot help but be permanently concerned with the idea that I may lose what I have. I worry about thieves, economic changes, revolutions, illness, death, and I am afraid of love, of disease, of where my own development may lead me, of change, of the unknown. I am thus perpetually in a state of worry, suffering from chronic hypochondria not only with regard to the possible loss of wealth, but also the loss of everything I have; I remain on the alert, tough, suspicious, solitary; I allow myself to be led by my need to always have more, in order to be better protected.[7]

9. The Quest for Power and Resistance to Power

The question of power is a rather touchy one. All of the ego's antennae spring out instantaneously, on red alert, at the mere mention of the word, for very specific reasons stemming from our own personal history.

Yet power is a genuine quality of the soul, but in order to recover it, one must be free of the ego's stranglehold, as the latter reacts very inappropriately and destructively to this energy.

Within the ego we find various mechanisms relating to power, which, different though they may be one from the other, are nevertheless all equally limiting and destructive.

The first of these is the raw hunger for external, material or psychological power. All of the personality's energy is then busy dominating and manipulating others for selfish purposes.

If we seek out the root of the power dynamic, we find an inability to connect with any real sense of mastery such as we experienced when we were still in contact with our essence (just as the need for stuffing stems from the ego's inability to experience fulfilment). The ego then tries desperately to recover this extraordinary sensation of power and freedom. At the level of the Self this experience is totally beneficial and respectful of everyone's well being, for the soul is genuinely all-powerful and it manifests this power through the energy of love. The ego, on the other hand, seeks power through separativeness and selfishness. Since it is impossible for it to really secure this experience of power in any permanent fashion, it is caught in a never-ending quest at this level, **and it always needs more**. We talk about "power hungry" people. We know how destructive the abuse of power can be, in various forms, springing from this state of consciousness, as it generates violence, injustice and suffering.

The quest for power in the form of control is also based on fear: fear of being conned, fear of being dominated, fear of losing one's territory, fear of losing one's identity, fear of losing in general. As far as the ego is concerned, security is not possible without controlling, dominating and manipulating its surroundings. The ego cannot see any other way of doing things, as it perceives others as potential enemies who are perpetually plotting to steal its territory or even to bring about its demise. We see here the primary mechanisms that were active when our identity was just being formed: these had a viable role to play at that time, but are no longer appropriate now that human beings have other conscious instruments with which to gain mastery in life.

This brings us to the second ego-limiting dynamic: resistance to power. It may be less obvious, but it is by no means less active. It can take two forms: resistance to one's own power, and/or resistance to other people's power. At the mere mention of the word "power", a whole assortment of negative associations immediately spring to mind. From the perspective of ordinary consciousness, the word suggests domination, manipulation, suffering, injustice, abuse, and misfortune. This is our past history, which is inscribed within our very cells.

From this viewpoint, we are first of all unable to recognize our own power. We are so afraid of it that we cannot allow our self to harbour even a small portion of it. Better to remain passive and useless, and thus to limit our creative potential, rather than run the risk of holding the least position of power. Many people, particularly those who follow a spiritual path, think they are practicing humility, while in fact they are merely tuning out of genuine power and acting out of fear.

As we reject this power for our self, we feel compelled to resist power in other people, or anything that can be interpreted as power. Under the guise of freedom, we resist any form of authority, whether real or imaginary. This produces automatic rebellious behaviours which block any possibility for learning and development, and which ultimately destroy any kind of freedom. For rebellious behaviour is determined by other people just as much as submissive behaviour. Instead of doing what other people want us to do (submissiveness), we do the opposite (rebellion). In both cases, our actions are based on what other people want from us. In both cases, we lose our freedom and our power, for we do not act as we would freely choose to. This mechanism sabotages our effectiveness and any personal or collective creative endeavour. We have explored some of its deeper causes in Volume 1 when we studied our unconscious structures, and we will better understand its fundamental mechanisms later in this book.

The fact that we confuse power and its vehicle prevents us from knowing the essence of the former. Now, to ignore the source of power is to be immeasurably weak. We do not have to conquer power since it has always dwelt within us. But as long as we do not see this clearly, we will pursue our pitiful efforts, and our false conquests will perpetually end up shipwrecked under the amused gaze of the gods. Corruption is not a by-product of power, but of an individual's appropriation of power, in a word, of the ego.[8]

◆ The illusion of power makes us subject to manipulation

Though this quest may appear to be aimed at gaining power over others (active manipulation), it makes human beings equally subject to manipulation. Indeed, the need to acquire power can be used by other manipulators in order to activate this inner mechanism. We can then be induced into doing anything in order to obtain power, and, since we can never get enough, we can be manipulated for a long while.

> We are never manipulated by anything but our own ego.

◆ ◆ ◆

In addition to the general behaviours just described, we can also identify certain attitudes which stem directly from the mechanisms of the lower mind, and which are all too familiar.

Indeed, when our consciousness is stuck at the personality level, we generally find two types of reaction: automatic reactions, originating primarily from emotional charges stored in the unconscious, and the more specific reactions of the lower mind. Both are closely linked. For people who are emotionally polarized, the mind is weak and programming is mainly activated through emotional mechanisms. The coachman is weak while the horse is strong; the quality of the journey depends on the latter's moods. This leads to behaviours like those just described. For people who are mentally polarized, and mired in lower consciousness, the separating, dominating aspect of the lower mind is more clearly obvious. The horse is more or less in shape; the coachman is the strong one, but he is locked up in rigid belief systems. He is cut off from the wisdom of the Master. One is then doomed to wandering on difficult paths that lead nowhere. In this case, the journey is not a pleasant one either. We shall examine some of the characteristic attitudes that stem from this mode of functioning.

Specific Dynamics Affecting the Lower Mind

Among the most common of these dynamics, the following are worth mentioning:

◆ Holding onto one's viewpoint

Wanting to have the last word on anything and everything: on how to make a salad dressing, how to raise children, how each politician or the latest popular singer should be rated, on the existence or non-existence of God, on the best brand of chocolate cookies—and most importantly, never changing our viewpoint, remaining closed to any possibility of seeing things in a different light. This is also about denigrating other peoples' viewpoints if they happen to be different from our own: the lower mind wants everyone to think, feel and act the same way as itself, in a bid to validate its own content. When we are caught in this mechanism, we get very aggressive the minute someone disagrees with our viewpoint, as this indeed constitutes a serious threat to the ego. Differences are insufferable. This is the source of all those narrow-minded behaviours we encounter on a daily basis, not to mention, on a broader scale, those fanatic behaviours and power abuses which have created, and continue to create, so much suffering throughout the course of human history.

This mechanism also generates many conflicts in personal relationships: parents who thrust their viewpoint on their children, spouses who demand certain behaviours on the part of their partners, arguments over trivia just to prove one is right.

Insisting on having the last word is a way for the ego to dominate others. This is where we can observe power games, not only in relationships, but also at work and everywhere else. As soon as a person has the least amount of physical or psychological power over others, the ego uses this power to impose its will, its perception of reality, and its ways of being and of doing things, on other people.

The following is a typical example of this type of behaviour:

This example is taken from an interview with Janine Fontaine M.D., as published in Chatelaine magazine.[9] Trained in standard medical approaches, Janine had many years of practice behind her in this field. Later on, she discovered healing methods, which might be called "alternative", where she worked at more subtle levels than the purely physical body, and she found that she had remarkable talents in this area. Her ability to heal people was greatly enhanced, to the greater benefit and satisfaction of those under her care. However not everyone agreed with this. In the course of her interview, she related the following anecdote: I recently saw a physician who was suffering from an illness affecting his extremities, an illness deemed incurable by classic methods. I agreed to see him on two occasions, even though he hadn't read my works—something I usually insist upon so that the people I treat understand what can happen. But since he was just passing through Paris—he lives in Brittany—and since his was a serious case, I agreed to treat him nevertheless. His condition improved dramatically, to the point where he could take up skiing again, a recreational activity that he had been forced to discontinue. He was in high spirits and decided to take a ski vacation, during which he took the opportunity to read my books. He had a third appointment with me. He came in and said, "This is a courtesy visit. I read your works. I don't go along with you. I'd rather live with my disease."

Some people would rather die than expand or let go of their point of view!

◆ Attachment to what is known, resistance to change

The lower mind abhors change, in the most inconsequential things as in the most momentous. It foresees and makes plans in a rigid fashion. An unexpected change will put it in an automatic state of stress, even if the outcome is something very positive. For example, we may decide to go visit some friends on Monday morning at 10:00, and it is such a big deal if this has to be postponed until the afternoon, even if, from an objective point of view, there is no problem with this.

◆ Comparison

When our consciousness is stuck at the personality level, we never cease to compare our self with others. Either we try to feel superior, which generates conceit—a source of many tensions and difficulties in relationships—or we shrivel up under a sense of inferiority that generates fear and suffering, which is no better.

◆ Criticism

Criticism is one of the personality's favourite activities, as is blaming others. Whether it takes the form of direct bad-mouthing or subtle criticism, it is a widespread attitude, in today's world, which makes people unhappy, negative and separate from one another.

We could extend this list of mechanisms and illusions in which we lose our self as human beings when our consciousness is mired in ego. The mechanisms would always have similar characteristics:

* they keep us bound in a perpetual state of stress and dissatisfaction;

* they make us vulnerable and subject to manipulation; and

* they bring on automatic behaviours that generate a lot of limitation and suffering, both on a personal level and on a planetary level.

Through all these mechanisms, we are just looking for a genuine experience of peace, fulfilment, joy, identity, power, freedom, and love. But in the context generated by these mechanisms, this experience remains beyond our reach. To compensate for this inability to experience fulfilment in life, human beings who are mired in lower consciousness will do what they can to try to meet such healthy aspirations through inadequate mechanisms, which could be summarized as follows:

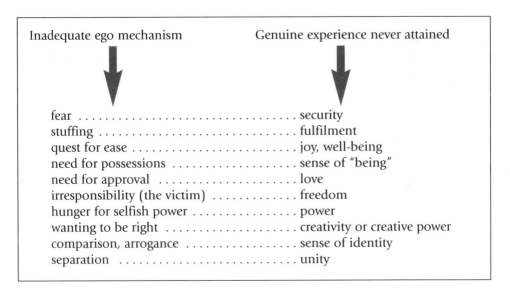

Inadequate ego mechanism	Genuine experience never attained
fear	security
stuffing	fulfilment
quest for ease	joy, well-being
need for possessions	sense of "being"
need for approval	love
irresponsibility (the victim)	freedom
hunger for selfish power	power
wanting to be right	creativity or creative power
comparison, arrogance	sense of identity
separation	unity

As long as our consciousness is imprisoned in ego, it will be impossible to experience an authentic, rich and fulfilling life; this is the way human nature is built. It is important to recognize this if we are to have any chance of finding our way to joy and freedom.

The foregoing descriptions are enough for us to understand the extent to which these mechanisms yield little happiness and lots of suffering. Yet even when we clearly acknowledge these behaviours and genuinely find them to be impediments to our own and other people's well being, nevertheless it is not an easy task to change them. In this sense, all the pep talks we may hear or give our self to inspire us towards "good spiritual behaviour" are just not enough. Indeed these behaviours are linked to deeper structures within the unconscious, and it takes more than just an intellectual understanding of them to be able to change them. A whole process of transformation, healing and liberation from the past must take place, for our behaviours stem from these old structures, which have hardened over time and become lodged in our unconscious, rather than from any conscious ill will or good will on our part.

On the other hand, when we know that these attitudes are not unavoidable, and that they are merely the consequence of a particular state of consciousness, this opens the door to deeper inquiry. We then ask our self questions such as: What is the source of these behaviours? How does ego work, and why does it work this way? Finally, how can one change such behaviours? This will be the subject of subsequent chapters.

In the course of the next chapter, I will present a history of human consciousness based on the finest esoteric traditions, which echoes the most recent scientific discoveries. As we understand the way in which our consciousness has developed over time, and the purpose for which it was built this way, this will enable us to approach subsequent descriptions of human reality in an even broader context and will facilitate our understanding of the structures by which our daily life is presently conditioned.

---

[1] Ego-driven behaviour is neither good nor bad; it is what it is according to the laws of the Universe. Mankind has become used to thinking in terms of good or bad simply because, at the time when the mind was taking shape, this was a (rudimentary) way for consciousness to differentiate between what was aligned with the evolutionary plan at that time, and what was contrary to it. For example, during the process of involution, it was perfectly "good" to learn to experience separation (individuation). It is now considered "good" to seek experiences related to sharing, love and unity. In fact this is neither good nor bad, with all the emotional charge that is attributed to these terms. It is simply what puts us in synch with the natural process of the journey we have undertaken. Going backwards or stalling is not satisfying. It is not "bad", it is just painful for us and for others.

[2] This process will be explored in greater detail in Chapter 3.

[3] The film entitled "For Better or for Worse" is a good illustration of this mechanism of separativeness.

[4] On this topic, it is worth taking a look at Barbara Ann Brennan's *Hands of Light*. This aspect is also explored in novel form, and very accurately at that, in *The Celestine Prophecy*, by James Redfield.

[5] Names and surnames used throughout this book are fictitious.

[6] Erich Fromm, *To Have or to Be?*

[7] Ibid.

[8] Jean Bouchart d'Orval, *Le secret le mieux gardé*, éd. Libre Expression.

[9] August 1984 issue, Montreal, Quebec.

chapter 3

A History of Human Consciousness

Having observed the ordinary inner workings of a human being in the foregoing chapter, we can now attempt to shed some light on the source of this condition. To this end, we could begin by using two different yet consistent and mutually reinforcing perspectives. One is simply more elaborate than the other.

The first is based on the simple model of the structure of a human being as described in Chapter I. Since this is already a widely accepted model (at the very least, it could be used as a working hypothesis), it can serve as a starting point for a more in-depth analysis. The second, more elaborate perspective focuses on exploring the various fields of knowledge in order to determine what is known about the evolution of consciousness throughout human history. Indeed, if the limiting behaviours most of us are familiar with spring from a certain state of consciousness, the following questions beg to be asked: Why do we live in this state? Where does it come from? Is it possible to change it?

To begin with, an overview of the history of humanity and of consciousness can be a very useful doorway to greater mastery over our personal and collective destiny. We have tried to get answers from scientists, biologists and historians: their answers are interesting, yet they only convey part of the picture. We then turned to the Masters of wisdom, as well as the most fundamental philosophical and spiritual traditions throughout human history, and found other answers which, for the time being, would appear to be more comprehensive while still being quite consistent with the way things are today. They give a perspective which is proving to be more and more accurate in the context of the accelerated pace of history that we are all experiencing these days. Furthermore, rather than being cut off from other aspects of contemporary knowledge, these answers tend to include them and broaden their scope. They are also totally consistent with a number of recent discoveries in the fields of science and advanced psychology.

These teachings have been dismissed, and even despised, in the context of our contemporary scientific/materialistic outlook, which chooses to describe reality and to build an understanding of "truth" strictly on the basis of physical data. This is just one of many ways of looking at reality, one that is certainly useful in the context of human knowledge, as long as we are aware of its limitations, which stem from the fact that the world is not simply material, as physical matter is just one form of universal energy. Open-minded scientists are rediscovering many other aspects. Nuclear physics is at the point of convergence between the material world and the world of energy, and several areas of materialistic science are now confronted with their physical limitations (molecular biology, genetic engineering, etc.). Thus contemporary research scientists,[1] those who choose not to hang onto the past but who are willing to turn their gaze objectively and without preconceptions towards uncharted realms, are taking materialistic science through a quiet revolution whereby the greatest esoteric teachings which have been handed down through the course of human history are now being rediscovered and confirmed.[2] So we have turned to them in order to offer a broader perspective on the history of human consciousness. This presentation has the advantage of demystifying many prevailing beliefs regarding humanity and its place in the universe, while at the same time providing a broad context in which to pursue our inner inquiry.

We shall briefly go over these esoteric findings, not as yet another theory, but rather as an interesting perspective from which to approach our most fundamental and practical questions regarding human consciousness: Why do we behave as we do in our daily life? Why are we not yet able to live in peace with our self and with others? Why are we both inwardly and outwardly engaged in war? Why isn't life beautiful more often than not? Why are we faced with all these limitations when in fact everyone longs for well-being and happiness? When and how is this ever going to change? We are no longer content with simplistic answers framed in terms of good and evil; we need a broader understanding of things.

What we are presenting here is a perspective on reality that will serve as a springboard to a deeper understanding of subsequent chapters.[3] In addition, this broader approach to the subject will naturally allow us to discover practical and efficient means of achieving a higher level of knowledge and mastery with respect to human dynamics as a whole. Finally, this information may trigger further research and thus become the seed for future discoveries.

Some readers are familiar with this kind of information. This will then serve as a review and an opportunity to clarify certain points, which often remain somewhat vague in esoteric literature. For others, this may be breaking new ground: the best approach would then be to treat these points as working hypotheses and to remain open to the possibility of a more expanded perception of things. It is not necessary to "believe" in these teachings. One can simply treat them as an arguable viewpoint and observe whether it is in tune with one's intuitive perception and one's common sense, as well as with the reality of the world as it is today.

As this chapter is a very succinct summary of some highly complex data, the following outline may make things somewhat easier to grasp:

Chapter Outline

- **Introduction to the esoteric perspective**
- **A history of the descent of consciousness into matter**
  The purpose of the journey
  The process of involution
  The process of evolution
  Modern times—a crucial moment in human history
- **Building the Self's instrument of manifestation from the beginning of individuation to the present**
  General principle: successive descents into the
    physical world
  The dissolution of the three bodies
  Permanent atoms
  How successive personalities were built
  We are not the outcome of our past
  The collective aspect of evolution
- **The motivations that prompt us to inner inquiry**

The questions we are concerned with are the following:

How did we get to where we are now?

Why is consciousness still mired in ego when this is so painful and destructive?

Is there a way out of this predicament?

And also:

Who are we?

Where do we come from?

Where are we going?

Introduction to the Esoteric Perspective

According to esoteric science, the universe is a vast energy system composed of various overlapping "worlds" or "planes", each vibrating at its own frequency. As far as we are concerned, the lowest frequency is that of the physical/etheric plane. Our body is composed of physical/etheric matter. Then comes another energy system, subject to different laws, which is commonly called the emotional or astral plane. This is the type of "matter" or energy that our emotional body is made of. Then comes the mental plane, our thoughts being the form taken by this mental "matter". There are also many other planes vibrating at even higher frequencies, bearing different names in different esoteric traditions though they all represent the same reality: a system of interpenetrating worlds, each vibrating on a particular frequency, each with its own laws and purpose.

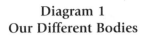

Diagram 1
Our Different Bodies

A human being is defined as a particular energetic unit within the universal energy field. Its vehicle of expression is composed of different bodies made of matter from each of the different planes.

Where do we get this information regarding the history of humanity?

How can we know the history of human consciousness? According to esoteric science, there is a place in the mental world where all the memories of nature are stored. The history of humanity is recorded here in minute detail: this is what Oriental traditions refer to as "akashic records". Rare are those who truly have access to these archives, for one must be able to reach this level of consciousness in order to comprehend these records. More often we have people who can intuitively connect with certain aspects of these memories and bring them down, in more or less distorted form, to the level of ordinary consciousness. I have examined a wide variety of sources, both ancient and contemporary, which convey information taken from this "logbook". I have retained a number of basic principles, which I found steadily recurring through different formulations. I have also kept what seemed consistent and inclusive in relation to other fields of knowledge, especially with regard to the latest discoveries of contemporary physics.

This will be an extremely succinct summary, in deliberately simple and general terms, of principles, which would require volumes to be adequately described. Consequently, this outline cannot even remotely convey the depth and precision of all the information that is presently available in this field, but it will be adequate for our purpose.[4]

Remember that this information is being presented not as the ultimate truth, but as a model to facilitate our grasp of reality. The same holds true for any description of reality, including that given by various scientific approaches. A model is interesting to the extent that it is consistent with our observation of concrete events, and that it encompasses previously available models and leads to a broader understanding of reality, and a correspondingly greater degree of mastery. It must be viewed not as ultimate truth, but as a working hypothesis that should be constantly tested in the crucible of experience, with an open and unbiased state of mind.

A History of the Descent of Consciousness into Matter

◆ The purpose of the journey

Generally speaking, according to esoteric science, the history of human consciousness can be perceived as the journey of a vast consciousness, one that exists at a very high level of vibrational frequency, which has chosen to experience certain aspects of itself through an exploration of worlds vibrating at a variety of frequencies.

The purpose of this journey is highly complex. To put it in extremely simple and general terms, one might see it as a great cosmic game with very precise rules. These rules cause this great consciousness to divide itself into billions of particles so as to be able to blend with the various worlds, right down to the physical. Thus this vast consciousness "strays" into matter, but only to open the door to its subsequent reintegration, and through this experience, to a merging of spirit and matter. Though it seems rather remote from our daily experience, this process underscores, both inwardly and outwardly, our personal and collective reality. From where we stand at the moment, this perspective may seem like an overly general outlook but it will prove quite useful, once explored in greater detail, in order to grasp the underlying consistency of the numerous psychological and physical challenges we now face in our daily life.

This long journey is unfolding in two major stages: an initial period called "involution", and a second phase called "evolution".

◆ The process of involution

In the beginning, billions of years ago, we were all one with this great consciousness that we humans have traditionally referred to as God. It was called divine simply to express the fact that it exists at a level far beyond that of ordinary consciousness, that it seems an inconceivable reality from the viewpoint of the average person. Its vibrational frequency is extremely high in relation to that of matter.

The purpose of the process of involution was to get divine consciousness to come down to the vibrational frequency level of matter. To this end, this great consciousness chose to emanate into a multitude of consciousness units, each bearing the totality of divine consciousness, in a way that is similar to the principle of the hologram. As these units gradually descended from one plane to the next, right down to the physical plane, they were subjected to a powerful gravitational pull towards matter. This force gradually caused them to lose sight of their divine aspect. Indeed, in order to make its "descent" possible, this consciousness had to become immersed in lower and lower vibrational frequencies, which limited and momentarily concealed its divine aspect, to the extent that it was eventually "forgotten" in order to delve more deeply into the physical plane.

Furthermore, in order for this process to be totally completed, these units had to also "forget" their fundamental unity. They learned to separate themselves more and more from each other in order to momentarily meet the requirements of the lower worlds and become immersed in them.

This descent down to the three worlds—the physical, the emotional and the mental—is what is called involution, the purpose of which is to attract the presence of these "divine" units into the world of matter.

How human beings were constructed during the process of involution

As these energy units—or consciousness units[5]—which were eventually to become human beings, made their way down from one plane to another, it was necessary to construct different "bodies" in order to allow them to explore and experience each of the planes they encountered along the way. At the end of the process of involution, the prototype human being had the following characteristics:

• it was composed of a vehicle of manifestation, which in turn was a composite of unfinished versions of the three bodies made up of matter from the three lower worlds (the physical, emotional, and lower mental bodies), which we now refer to as ego, or personality, or lower self;

• it was host to an indwelling divine spark, which in turn had three bodies (the higher mind, buddhi and atma), which we refer to as the Self, the higher self, the soul, etc. This descent took place over billions of years, in a systematic, and thoroughly structured manner.[6]

Throughout this process of involution, as consciousness descended into matter, these energy units were entirely under the direction of entities existing at a higher level of consciousness than that of humanity. This descent occurred smoothly, in keeping with divine Will; these units were not yet endowed with a will of their own. The goal was simply to construct a sufficiently functional prototype of the three bodies—physical, emotional and lower mental—and of the three aspects of the Self.

This process required a **momentary identification with matter.** Indeed, in order to construct these different bodies, it was necessary for divine consciousness to "lose itself" momentarily in total concentration on the three bodies, and to forget its primary source. The force prevailing at that time was the gravitational pull towards matter, and these energy units had no choice but to follow its course—such was the prevailing order of things. This is how the lower mind, in particular, was constructed (that part of the mind which belongs to the personality), with basic primary mechanisms fulfilling the requirements of the process of involution. The goal was to ensure the immediate survival of the personality, until the time came for a renewed link-up with divine wisdom via the higher mind and the soul. These requirements, as it turns out, have generated those primary mechanisms which we are all too familiar with: fear, separativeness, the quest for power, the pursuit of pleasure, selfishness, materialism, denial of our spiritual nature, etc. So there is nothing bad about these mechanisms per se: they were essential for the construction and survival of the ego during the whole period of descent. On the other hand, what was once a necessity for involution is now an obstacle to evolution.[7]

Diagram 2
Involution–Evolution

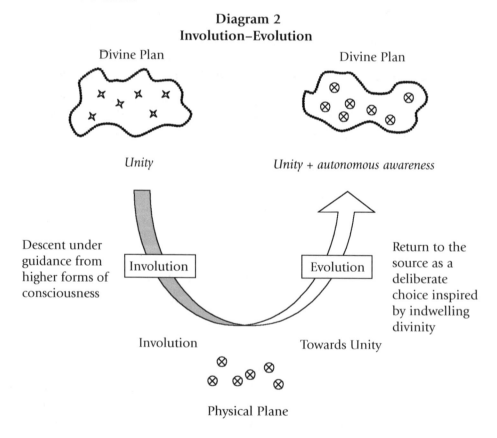

Divine Plan

Divine Plan

Unity

Unity + autonomous awareness

Descent under guidance from higher forms of consciousness

Involution

Evolution

Return to the source as a deliberate choice inspired by indwelling divinity

Involution

Towards Unity

Physical Plane

◆ The process of evolution

Eighteen million years ago, the process of involution was reaching the point of completion while the process of evolution, the return to our divine essence, was set in motion. Considering the billions of years of involution, this event is a relatively recent one in the history of humanity, even if it seems extremely remote by human standards.

The goal of the process of evolution is to allow these units, whose consciousness has descended down to the level of matter taken from the three worlds, to explore this level with increasing awareness in order to gain complete mastery over the physical, emotional and mental worlds, to bring concrete manifestations of divine consciousness into them, and to recover a perfect state of <u>freedom</u> within these three worlds.

We have quite a way to go yet in order to reach this goal. In fact the dynamics of evolution have only just begun to take effect. We are still subjected to the powerful gravitational pull of matter, and feeling separate from one another. In order to recover our unity and freedom, we will have to meet the following challenges:

- **Set our self free from the gravitational pull of matter,** which served to build the ego, with the lower mind as an instrument. The workings of the lower mind, which is not connected to the Self, are based on a set of primary functions that fostered the involutionary movement towards the world of matter, and are at the root of human behaviours such as described in Chapter 2. From this perspective, it becomes much easier to understand the mechanism of the lower mind and its effects on day-to-day experience, which we will explore in greater detail in the next chapter. This new level of understanding will enable us to dispel the sense of guilt which has become culturally embedded as a result of religious and/or moral teachings, and thus to initiate a more rapid and more effective process of conscious transformation;

- **Recover our divine essence,** which had to be "forgotten" during the process of building our instrument of manifestation;

- **Develop autonomous awareness** so that the process of evolution can be set in motion through a **deliberately chosen** thrust on our part.

Individuation and free will

A major factor (a rule of the game, so to speak) comes into play at that moment. Indeed the process of evolution—the return to divinity—can only occur through the exercise of free will on the part of all these units. It could be said that God, in an act of pure love, gave these particles of Himself total freedom to recover their own divinity and return to Him. As this great consciousness explores the world of matter, these units, which represent it, can thus decide, in no other way but of their own free will, to return to their divine essence and thus achieve the union of spirit and matter, in accordance with the divine Plan.

This is the reason why, eighteen million years ago, as the process of involution was drawing to an end and the process of evolution was being initiated, human beings went through a process of individuation. This process mostly involved the lower mind, separating human beings even more as entities, which nevertheless remained endowed with divine consciousness as well as with the ability to develop complete freedom of choice. Thus liberated from any collective divine tutorship, human beings then began to work on developing complete autonomy.

This apparent separation from divinity and from each other was necessary for us to have total freedom of choice with regard to reconnecting with the divine in-dweller in all of us and manifesting this divinity in the world of matter.[8]

Esoteric science offers a very precise description of this process of individuation. Let us simply mention that this freedom of choice was granted to the human race at the moment when the connection was sufficiently established between the three bodies of the Self and the three bodies of the personality, via the mind. This is where we are now. Throughout the process of involution, "mankind" gathered all the necessary material to construct its instrument, the ego. At the moment of individuation, human beings were granted the freedom to use the latter as they saw fit, in order to experience the physical world, and on the basis of such experiences, to complete the building process and then gain mastery of the instrument in order to foster the manifestation of the Self. During the process of involution, mankind had to **focus its consciousness on the construction of the ego;** in the course of the process of evolution, which is now taking place, mankind will be impelled by the force of evolution to **refocus its consciousness on the Self,** with its divine vibration. This new impulse makes us want to disengage our consciousness from the bonds of ego so that it can become strictly an instrument of divine Will, via the Self.

Eighteen million years ago, human beings thus found themselves endowed with an instrument, which is quite similar to the one we now have, only less developed physically, emotionally and mentally. Since then, we have had to perfect this instrument in order to increase our knowledge and mastery of this world, thus getting ready to take responsibility for our destiny and our actions.

The forces of evolution

From the outset, what is it that moves human beings towards learning to use free will in the direction of evolution? The answer, of course, is suffering. It would be nice to have a more pleasant answer to this question, but such is not the case. However, this awareness leads us to the realization that suffering is not unavoidable. We have the option either to remain caught up in those ego forces that keep us mired in the world of matter, which generate suffering, or to make the effort of deliberately elevating the vibrational frequency of our consciousness, of learning to master the three lower aspects of our personality vehicle, and thus gain access once again to the happiness, freedom and power that are part of our divine nature. As we become more and more aware of the fact that our personality mechanisms are a source of suffering and loss of freedom, we gradually come to the point of choosing the dynamic of the Self. Thus our stay on earth is akin to attending a school for the development of intelligence and wisdom. And the more we develop these qualities, the less we need the proddings of suffering to motivate us to advance along the road to a full manifestation of the soul.

Diagram 3
Humanity today
Both dynamics (involution-evolution) remain active.

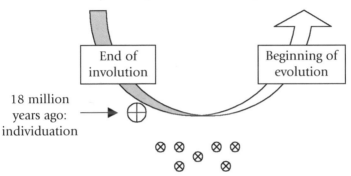

◆ Modern times—a crucial moment in human history

Our day-to-day problems, our lack of mastery as well as our personal and collective limitations stem from the fact that we are still in a transition period where the growth process is being reversed: involution is ending, while evolution has begun.

Eighteen million years ago, the process of involution did not suddenly come to a standstill in order to make way for the process of evolution. As we have already noted, eighteen million years is a relatively short period of time in the history of human consciousness, and **we are still in the period of inversion of the process**. The forces of attraction drawing us towards matter are weakening though they remain active, while the forces drawing us back towards divinity are also active, yet far from having reached their full intensity. We are at a very unique juncture in human history, as we find our self in the middle of a major course change, from a descent into the world of matter to an ascent towards a renewed expression of divinity. If we look at any other similar dynamic in nature, there is a moment of inertia, which translates into a great deal of tension, as when an airplane flying at treetop level noses up towards the sky. This inversion requires a large amount of energy, and that is where we are at this point. This explains the great tension, which can be felt in all areas of human endeavour on the planet, and the battle that seems to rage between "good" and "evil". There is neither good nor evil; there are simply two opposite dynamics which are presently juxtaposed: one (involution) which has come to the end of its course since its goal has been achieved (the descent into the world of matter); the other (evolution) which is taking off with increasing power and momentum (the return to divinity, having mastered and "divinised" matter, and gained autonomous awareness).

It is therefore pointless to lament over "paradise lost" or over the lost wisdom of ancient traditions, which seem to us endowed with more wisdom, more spiritual knowledge and more power than our own (oriental, native, Atlantean, cabbalistic traditions, etc.). These very inspired traditions were needed to guide and support humanity for a time. But our apparent momentary loss of wisdom was totally appropriate in order to allow us to learn what we needed to learn, particularly in the area of mastering our higher mental faculties. Esoteric teachings are reassuring on this point as they emphasize what needs to be learned during this day and age, when the lower mind seems to have taken over with its flock of miseries. We are now ready to reconnect with this wisdom and this ancient knowledge, by integrating it within a broader experience of awareness, which involves, among other things, the need for each of us to turn to his/her own soul, our indwelling Master, for guidance.

Certainly, along the path of evolution, even though we are no longer under the automatic guidance of "the gods", we still need genuine teachers to inspire us, to help us discover our hidden potentialities, to point us towards the right path. But these teachers do not impose any form of authority whatsoever. Such genuine teachers suggest and inspire while allowing each person the freedom and responsibility to discover his/her own truth. Of course we are still influenced by the fallout from the dynamics of involution, which produces systems based on the authority of one or several individuals, systems that are still attractive to those who do not want to take responsibility for their life. These systems exist in a wide variety of forms, from cults where a pseudo-spiritual "Master" is surrounded with a blissful and submissive group of devotees, right down to the immense power of influence exerted by the media which, for the most part, program people to behave like sheep, in a state of passive apathy, while grinding individual creativity down to nothing. These systems are headed for a rapidly accelerating rate of extinction, as the process of evolution gains momentum and mankind develops wisdom, intelligence and discernment as a result of securing a more and more constant direct contact with the soul.

Nothing happens without a reason, and we will have gained something from our journey through the darkness of the lower mind. We will be able to experience this ancient knowledge with a far more sophisticated level of mastery, in ways that will manifest an even deeper level of integration. There has been no mistake, only a long journey with many twists and turns, some of which might perhaps have been avoided. But the fact that they have not been avoided can only yield an even more fulfilling experience of our collective psyche.

Such is the history (or experience, if we want to avoid speaking in terms of a time continuum) of the journey of consciousness through the construction of a vehicle which has allowed us to experience the world of matter to this day, to read these words, and to continue with our exploration. We are now coming to a crucial moment in this building process, where the collective consciousness of humanity has reached a point of development such that a number of individuals now have the opportunity, by making a deliberate choice, to re-establish a more complete and open connection with their soul. They will thus have a more and more refined instrument with which to manifest the will of "God" on Earth. As this happens, they will give humanity a powerful thrust resulting in a collective shift in the direction of evolution, of a common, concrete manifestation of divine energy in all its beauty, its fullness and its boundless love.

We are therefore now in a very unique situation: we have not yet fully recovered our connection with our original source, our Self. Our consciousness is still mired in our ego, which we are trying to master even as it keeps us bound to the dynamics of involution, yet an inner force is pushing us into the opposite dynamics of evolution. Indeed, besides suffering, what compels us to move on in our quest is the memory of a divine source of freedom and joy, a deep conscious or unconscious desire to re-enter that state of grace which was ours at the start of this great journey, and which we had to temporarily move away from. Eventually, when it is fully achieved, this union will most certainly bring mankind to a great cosmic orgasm!!!

This process of separation and identification with the world of matter, which was needed in the context of involution, is the reason, in particular, for the almost hypnotic attraction that material objects still exert on human consciousness. The ego's need for possessions, coupled with our identification with material things, produces an exaggerated sense of the importance of the physical world. Thus we see individuals spend their entire life working very hard to earn money, which they then spend on material things: make house renovations (or dream of them), buy a new car, a new lawn mower, a stereo set, a fancier bed, upgrade their secondary residence, their cookware, etc. Their energy is almost entirely invested in material concerns. The kind of over-consumption of goods that we see in large commercial centres is an expression of this collective hypnosis.

Yet on the ego level, we just can't help our self: it's our nature. Only through the energy of the soul can we hope to liberate our self from this influence, to achieve that state of "detachment" mentioned by so many spiritual teachers. We are in a better position now to understand the source of that attachment. Here again, there is no right or wrong, just an evolutionary process that we would do well to speed up if we want to bring an end to our suffering and recover a state of peace and freedom.

This course change in the evolution of consciousness also explains why so many individuals are now striving to define a new set of so-called spiritual "values". When we are involved in a process of inner inquiry—because we sense that there has to be a better source of satisfaction than the material world—what we are actually doing is intuitively responding to the process of evolution which is being activated more and more intensely for all mankind.

This perspective also leads to a better understanding of the hurdles we may encounter in our desire to achieve a higher level of mastery in our life. We have a clearer perception of why so many individuals have tried for so long to "find" God, why vast numbers of people are seeking a more open and authentic experience of life, either within a traditional context or outside of any philosophical or religious affiliation. Conversely, we can also see why so many people are still caught in a narrowly materialistic level of awareness, a remnant of the process of involution. This is a natural movement of human consciousness, whereby old mechanisms are being cast aside in order to proceed towards building a concrete world of peace, justice, abundance and freedom for all human beings on this planet.

With this new understanding, what can we do in concrete terms in order to be rid once and for all of the influence of involutionary forces, and to speed up the process of evolution towards divine manifestation? What can we do to free our self from limiting behaviours such as those described in Chapter 2, and get back in touch more quickly with our "divine" essence, thus clearing the path toward genuine well-being? As we consider our situation in a broader context than that of "good and evil" or that of a self-centred pursuit of personal well-being, we will empower our self to find concrete and conscious means to speed up the work of discarding the bonds of ego. This, in a very real way, will be a positive thrust towards making one of our innermost dreams come true: that of living free, in a world of beauty, abundance and love.

The work initiated at the time of individuation is far from finished. In the course of the next few centuries, we will be able to speed up this work and bring it to the point of completion. To this end, two things must be accomplished:

- Continue to perfect and to **master the three lower bodies** so that they become a well-coordinated, flexible and efficient instrument for the manifestation of the Self. This is done by developing the higher mind (intelligence, intuition, capacity for creative thinking and objective observation), while at the same time working on deactivating the mechanisms of the lower mind (mastering the emotional body). Indeed the latter is loaded with past memories and unable to control the emotional body, thus limiting an individual's consciousness to a machine-like state, as we will see in the next chapter. (The coachman must learn to stay in touch with the Master, and to control the horse in an appropriate fashion.)

- Link up **the ego and the Self.** With a well-built, receptive and coordinated ego, build a reliable and strong enough connection so that the personality can tune in to the will of the Self, which is the perfect instrument of the will of the original Great Spirit. This is also achieved by putting the lower mind in its proper place, defusing inadequate knee-jerk responses, and developing the higher mind since the latter is the bridge between the soul and the personality. It will thus become possible for Divinity to manifest its will in concrete ways in the world of matter, the physical world, and the great process will have reached its goal.

In very broad terms, these "tasks" are a summary of the program in which any authentic spiritual seeker is involved. As one can see, this process can be presented in a far broader perspective than that provided in the context of religious systems (which are not excluded), and it can be used as a fusion of all forms of human inquiry (scientific, artistic, religious, psychological, ethical, philosophical, etc.)

To get a better grasp of the present general state of consciousness, it might be helpful to take a closer look at how the ego—the personality—was built since the time of individuation. How did we get to this aggregate of physical, emotional and mental components? What has happened since the moment when human beings became individuals? As we observe how the building process developed up until now, it will be easier for us to understand **why human beings are structured as they are today,** and what specific work remains to be done.

Building the Self's Instrument of Manifestation from the Beginning of Individuation to the Present

Or, from the perspective of esoteric tradition, how we bring our history with us; how both the treasures of acquired wisdom, and the hang-ups stemming from a past which has yet to be mastered, remain with us as we proceed along our evolutionary path.

◆ **General principle: successive descents into the physical world**

Since the time of individuation, mankind has been working on the progressive construction and alignment of the ego through a specific process, which mainly unfolds through a series of "journeys" into the world of matter, a series of successive "lifetimes".[9] Through these forays into the three worlds, we keep perfecting our instrument for the expression of the will of the Self.[10]

As we complete each journey, we gain more knowledge and mastery, and bring along some very useful baggage, and some that is downright useless and cumbersome (hang-ups, negative memories, failures, suffering, etc.) as well as aspects that have yet to be mastered.

The fact that we have the opportunity to make several journeys into the world of matter, rather than just one, in order to construct and perfect our instrument and its alignment with the soul, has become more widely accepted in our collective consciousness over the last few decades. "Reincarnation" is the term used in reference to this phenomenon. Though it is gaining widespread recognition, this phenomenon needs some clarification, as there is still a great deal of confusion surrounding this issue.

What is it that actually reincarnates?

In simple terms, let us be clear on the fact that it is not the ego that reincarnates. With each reincarnation, the former personality is dissolved and the Self rebuilds another one that is completely different from all previously experienced personalities, in order to perfect its instrument. It is true that past life experiences will have a bearing on the constitution of the new personality, in the sense that what was gained through preceding incarnations will be used, but not in the sense of any continuum on the personality level. We are immortal at the level of the Self, but quite mortal in terms of our personality, and, to the extent that we remain identified with our personality, we will in fact pass away. Pity, just when we thought we might have found a great theory to reassure our ego.[11]

In this context, therefore, we will view the phenomenon of "reincarnation" as being **the process of constructing our instrument for the manifestation of the Self in the three worlds, rather than as an illusion of permanence for the ego.**

In order to avoid this pitfall, where the ego can easily stray, some spiritual traditions simply refuse to dwell on past lives, though they implicitly recognize reincarnation as a matter of course. They refer to the latter as a return to universal consciousness, after each "death", where material that needs to be worked on is selected not on the basis of personal experience, but from the collective treasury of experience belonging to humanity as a whole. There is some truth to this approach, which has the advantage of making it easier to avoid ego identification, for indeed the ego does not reincarnate. We would prefer an even more global perspective, which includes both the aspect of "individual" lives (from the viewpoint of the soul) and the possibility of drawing from the totality of human experience.

Based on our observation, it would seem that it is initially quite helpful to view things from the perspective of "individual" successive lifetimes. Indeed, each unit is responsible for working on its own transformation. This angle makes it easier to identify with the soul, since the latter draws from the sum of experiences accumulated by the different personalities. If we reject the perspective of a series of individual "lifetimes", we automatically sidestep any possibility that we might engage in inner work aimed specifically at what needs to be done on the level of the unconscious. There are pitfalls to be avoided on many different levels, and it is important to remain vigilant so as not to reinforce the personality, so that we can in fact make it less rigid, and make our own detachment from it easier to achieve.

All that is needed is to simply avoid taking these lifetimes "personally", at the ego level: these different lifetimes do not belong to our present personality, but to our soul, as part of the material it has to work with. And since, at the soul level, we are not separate from one another, we cannot really say that these lives are our own. Both approaches eventually converge into what seems like a paradox, as is always the case when we attempt to describe reality at the soul level, rather than at the ordinary mind level, with its obvious limitations; the reality of the Self can hardly be described through concepts belonging to the personality. Yet once we have integrated the paradox, what remains is the fundamental reality that the soul is building an instrument through successive experiences in the world of matter. **These lives are not us: they are merely experiences of our Self.** On the other hand, we have a responsibility to do something with these experiences.

We shall now describe how the three bodies are perfected through the experience of "successive" lifetimes. This will allow us to have a clearer grasp of what, in fact, goes through the process of reincarnation, and what disappears once and for all. What follows is a simple presentation that is nevertheless adequate for our purposes.

◆ The dissolution of the three bodies

At the end of any given lifetime, the physical body "dies", as we all clearly know. We also know that the substance or matter constituting this body disintegrates and becomes absorbed as earth matter. The physical body is thus completely destroyed. At that moment, according to materialistic science, we have disappeared for good. And indeed it is true that the physical body has disappeared for good.

However the consciousness, which dwells in that body has not ceased to exist. In fact, after leaving the physical body, the soul's consciousness continues to have experiences on the emotional plane (also called the astral plane) as well as the mental plane. "We" thus continue to exist, for a while, in the astral world, with all the thoughts and emotions we had during the physical lifetime from which we have just departed. The body of our personality is then made only of emotional and mental matter.

Then comes the time to leave the emotional world, having done what was needed at that level. We are now "dead" to this emotional world, we depart from our emotional body which then merges with universal astral matter, much as the physical body merges with universal physical matter upon physical death.

We then find our self existing only in the mental world. The process is the same as for the previous levels: after some time spent having experiences at this level, we depart from our mental body, which then merges with universal mental matter, and we now find our self at the level of the soul. The personality, which was used by the Self as a medium of experience, has now completely dissolved. The ego has died and will never reappear as it once was. What remains then of the journey through this lifetime that has just ended? Where, at what level is there some form of continuity?

◆ Permanent atoms

When our consciousness departs from the physical/etheric body, all the information related to this body's experiences in the course of this recently terminated lifetime is recorded in a unit of consciousness called a *permanent atom* (or *seed atom*, according to tradition). This permanent atom is transferred into what is left of the personality at the emotional and mental levels. The process is then repeated, in turn, at both of these levels as well: when our consciousness departs from our astral and mental bodies, it takes with it permanent atoms that carry the essence of our experience at the emotional and mental levels. When the personality is completely disintegrated and its indwelling consciousness has fully returned to the Self, what remains is these three permanent atoms in which the Self can access all the information related to the accumulated experiences of this lifetime in the three worlds. This is then added to the experiences gleaned over past lifetimes.

At that moment, the Self takes stock, so to speak, of what has and has not been mastered, of the ability or inability of its instrument to manifest its will in the three worlds. On this basis, it also determines what "lessons" remain to be learned and selects an appropriate time and sets the conditions for the recreation of a new instrument in a context that is conducive to further learning. This is a complex process, which occurs more or less consciously, depending on the level of evolution attained thus far. So it is not the form (whether physical, emotional or mental) that reincarnates, **it is not our latest personality that reincarnates, since it no longer exists**. The Self simply constructs another instrument, in the light of past experiences, another "personality" to undergo a new set of experiences. The latter is not completely independent of previous personalities, since it is based on all the learning acquired thus far, on all the aspects of consciousness, which have already been developed, on all the lessons learned or missed.

◆ How successive personalities were built

What we call "a descent into a new incarnation" is in fact merely the reconstruction of a new instrument. First of all, the Self projects its consciousness into the mental world and attracts material based on mental matter that will be integrated into the new personality. This material is not attracted by chance: it is a function of all the experience and knowledge—sometimes mastered, sometimes not—that was accumulated in the mental worlds. It will thus include some aspects of the former personality as well as previous personalities, plus some collective aspects, as the case may be. All of this mental material, on the one hand, is refined through the whole process of integration which occurred at the level of the Self, and, on the other hand, is selected on the basis of what the Self deems appropriate as a learning program for the lifetime that is about to begin. We therefore do not necessarily carry with us all of the material from the lifetime that has just ended. The essence of the experience of this lifetime is blended with the essence of the experience of all kinds of other lives: our own, and as the case may be, that of other souls. This creates a very different potential from what was available to us in our former lives.

Once this process is completed, our consciousness descends into the astral plane and, through a similar process of energetic attraction, pulls together all of the emotional material that will prove useful to the new personality; this material is also attracted as a function of the essence of past emotional experiences and of what the Self wants its instrument to work on in the course of this next incarnation.

The same process will occur at the physical/etheric level, especially when it comes to parent selection. The Self "chooses"[13] the parents through whom this soon-to-be-incarnated being will be able to gain a physical/etheric body (along with specific genetic baggage) that is in keeping with the essence of all the experiences that this being has encountered in the past on the level of the physical/etheric body, as well as with all that this being needs to learn in this new lifetime. The process of choosing parents therefore does not occur at the level of the personality, but rather at the level of the Self, which has its own requirements based on its own program.

By the way, this process of "choosing" parents comes into play not only at the level of putting together a physical/etheric body, but also at the level of the material constituting the other bodies as well. Indeed, during the intense parent-child interactions that will take place throughout childhood, the parents' emotional and mental make-up will have a major impact on the development of the child's character. This, of course, is taken into consideration when parents are chosen, as well as the positive karmic relationships and negative karmic bonds that need to be resolved.

Thus a being's physical birth is endowed with a relatively well-defined potential, at the mental, emotional and physical level, resulting from the integration, by the Self, of all past experiences as well as experiences that have yet to be encountered in this new lifetime. This potential carries all the conscious realizations, the positive wealth of acquired knowledge on the level of physical, emotional and mental mastery: a whole dynamic of mastery that the Self will be able to use directly to manifest its will on the worldly plane. This constitutes the part of the ego that is flexible, intelligent, creative, free and serene, and that makes it an effective instrument. On the other hand, since the process of evolution is not yet completed, **this being also carries with it those parts of the ego that are still at a low stage of development or that have solidified or become blocked as a result of past experiences.**

Indeed, the process of building the ego with its three bodies is a complex one that develops according to natural laws, not in a linear rational manner, but rather through successive approximations.[14] A useful comparison could be drawn with the construction of a house. The house is the flexible and transparent personality we want to build as a dwelling for our soul. But as we build, there is a gradual accumulation of debris, excess materials, dust, empty paint cans, etc. There are some finished parts and others that are built but have yet to be tidied up.

What this means is that we now possess a certain number of positive experiences in terms of knowledge and wisdom, from which we derive some degree of mastery in the three worlds (some parts of the house are beautiful, clean and well-built: this is our "light" side). But we also still carry a heavy load of unused materials and psychological garbage as a by-product of the construction process itself. From these parts of the ego spring our lack of mastery, as well as all our suffering and limitations.

Thus, through our experience in the world of matter, we have developed knowledge and a certain level of mastery, but at the same time we have accumulated a whole slew of unintegrated experiences, blocks, and defence mechanisms that separate us even more from one another. These are recorded at the lower mind level, which builds its operating system on the basis of these defence mechanisms. This is why it is so important to defuse the emotionally charged memories of the lower mind.

This perspective allows us to better understand how the lower mind and the general mechanisms of the personality work, and we will examine this in the following chapters, along with the typical human behaviours that we can observe today, as these are but the expression of whatever level of awareness has been attained. We will see, in particular, the extent to which these non-integrated memories, these hardened defence mechanisms (this non-recycled garbage), condition our behaviour on a daily basis. Yet the belief that we are the outcome of our past is a major misconception prevailing in certain contemporary psychological approaches, and which we now have a good opportunity to dispel.

◆ We are not the outcome of our past

Contrary to the claims we find in certain psychological theories, which tend to explain everything in terms of a linear stream of cause and effect, and notwithstanding the fact that we are talking about "evolution", we are not the outcome of our past. The behaviour of some individuals may tempt us to think along these lines, but this is a superficial outlook, which gives us little chance of liberating our self in any real sense. As we will see further on in this book, the past conditions the structures of the ego, and thus the behaviour of most people who are hung up in these structures, but the ego is not the essence of a human being. This distinction is of primary significance, for it will influence our whole approach to inner work as well as the effectiveness of this work. **The past conditions our instrument of expression, not the source of our being.**

We have chosen to start from the premise that the very essence of a human being, what is truly ours, is the soul, a higher, perfect divine consciousness. In essence, we are all free and divine beings: this is what we have always been since the dawn of time and will be for all eternity. We are not the outcome of our past. On the other hand, our instrument of manifestation, as it evolves through each

> To say that we are the outcome of our past is like mistaking the instrument for the owner of the instrument.

incarnation, is to some extent a product of our past, a product of what we have learned. To identify our self with our ego is to forget that we are essentially a soul.

If we as human beings often behave in ways that are not very intelligent, or down-right discordant and destructive, if we seem unable to live each day at peace with our self and with others, it is not because we are imperfect or incomplete, it is simply because our expression of our inner divinity in the physical world is undermined by the limitations of our instrument which is, for the time being, imperfect and incomplete.

Our past has given us the opportunity to build our instrument, yet at the same time, because the building process is not yet completed, it is the yoke that prevents us, at this stage, from freely manifesting our divine nature in the three worlds. It is during this process of building and learning that we acquired these limitations, and momentarily lost sight of who we really are, precisely as a result of ego identification. This was part of the plan. What we need to do now is to move on to the next stage. To this end, we must now start from a perspective where the essence of our being is recognized as being independent of time, and where the ego is put in its proper place.

Many of us have now reached the stage where the point of identification of our consciousness is changing, as our personality has reached an advanced stage of construction. But, as is the case in home construction, in order to be able to fully enjoy its benefits, we have to do some housekeeping along the way and get rid of the garbage. We will need to eliminate debris such as the psychological blocks and defence mechanisms we have accumulated during our learning process, and which are now a hindrance to further progress. Otherwise, though it may be well-built, this beautiful home will remain unusable because of all the useless piles of building materials, the scaffolding that blocks the entranceways, the old broken tools left strewn on the floor, the dust and the rubbish cluttering every room. This trash prevents us from fully enjoying our acquired knowledge. It also prevents us from moving ahead in the building process, for when there is too much trash lying around, it becomes impossible to work.[15] If we take the trouble to remove the debris, knowing that something very beautiful lays hidden underneath it all, we know what we are doing, and we quickly rediscover and let loose the wonders we had already built into our home.

However, this outlook should not translate into a denial of the past, of our shadow, such as we find in some New Age spiritual approaches. Indeed another seed of confusion often takes root here, whereby we say that all is well, since we are perfect and divine, and we overlook the fact that there is some serious tidying up to be done. This is yet another way for the ego to appropriate and interpret truth to its own advantage. This attitude leads one to avoid the work involved in inner liberation while deluding oneself into thinking this is some form of spiritual practice. Our day-to-day experience does not support this perspective; our behaviours are far from divine. Though we are perfect in essence, we also have an instrument of manifestation that is still under construction, that still needs to be set free from the limitations of the past, if we truly want to manifest our divinity in any concrete manner.

We do not become enlightened by imagining beings of light,
but by making the darkness conscious.
—Carl G. Jung

To continue with the previously used analogy, the purpose of this book is to foster a clearer understanding of the structure and of the present state of our instrument (the home), and to clear the way for the arrival of the real owner. In particular, we will observe all this accumulated debris left over from our past, determine its place in our psyche and try to understand the way it works, so that we can get rid of it more quickly, or better still, find a way to recycle it. We will then be able to give our soul a nice home, so that it can dwell in this world and bring to it the full radiance of its joy, its love and its beauty.

◆ The collective aspect of evolution

Another clarification is needed here so that the following chapters can be more fully understood. Though we may appear to perceive each individual's evolution as being independent of others, the truth of the matter is that things are not that simple. We will approach the process from this angle, for it allows each individual to take responsibility for some stages he or she needs to go through, and for specific work that needs to be done. On the other hand, let us not forget that we are all intimately connected, in essence, and that our individual history will have to make way at some point for greater involvement in the evolution of a more universal consciousness. In reality, humanity is progressing collectively, and each of us carries all of the experiences of all other human beings. We will have to take this into consideration at a more elaborate level.

Yet this aspect naturally emerges when the time is right, and there is no point in rushing into things. In order for the process of transformation to occur in any real sense (not just in the form of vague hopes or intellectual theories), in order to dig deep and manifest this transformation in the form of action in this world, it is helpful to start with our history as we perceive it at an individual level (which does not necessarily translate into separation, the way the ego would tend to interpret this). This is just an indispensable first step that is often overlooked in a number of spiritual practices.

Based on observations emerging from my own personal experiences and those of many people involved in advanced consciousness work, when an individual takes full responsibility for his/her own destiny, becomes aware of his/her own inner structures, both conscious and unconscious, and gains enough mastery over them, a window on the collective consciousness natural opens up. He/she begins to experience a more universal dimension of consciousness and, rather than turn this experience into an ego inflating disconnection from reality, will want to make an even more significant concrete contribution in the real world. We are no longer in the realm of theory, nor is this a transcendental experience that is disconnected from reality. This is a practical experience of the expansion of individual awareness into collective awareness. But we must reach the point where we have defined, constructed and liberated our individual aspect, which paradoxically will foster our detachment from individuality, before we can experience this expansion. There is no contradiction in this, quite the contrary: this is the core of our work. If this stage is not adequately completed, we run the risk of getting lost in vain fantasies and philosophies, in states of awareness that are disconnected from reality, and, finally, of wasting our potential for personal and collective transformation.[16]

When an individual manages to fully establish a connection with the soul through personal work, he/she then recovers a full measure of power and freedom, while at the same time becoming an antenna so that the rest of humanity can make this transition more quickly and easily. At that point, through a natural dynamic that we will explore in detail further on in this book,[17] the person becomes not only an agent of transformation for his/her own individual consciousness (for the latter, while in contact with the soul, undergoes a transformation and expansion such that the very concept of individuality becomes obsolete), but also an agent of transformation for the collective consciousness of humanity. As we work on our own transformation, we are simultaneously working for all those brothers and sisters who, for some reason or other, do not necessarily have the opportunity to do this work.

We shall therefore approach this work from the angle of individual transformation. Nevertheless, even though this subject may seem to be focused on each individual's personal history, we shall never lose sight of the fact that this is not just about individual salvation, freedom and power, but ultimately about liberation for all humanity, for there can be no salvation that is strictly individual.

The Motivations that Prompt Us to Inner Inquiry

Driven by this great force of evolution, mankind is advancing towards a radical change in collective consciousness, a change that will take us from the kingdom of Man (the fourth kingdom of nature) to the kingdom of the Spirit (the fifth kingdom of nature). Though we use the term "spiritual", we are not referring to any specific religion. True, all religions have worked more or less effectively on awakening our spiritual nature. The basic principles of any religion are certainly helpful within the context of spiritual inquiry, as they are generally excellent in essence and ultimately point to the same truth. At this level, all religions are one; they are united in that they reflect a desire to help us find our true nature as a spiritual being.

Unfortunately, these religions have become biased to a very large extent by the human mind in terms of presentation and form, and have been subject to serious appropriation by our separative ego, so that what should have led to our liberation from ego bonds has often ended up reinforcing these bonds. Given the level of awareness of mankind at the time, this is hardly surprising. We have certainly learned many lessons along the often-tortuous paths of the world's great religions.

Consequently, as we engage in spiritual practice in the present context, we can appreciate the value of these religions without necessarily subscribing to any one in particular. In the light of esoteric science, we can develop an understanding of our spiritual nature and of our destiny without getting involved in any dogma, and we can put all previous religious or spiritual teachings together in a broader perspective.

Putting aside all religious teachings or esoteric knowledge, the process of evolution is being accelerated to such an extent nowadays that vast numbers of people are seeking a more fundamental core around which to build their lives. They seek to bring meaning to their existence, beyond mere survival and acquisition of material goods. This is fertile ground for genuine transformation. While there are a great variety of reasons that might motivate us to engage in this process, the fundamental reason is that we are responding more or less consciously to pressure from our soul, as it demands an outlet through which to manifest itself more fully.

Sometimes we are propelled into a process of inner inquiry when our life falls apart. Nothing is working anymore in our relationships, which are becoming increasingly difficult (spouse, family, work environment), in our job, which seems more and more devoid of meaning (we are no longer satisfied with mere subsistence work), and in our physical body, which is prone to lack of energy and illness. In some cases it takes the form of a crisis in a particular aspect of our life, while in others everything seems to crumble all at once. These moments of tension are not necessarily a bad sign—quite the contrary, in fact. These are often the warnings of the soul, designed to wake us out of our slumber, out of this relatively comfortable stupor nurtured by a materialistic environment that turns human beings into automatons, so that we can reclaim our creative power and our freedom. The moment the soul awakens in us, it can no longer tolerate that we live our life like robots, locked into outdated mechanisms and manipulated by the powers that be. It demands that we reclaim our power and freedom, and if we do not awaken willingly, it sends us these times of crisis, which are actually blessings in disguise even though, at the time, they may seem very painful to endure.[18] It is important to look at such times of trial from this angle, and avoid blocking the process by trying to put our self back to sleep and going back to our ordinary ways, for it is pointless to resist the force of evolution that is presently gaining momentum among all of us. This is the reason why a growing number of people are looking inward for answers in order to bring harmony and a more authentic sense of existence back into their lives.[19]

Sometimes there is not necessarily any need for a crisis, and we initially seek the experience of inner transformation simply because we are no longer really satisfied with our ordinary life. We feel as if something essential is missing even if, or especially if, on the material plane, everything seems to be going well. In fact, it is often when we have mastered our ordinary life to some extent that the real work begins: that is when we realize in concrete terms that genuine happiness and freedom go beyond what mere materialistic concerns and relative comforts can provide. Thus, initially, a feeling creeps in that we have yet to address some essential issues in life. This feeling of dissatisfaction is eminently positive and beneficial, for it shakes us out of the collective state of hypnosis generated by the materialistic addiction that characterizes our world. We then begin to seek out and confront these essential issues.

This feeling grows as an individual evolves. There is intensified pressure from the soul, compelling us to pursue our quest through any means available to us. Up until now, those who clearly felt this inner calling were few in numbers. Nowadays the collective spiritual pressure of the soul, fostered by all those individuals who have already blazed trails towards self-realization, has reached a level of such intensity that growing numbers of people are feeling this inner calling, with varying degrees of clarity. This explains why we see this awakening of consciousness taking place everywhere in the world, and manifesting itself slowly but surely in all areas of human endeavour—be it political, social, economic, medical, or educational—and in the rising public interest in a great variety of activities which deal more or less in depth with personal growth and subtle realities, such as courses, workshops, training sessions, books, and publications. This is experienced with varying degrees of awareness, of course, but it is a sure sign that all of humanity is seeking for a way out of constricting materialism. We are about to find our way towards a greater level of awareness…a greater level of freedom.

Afterwards, we may notice that we are less and less motivated by personal interest; as we tap into the energy of the soul; the desire to contribute becomes our profound natural motivation for this inner process. We spontaneously seek to help others, to create original work, to manifest beauty and love in a concrete fashion, through **service to humanity**. This is now done, even at the cost of personal discomfort, in a free and joyful spirit of dedication, which allows the soul to take an even more active part in the manifestation of the "kingdom of God" on Earth.

This perspective is important, since it allows us right away to avoid the pitfall of "spiritual selfishness" ("I am concerned with my own growth, and the only thing that matters is my own spiritual self-realization."), which contradicts the very process of evolution and thwarts any subsequent work we may do. However we must also be careful to avoid "spiritual pride" ("I am spiritually ahead of the game, and I have a great mission to fulfil in the world."), or "spiritual guilt" ("I should be a better person."). These distortions stem from the ego and its attempt to reclaim the process of inner inquiry for its own advantage.

Nevertheless, even in these mistaken attitudes, there is a grain of truth. Indeed, working on one's own spiritual transformation is, in a sense, the only thing we can do. We cannot take anyone else's place and do their work for them, for they have their own path as well as the spiritual responsibility that they have chosen for themselves. We can be an inspiration, an example and a supportive role model for them, but each individual must advance through his/her own personal efforts.

A great musician can be an inspiration for music students, and a good teacher can provide a good measure of support, yet the student will have to put in hours of personal practice if he/she is ever to master the instrument and create beautiful music. In addition, each of us has a particular musical score to play in the great orchestra of humanity: the pianist does not play the part of the cellist. Musicians can offer support and encouragement to one another during practice sessions, but when the time comes to play, each is responsible for his/her own score. And if we play our part well, it will make a difference in the overall musical performance. We can take this a step further when we deal with transformation. Indeed, as we are all part of a great collective consciousness, there comes a point where our own virtuosity allows other musicians to achieve perfection more quickly. We will examine this dynamic further on in this book. Thus there will come a time when, thanks to each individual's personal work and everyone's mutual help, the music we create on this planet will be marvellous indeed. Our focus will be on playing beautiful music, rather than on who gets the spot as first violin or who plays the clarinet. At that moment, we will be happy each in our own place.

By the way, the most evolved people are not the ones who brag the most about following a spiritual path, far from it. We may encounter people who are spiritually very awake in all walks of life, and they often have no notion of taking part in a major transformation of consciousness. Yet these are all people who are making a concrete contribution, in one form or another, to the welfare of humanity, whether they be artists expressing beauty through their creations, scientists conducting ethical research, engineers producing positive inventions, housewives radiating love and tenderness, teachers being attentive to their students' needs, house maids performing their work efficiently and joyfully, spiritual teachers sharing the wealth of their knowledge, doctors dedicating themselves to healing their fellow human beings, etc. These are generous beings of impeccable integrity, who excel in their field of work and dedicate their lives to service. Spiritual advancement is not a matter of philosophy, but of **the quality of service and love that we can bring into the world, for this is a sure manifestation of the soul.**

As we look at the history of the evolution of consciousness, we can see a continuing process of transformation. Nowadays, for most of us, the ego is part flexible, part rigid, and our different bodies are more or less coordinated. We have a more or less firm connection with the Self. Our consciousness is somewhat developed, but there is still work to do in order to gain complete mastery of our instrument in the three worlds.

In this respect, it is helpful to know how this instrument works, as it is mainly conditioned by the lower mind. It is important to understand why we have such a hard time feeling free, happy, and at peace with our self and with others, despite our best intentions.

In the following chapter, we will examine the workings of the lower mind. This knowledge will enable us to move towards mastering this inner mechanism, and to use it to serve the designs of our soul.

---

[1] Fritjof Capra, Robert Dutheil, Rupert Sheldrake, David Bohm, Valerie Hunt, Hubert Reeves.

[2] From the most recent, as found in the works of Alice A. Bailey, Max Heindel, Rudolph Steiner, and H. P. Blavatsky, to the most ancient, as found in such treasures of wisdom as the Bhagavad Gita, the Kabala, the Vedas, etc.

[3] The reader can, of course, skip this chapter and move on to the next. One can then simply observe the workings of the personality as they are, on the basis of the model presented in Chapter 1.

[4] For a more precise and far more elaborate study of this topic, the reader can refer to the works of Alice A. Bailey, particularly *A Treatise on Cosmic Fire*, Lucis Trust, or, for a more accessible approach, *A Rosicrucian Cosmography*, by Max Heindel.

[5] Consciousness and energy are synonymous, as science is now beginning to discover.

[6] For a precise description of this process, please refer to the works mentioned in note #4.

[7] To go back to the analogy of the violinist and his violin, which we presented in Chapter 1, each "human being" has constructed its "violin" during the process of involution. Now each must remember his/her primary identity as a musician, and learn to master the instrument in order to be able to manifest the beauty of the music, which flows deeply within each being, in the physical world. He/she will then remember being part of a gigantic orchestra composed of billions of fellow musicians.

[8] The symbolic significance of the Garden of Eden and the "fall" of Adam and Eve become obvious as we probe deeper into this aspect of the history of human consciousness. The Garden was that time when the energy units were totally guided by the gods, and all was order and harmony. The so-called fall is a symbolic representation of the development of the lower mind. The original "sin" is that of separation, and generally speaking, is nothing more that the takeover of the personality by the lower mind, with all its limiting mechanisms. This takeover was necessary in order to allow human beings to cut the umbilical cord of divine tutorship, and to become free and responsible for their actions and their evolutionary choices. **Our task then was to learn to live autonomously, under the inner guidance of our soul (to freely reconnect with our divine essence) without any outer direction from the gods** (expulsion from Paradise). Many mistakes will be made, of course, with this freedom of choice, creating a great deal of suffering, but this is how we learn. There was never any "sin"; the evolutionary Plan simply includes a dynamic which involves momentary suffering, to the extent that the higher mind has not yet reached that point of development where the personality is in alignment with the will of the soul.

[9] On this issue, esoteric science now provides cross-references to a number of experiences and observations of advanced psychology. See *Other Lives, Other Selves* by Roger J. Woolger, Bantam New Age Books. A Jungian psychoanalyst rediscovers the phenomenon of "past lives", with all the scientific rigour of his training.

[10] In addition to these "individual" journeys, there are also some broader processes at work, which involve the collective consciousness, and which we will refer to later on.

[11] The ego, in its unceasing efforts to give itself a definition it can never attain, may appropriate the process of reincarnation to delude itself into the belief that it is somehow immortal. This is why the term "reincarnation" seems suspect to many, as being just another simplistic "New Age" fantasy. We can indeed appreciate how stories of previous lives as an Atlantean priestess or as a member of the British royalty seem irrelevant, especially since these stories generally cast the individual in flattering celebrity roles, rather than as a beggar, slave, crook or tyrant. To refer to such stories as evidence of personal importance only serves to keep people mired in the illusion of ego.

[12] In order to have a model that is workable in concrete terms, it is practical to view this story from a temporal perspective, even though the actual process occurs beyond time. This approach facilitates real changes in awareness, leading to genuine healing and opening the door to potential ego liberation, which is essential if we are to recover our freedom in practical, day-to-day terms.

[13] This choice is made through a process of energetic attraction rather than through a rational process springing from a limited mind.

[14] This process bears some resemblance to an artist's creation of a painting. He will start with a base coat, then add broad strokes, then more and more precise dabs with smaller brushes which will refine or even cover up his initial ideas. The artist does not begin his painting at one corner of the canvas and gradually fill the space until the finished work appears as he gets to the other side: there will be many touch-ups and adjustments before the work is finally completed.

[15] This accumulation of debris can reach such proportions that some of us believe we simply do not have a home, and that, instead, all we have is a pile of debris (some therapies only focus on problems, overlooking the power and beauty of the soul laying hidden behind all this stuff).

[16] We will note that, now that we have developed our individuality, each of us is now proceeding at our own pace along the path of evolution. This is why, at this stage, we can speak of "levels of evolution". Indeed while, at the level of the Self, all beings are equal, and equally divine, this not the case at the level of the personality. Some beings that have reached an advanced stage of evolution have acquired a level of intelligence, knowledge, intuition, wisdom, and mastery in emotional, mental and even physical terms that others are still far from achieving. Some have arrived at the level of the University of Life, while others are still at the high school level. There is no inequality in essence, but a multiplicity of levels of awareness that each individual reaches at different times. It is important to bear this in mind so that those who are more advanced will use their knowledge and wisdom, instead of wasting it on ego inflation, to help those who are at a less advanced stage, knowing that the latter may far surpass them once they graduate to the University of Life. Also, those who are less advanced must humbly recognize that fact and welcome whatever appropriate help they may receive from those who have a head start on them, without turning this into self-deprecation and without insisting, out of misplaced pride, on **claiming a state of equality which is non-existent at the level of the ego.**

[17] The morphogenetic fields of information, as described in Chapter 14.

[18] Christiane Singer, *Du bon usage des crises*, éd. Albin Michel.

[19] It is interesting to note that the word "crisis" is a derivative of the Greek word "krisis", meaning *decision, choice*.

chapter 4

The Lower Mind

WHAT IT IS MADE OF AND HOW IT WORKS

*Man therefore is utilising the lower mind, the reasoning mind,
whilst the soul is utilising the higher or abstract mind.
Both units are working with the two aspects of the universal principle
of mind, and on this ground their relation becomes possible.
Man's work with his mind is to render it... receptive to the soul.*[1]

The great journey of consciousness we have just described has taken us to the point where we have this remarkable instrument called the ego (or personality), so as to give the Self an instrument through which to experience the world of matter and to express itself on that plane. But this journey is not over, for the ego has not yet reached a high enough level of development, flexibility and harmony to be the perfect instrument required by the Self.

If we go back to the image of home-building, we realize that this home is not yet finished; everything is still far from being neat and tidy. It is still not very pleasant to live in, and we can't help but wish for something better, which is only normal. In fact, this is evidence of the will of the soul, driving us to want a life full of beauty, harmony and freedom. For this reason, it would be against our nature to stop there, without continuing to build and to complain about our lot (as victims); or wanting to leave the house claiming that it is not fit to live in (refusing to play the game of life); or getting used to a life of mediocrity and passivity (getting discouraged and dying before our time). Nor would we be any better off if we pretended that everything is fine while we shiver in cold drafts (becoming rigid and unable to feel anything); or that our house is perfect and should be a model for others to emulate (arrogance, pretentiousness, rigidity); or if we tried to invade someone else's house in order to compensate for our own sense of emptiness and discomfort (domination, exploitation, manipulation, parasitic behaviour). If we want a more pleasant house, obviously we will have to get to work, consciously and deliberately, to clean up our act, tidy up the space, and get on with construction. This is the goal of any form of inner work.

We have seen how our consciousness, in its effort to create a suitable instrument, has chosen to lock itself in the mechanisms of the ego, for a time, and to focus solely on experiencing the three worlds. We shall now specifically examine how it has moulded itself in the confines of our personality, and how it functions in this process, for this is what directly conditions the quality of our daily existence. This is also what we will have to liberate our self from if we want to recover our freedom.

Indeed, for many of us, the time has now come to move from an outdated, limiting, and painful mode of functioning to a different mode, one that has the potential to bring the full light and power of the soul into this world. This transition produces a state of inner tension that many people are presently experiencing, though they may not quite understand where it comes from.

In order to be able to get through this transition as efficiently as possible, it is helpful to find out more about the ultimate goal of this whole mechanism, and to understand this old way of functioning as well as the new dynamic we want to install.

As we have seen through the model outlined in Chapter 1, the ego is essentially directed by the lower or automatic mind, in close connection with the emotional mind (the coachman and the horse). This part of the personality, which oriental traditions refer to as the *kama mana*, is where the major difficulties lie (the coachman is not receptive to the Master's instructions and wants to do things his own way), but also where a new way of functioning might possibly be created.

When we refer to the lower mind, we are not just talking about our conscious thoughts, which can spring both from the lower and from the higher mind. This is mostly about the unconscious layer of thought, which is an aggregate of all the thought systems that we have accumulated over time, and that carry a powerful emotional charge. We shall attempt to examine the precise structure of this unconscious layer of our personality.

In order to better understand the mechanism of the lower mind, let us first go over this mechanism's intended purpose—its correct function within a human being—so as to foster a direct expression of the will of the soul. For there is no useless element in human nature, and this mechanism has its place in the way a fully transformed personality will eventually function. We will then describe its past purpose—its primary or intermediate function during the construction phase of the ego—a function it still holds in most of us.[2]

The Ideal Way to Function or the Ultimate Goal

The ULTIMATE function of the lower mind is to be:

- **a perfect instrument to record and transmit information from the three worlds to the Self,** and

- **a faithful tool for transmitting responses from the Self** to the personality so that the latter can perform the will of the Self in these three worlds (this is where the coachman becomes totally subservient to the will of the Self).

The lower mind is that part of the personality which records information from the environment via the five physical senses. Ideally, it should remain silent and simply transmit this information without distortion to the higher mind, which relays it to the Self. The latter issues a response, which is received by the higher mind in the form of ideas and intuition, and then transmitted to the lower mind, which remains **silent and receptive**, and translates this response into thoughts that activate the emotional and physical body. We then act appropriately and wisely, as we manifest the will of the Self in the world. In this ideal model of functioning, **the lower mind is just a flexible and reliable intermediary between the physical world and the soul,** via the higher mind. The emotional body is completely under the control of an active higher mind and a neutral lower mind. It remains permanently calm, wastes no energy, and no longer has any impact on the way the personality reacts to situations (the horse is thoroughly trained by a now intelligent coachman, who is totally tuned in to the Master and obediently carries out his orders). The will of the ego and the will of the Self have become one. At that point, the personality becomes a supple, perfect medium of expression for the Self (see diagram 1). Today very few people have reached that point of mastery. Many, however, are actively working towards that goal.

Sometimes we do, in fact, function in this manner, which goes to show that this is not beyond our reach. Human consciousness has evolved through thousands of years of learning. Circuits have already been installed, directly connecting the personality to the Self. Thanks to these previously established "pathways" to higher consciousness, we can access all the qualities that the personality has already integrated in the past. Mozart incarnated with a lower mind that was very receptive to the great music of the Self, and practical skills embedded in his consciousness that enabled him to manifest this music in concrete form in the physical world. This wealth of abilities is not the outcome of accumulated memories, but stems rather from the capacity of the personality to establish a direct connection with the Self. It may have taken some time, perhaps thousands of years, to build this connection and this receptivity, but once the connection is established, knowledge flows through instantaneously. This is not acquired knowledge, as it can be accessed at any moment (to the extent that the lower mind remains silent).[3]

> Genuine knowledge comes directly from the Self, not from an accumulation of memories.

We sometimes experience such moments of grace, where we find our self in a Self-induced state of serenity, love, and inspired creativity.

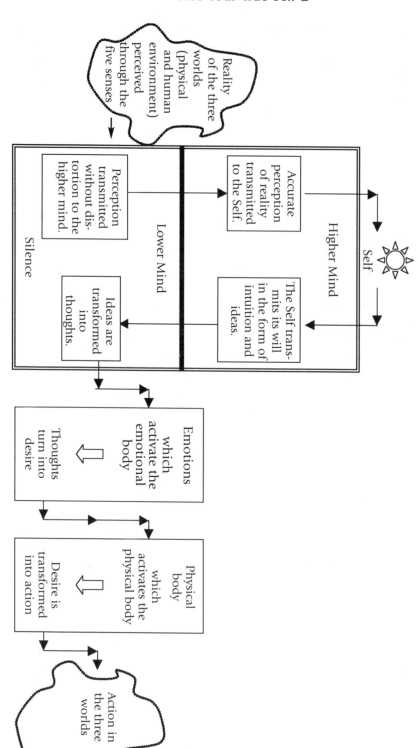

Diagram 1
The Ideal Way of Functioning

Reality of the three worlds (physical and human environment) perceived through the five senses

Perception transmitted without distortion to the higher mind.

Accurate perception of reality transmitted to the Self.

Lower Mind

Higher Mind

Self

Silence

Ideas are transformed into thoughts.

The Self transmits its will in the form of intuition and ideas.

Emotions which activate the emotional body

Thoughts turn into desire

Physical body which activates the physical body

Desire is transformed into action

Action in the three worlds

However, there are moments when our behaviour is anything but harmonious and effective. At such times, peace, joy, energy, and mastery remain out of reach, and life becomes difficult and unsatisfactory. Our higher mind is not yet fully developed, and we still carry a lower mind that is cluttered with all kinds of unintegrated memories of past experiences. These memories, which fuel the independent will of the ego, will impede any experience of well-being and freedom. This mechanism concerns us all, and we will therefore describe it in detail. For if it is not recognized and defused, it will ruin any effort we may make in order to progress along the path towards spiritual realization.

The Mechanism of the Lower Mind Left to Its Own Devices

> *If you can clearly know your prison,*
> *you can design and plan your escape.*
> —*Lazaris*

◆ The Primary Structure of the Lower Mind and its Purpose

Before the process of individuation took place, human beings were endowed with instinctive automatic responses designed for basic survival: these instincts had to do with safety, food supply, and reproduction. At the time of individuation, a new dynamic was installed leading to the development of intelligence and free will, creating the potential for a deliberate return to higher consciousness. Thus mankind was endowed with a lower mind functioning on the basis of a system of memories. This is what we are now focusing on.

In order to foster the construction and survival of the ego, until the time comes when the higher mind and its connection with the Self have reached an adequate stage of development, the lower mind has been endowed with a mechanism that allows it to function **independently of the Self and to take charge of the way the personality functions on a daily basis**. Thus, for a very long time, as it was totally engrossed in the construction process, human consciousness was simply not concerned with any form of guidance coming from any other source than this primary mechanism.

This primary system of the lower mind is still very active in most people: instead of transmitting clear, undistorted perceptions directly to the Self, and silently waiting for the right response, the lower mind short-circuits these perceptions and uses them independently, according to its own parameters, and its own **self-sustaining will**. How does this short-circuit occur, and what are its consequences?

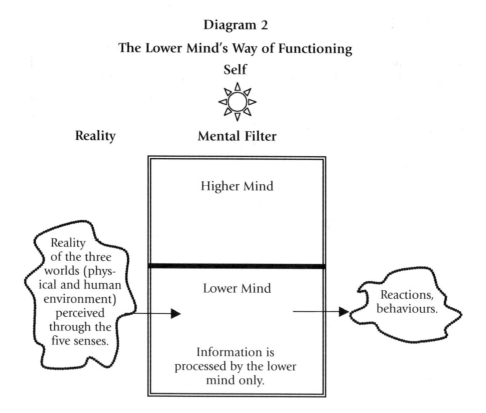

Diagram 2

The Lower Mind's Way of Functioning

The computer

The mechanism of the lower mind can be compared to a computer. Indeed, in order to function on its own, without any connection to the Self, the lower mind has been given a primary memory storage system as well as a program designed to process these memories automatically and reprogram itself on the basis of these memories. This system is what gives it this self-sustaining will that functions according to certain basic and relatively simple principles that we will examine shortly. This is what is commonly called **the will of the ego**.

This made it possible for the ego to:

- experience whatever was needed to further its construction, definition, and individuation;

- begin to build a bridge between the personality and the Self; and

- ensure the survival of the personality in the physical world, until the time comes when this bridge is solid enough so that survival can be ensured by a higher level of consciousness.

This way of functioning, which was appropriate and necessary for a very long time, is now a hindrance that must be overcome in order for us to recover our true nature.

The false self

Without the knowledge and wisdom of the Self, the primary workings of the computer must not only ensure the physical survival of the personality, but also its own survival, **the survival of what the ego (especially the lower mind) identifies with**. This includes its ideas, opinions, beliefs, automatic emotional responses, defence mechanisms based on conscious and, especially, on unconscious mental systems. Thus the purpose of the lower mind, in particular, is to maintain all its recorded past memories, since, as a computer, its existence hinges around this accumulation of memories.

As a result of its momentary identification with this mechanism in order to foster the construction of the personality, human consciousness has generated a pseudo-identity, a temporary false self which is controlled, and whose survival is ensured, by the lower mind. At the moment, most of mankind still identifies to a large extent with this false self.

The Lower Mind's Automatic Responses

What are the mechanisms of this false self? How does it program itself, and how do we react when we are caught up in this mechanism?

There are two stages to this: 1. the computer collects a data bank and 2. the computer processes this data.

1. Collecting the data bank

To begin with, any experience is permanently recorded and stored in memory, in all its aspects: conscious physical reactions (gestures, actions); automatic physical reactions (hormone secretions, heartbeat, muscular tension, etc.); physical sensations at all levels (sight, hearing, smell, taste, kinaesthetic perceptions); and emotional and mental reactions. Everything, absolutely everything, is recorded and stored in memory, at an unconscious level. Our conscious memory recalls relatively little of this information, **but everything is imprinted in the "unconscious"[4] part of the computer.**

During the recording process, there are two basic possibilities: either the experience is a "pleasant" one, which does not generate any stress or tension or it is an "unpleasant" experience, which is stressful and threatening to one's survival from the ego's perspective. The computer records both types of experience in two different forms of memory, which will be processed differently.

Active memories

The painful experiences that the personality is unable to integrate—to take in naturally without stress or resistance—are recorded as memories that we will describe as **active**. These are experiences where fear is activated, in one form or

another, where the personality feels physically, emotionally or mentally assaulted, where its survival, in a broad sense, is threatened. This can be caused by genuine shock (or what is perceived as such) in relation to physical survival (accident, physical assault), or some unexpected emotional shock (abandonment,
rejection, loss, powerlessness, shame, guilt). There may not necessarily be any real
shock, but a continuous recurrence of painful experiences which are either physical (illness, lack of adequate care, poverty, daily physical abuse), or emotional in
nature (loneliness, despondency, repeated psychological abuse, emotional deprivation, suffering in one form or another), and that the person is unable to integrate. Whatever the nature of the pain, if the ego is unable to deal with it in a
serene, relaxed and open manner, it resists, contracts, and snaps into a state of
protection and defence. An energy block is created, loading an **active memory**
into the computer—**an unresolved area of tension**—that will subsequently be
used to fuel a specific **defence mechanism**.

The shocks and traumas experienced at the moment of physical birth, during
childhood, and at the moment of death, will have a tendency to lodge themselves
more deeply within our consciousness. Yet this can also happen at any moment
of our life. What matters most in terms of memory imprint is either the intensity
of the shock, or the duration of our suffering.

*Joseph, a young peasant's son back in the Middle Ages, is playing in the woods while
the Lord of the county is involved in a hunting party in that area, which is forbidden to
peasants at such times. Joseph knows this, but he has decided to go out and gather fire-
wood nevertheless. At one point, he hears the hunting dogs bearing down upon him, and
tries to hide. The hunting party spots him and the dogs are sent charging after him.
Joseph tries to outrun them as fast as he can, but the dogs catch up to him, and tear at
his flesh until the noblemen arrive. They laugh at his cruel fate, then move on with their
dogs. Joseph lays on the ground, in terrible pain from his wounds, until his family finds
him several hours later. Joseph's unconscious has recorded everything: the fear and stress,
the threat to his physical survival, the shock at being physically attacked, everything is
stored in memory with a heavy physical and emotional charge.*

*Mary Beth is eleven years old, a lovely girl who looks older than her years. One day,
she happens to be alone in the house when one of her older cousins, in his twenties,
arrives with a friend to visit her brother, who is out. The young men begin to joke with
Mary Beth, who doesn't understand what is going on. Then her cousin's friend tries to
kiss her, and she pushes him away. He responds angrily, while her cousin laughs. Then
both boys move closer to her and end up sexually abusing her. Afterwards, they leave as
quickly as they arrive, telling Mary Beth not to say anything to anyone, otherwise they
would do it again, and beat her as well. The poor girl is devastated and terrified. She
will say nothing, of course, burying the fear and shame deep inside of her; yet everything,
the physical aggression, the fear, the shame, has been recorded in her unconscious.*

In both of these examples, an active memory is recorded, and from that moment on it will be used automatically and unconsciously according to a specific dynamic that we will describe further on in this book.

An active memory can be created even without the occurrence of a major event. What determines the intensity of the shock is not the external magnitude of the event, but the vulnerability of the person at that moment. This vulnerability varies greatly, depending on the person's level of evolution and, as we shall see in the next chapter, on the types of memories from a more distant past that such apparently innocuous events can evoke. Let's take Benny's story as an example:

Benny is eight years old. Annabelle, the neighbours' daughter, is in the same class as him in school. He finds her incredibly beautiful, with her long curly hair and green eyes, and dreams of marrying her some day. He has a major crush on her but has never dared to tell her about it, being naturally quite shy. One day, as an exercise in written and oral expression, his teacher asks each student to write a poem on the subject of his/her choice, which he/she will subsequently read to the class. Benny wonders what subject could inspire him enough to do this assignment. Then an idea springs to his mind: he will write a poem celebrating Annabelle's beauty, so that she will understand how much he loves her. On the day scheduled for the presentations, Benny's turn comes and he goes to the front of the class and begins to read his poem. Feeling choked with anxiety and emotion, he fumbles through to the end, where a slip of the tongue turns his most beautiful line into a grotesque parody. Everyone laughs at him, as he goes back to his seat feeling terribly mortified and miserable. For several days afterwards, his classmates continue to jeer at him, which cuts deeply into his soul.

Here again, the experience is recorded into the unconscious, and an active memory is installed. These examples portray memories forming at a specific moment in time. Yet our day-to-day life is filled with hundreds of opportunities that load the automatic unconscious portion of our lower mind. It is easy to imagine the number of shocks absorbed during childhood, both psychological and physical, even in the context of what might be termed a "happy" childhood. Since nothing is done to defuse these tensions and these memories, they remain lodged in the unconscious, conditioning most people's behaviour.

It must be noted that the more painful the wound, the more strongly the memory will be imprinted, and the more deeply it will lodge itself in the unconscious. **The memories that most potently condition our behaviour are generally the most unconscious ones**, i.e. the memories we least remember, or which we have forgotten altogether. Remembering these painful moments would simply hurt too much. A primary protective mechanism makes sure that we "forget" on a conscious level. But nothing is forgotten at the unconscious level. As far as our present day to day experience is concerned, since the bulk of these scars were sustained during the first five to seven years of our life, many of us remember little of this period. A veil of forgetfulness has been drawn over it all in order to suspend the suffering. Yet there is a price to be paid for that, as these memories remain active, conditioning our adult life in very specific ways, and ultimately preventing any possibility of a lasting experience of happiness and freedom.

Thus, an accumulation of active memories builds up in the lower mind. These will form the core around which a more and more separate entity will crystallize, a false self endowed with its own will, its own operational laws, and its own way of perceiving reality.

It must be noted that what solidly anchors an active memory into the inner workings of the computer is its emotional charge. Even where physical aggression is involved, the emotional charge of fear is the hook that buries deep into the unconscious. So this is not just a mental mechanism. It involves a primary response mechanism of the mind combined with an emotional energy charge. The lower mind functions as a recording device.

Every human being is thus subject to an emotional mechanism that is not yet mastered, and a lower mental mechanism whose purpose is to ensure the survival of the false self at any cost. The soul, of course, has no way to express itself in such a context. It is interesting to note that our definition of active memories includes many aspects of what is commonly called "complexes" in classical Jungian psychoanalysis:

> The *Dictionary of Psychoanalysis* (Larousse, 1974) defines a complex in the following manner:
>
> **Complex:** ... *The initiative for this concept is, to a large extent, attributable to the Zurich school of psychoanalysis—especially Jung—who define it as "detached bits of personality, groupings carrying psychic content, which have become separate from the conscious mind and which* **function in an arbitrary and autonomous manner**, *having a discrete existence within the sphere of the unconscious, from whence they can, at any given moment, hinder or foster certain conscious outcomes." According to Jung, it is composed of an unconscious and autonomous core, which is nevertheless charged with meaning, and an aggregate of related associations* **which retain an emotional charge** *and reflect the schematic network of behaviours to which the subject is* **unwittingly and unwillingly** *predisposed. It is further identified as the nuclear organizational force behind functional disturbances, the veritable "nerve centre" of an individual's psychological life. When a complex becomes manifest at the conscious level, it acts as a foreign body that cannot be either assimilated or dissolved. According to Jung, a complex is therefore* **"whatever remains unresolved within an individual**, *the weak point in every sense of the word."*
>
> And following is a quote from Carl Gustav Jung's *Man in Search of His Soul:*
>
> *Scientifically speaking, what is an "affective complex"? It is a vivid emotional image of a definitive psychic situation, an image that is, moreover, incompatible with the individual's usual attitude and conscious space; it is internally highly cohesive, as it is endowed with a kind of wholeness all its own, and with a relatively high degree of autonomy: it is only fleetingly subservient to the dictates of consciousness, and subsequently behaves as a* **corpus alienum**, *with a life of its own, within the individual's conscious space.*
>
> *[...]*

The hypothesis whereby complexes are seen as split and compartmentalized psyches has now become a certainty. Their origin, their etiology, can often be traced to an emotional shock, a trauma or some such incident, that has the effect of separating a compartment of the psyche. One of the most frequent causes is the moral conflict stemming, ultimately, from the apparent impossibility for the individual to totally accept human nature. By the mere fact of its existence, this impossibility leads to an immediate split, which may or may not escape the individual's awareness. This remarkable unawareness of complexes is in fact generally the rule, which, of course gives them that much more latitude to influence perception: their assimilating force then becomes amply evident, as the individual's unawareness of a complex enables it to assimilate the conscious self, which creates a momentary and unconscious alteration of the personality called **identification with the complex.**

[...]

Thus I am inclined to suppose that autonomous complexes are the normal manifestations of life, and that they are responsible for the structure of the unconscious psyche.

Here another major fact should be noted: **the extent to which an active memory will be deeply embedded in the unconscious**—and thus its power to influence an individual's subsequent behaviour—**depends far more on the level of evolution of the individual than on the actual situation.** Given identical "traumatic" situations, a less evolved person will tend to have a stronger emotional reaction than another more evolved individual who has gained proper mastery over the physical and emotional bodies. For example, an experience involving rejection or public embarrassment can produce a highly charged memory for a less advanced person, while another person might take this same situation in a more impersonal manner, without creating any active memories. Nevertheless, given the average level of evolution where most of us are, our mastery over the three bodies (mental, emotional and physical) is relative at best, and we all carry an aggregate of active memories, which greatly limit our access to freedom and well-being.

Loose memories

Situations in which we feel free to do as we please, naturally accepting whatever is happening without resistance, are recorded as **"loose memories"**. Essentially these are situations where we experience a sense of well-being and security. There is an easy flow of energy, on the physical and emotional levels as well as the mental level. There is no energy block to be loaded into the computer's memory.

For example: I am travelling through Colorado with two good friends. We visit the Grand Canyon, along with a guide. I marvel at the beauty of everything around me, I learn some very interesting facts about how this particular landscape was formed. My mind records this reality in a supple manner, and there is no emotional charge attached to it.

These loose memories are the guardians of a stock of genuine learning leading to greater flexibility and openness of the personality. **They will foster the development of the higher mind.** Since they do not carry any emotional charge, they will not be used by the automatic program, which we shall now describe.

2. Processing the information: activating the automatic program in two phases

In any given situation, the automatic mind (which is not in touch with the Self) has no reference point by which to gage the reactions of the physical and emotional bodies and thereby create the best possible conditions for survival. The only thing it has is, on the one hand, its database of active memories, and, on the other hand, a program it can use to process this data. At each moment of our life, the lower mind receives information coming from the outside. **In order to ensure the survival of the personality according to its own logic,** if the individual's consciousness is operating at this level, the computer will automatically be activated in two stages:

- **it compares,** moment by moment, the present situation with the entire stock of past experiences recorded in its memory bank, so as to find situations which might be similar to the present one; and

- **it automatically activates** the personality: the results of all these comparisons are processed in a way that conditions the reactions of the personality and leads to automatic behaviours that provide for protection and "survival" based on built-in criteria within the computer. Thus the entire physical, emotional and mental system is activated on the basis of a principle we shall call the "principle of closest resemblance".

The principle of closest resemblance

If the computer manages to locate a memory of a situation that is identical to the present one, then all the previous reactions at the three body levels are activated in the same manner as they were during the previous situation, according to a very simple logic: "If, in the past, I survived thanks to this response, I have a better chance at survival now if I activate the same response." The physical body is activated to generate the same reactions in the nervous system, the same heart rate, hormone secretions, and muscular tension. The emotional body is automatically caught in the same emotions: fear, anxiety, anger, excitement, pleasure, enthusiasm.[5] The mind is automatically flooded with the same negative or positive thoughts: judgement, interest, appreciation, attraction, suspicion, or calculations. The lower mind thus provides the best chances for its own "survival", based on its intentions and resources. In such cases, we are automatically led to replaying previous scenarios, without any chance of reacting in a new way.

Yet very rarely do present situations exactly replicate past ones. So, just to be on the safe side, even in the absence of total similarity, the computer checks if there is at least a partial resemblance. If there is **just one little detail** that is reminiscent of a past situation, that is enough for the computer to latch onto it, in the absence of any other data, and spring into action. At this point, it processes this situation in exactly the same way as it did in the past with the one found in its memories, even though it is generally quite different. **This is not at all the same reality, yet the computer treats the situation as if it were the same.** When we allow our consciousness to identify with it, this mode of functioning of the lower mind completely conditions our quality of life. We shall examine some of the most direct consequences of this.

A Distorted Perception of Reality: The First Consequence of this Mechanism

When our consciousness functions at the lower mind level, we are obviously unable to perceive a situation as it really is, since we equate this situation with a past experience that generally bears little resemblance to the present one. However we do react as we did in the past, even on the basis of a minor detail, **in the belief that we are indeed perceiving reality when we are in fact projecting a past situation onto the reality of the present moment.**[6]

Robert is five years old. Today, his mother has organized a family reunion to celebrate her sister's return from a long trip. This lady is very famous in the world of journalism. She has long blond hair curling down to her shoulders, large gold-rimmed glasses, and a strong personality. Everyone listens to her in rapture. When dessert is served, the children get a glass of chocolate milk to go with the cake. Robert gets his glass, and Mary, his cousin, accidentally bumps him as she reaches excitedly for hers, so that Robert spills his glass of chocolate milk all over his fine white shirt. Mary cries out when she sees the mess, and all eyes turn to Robert who pitifully watches his beautiful shirt turn to a rather inelegant brown. At that point the aunt, who was beginning to find the kids much too rambunctious, wades into the general silence and slings a few cutting words at Robert, making him look totally ridiculous. Everyone laughs except Robert, who quietly leaves the table and locks himself in his room. The party's over for him. Even though he knows that there will be games for the kids later on, and a film on lions, taken during his aunt's latest journey, he will not leave his room for the rest of the day.

Robert has just gone through an emotional shock, and his lower mind has recorded everything: his aunt's appearance and face as she spoke to him, her long, blond, wavy hair, and her gold rimmed glasses. The event itself will soon be forgotten, that is it will no longer be consciously accessible. But the mechanism of the lower mind has consigned everything to memory and, from that moment on, it will condition many of Robert's future reactions and choices, without his realizing it. Here, in particular, is one example of what happened later on in his life:

Having completed his education, Robert starts looking for a job. One morning, in answer to one of his applications, he gets a note in the mail inviting him to an interview for a position that seems extremely appealing to him. Filled with excitement, he picks up the phone, and contacts the person in charge, a lady who will be conducting the interview with him. The telephone conversation is most pleasant. Why wait any longer? He schedules an appointment that very afternoon. He gets physically prepared, putting on his finest business attire, and mentally psyches himself by going over all his relevant knowledge and qualifications for the job. He feels quite self-assured, as his competencies are a perfect match for the requirements of the position. He arrives at the meeting feeling calm, cool and confident. He is ushered into the office of the person in charge of hiring. The lady he had spoken to that morning turns out to be a middle-aged woman who welcomes him in very nicely and asks him to take a seat. Despite this friendly welcome, Robert suddenly feels very nervous and ill at ease. The lady begins to ask questions, and he fumbles for answers. He really feels out of sorts, and gradually loses all his usual aplomb. Though he had come prepared to make a great impression, and usually has great interpersonal skills, he begins to ramble, contradicting himself, going off track with unnecessary explanations, and eventually coming across as someone who really isn't sure of what he wants. As the interview ends, Roberts feels devastated. He realizes that he has made a fool of himself. He even forgot to mention some specific professional experience he had which would have been a major asset for this position. Yet he had come to the interview feeling together and in great spirits. What happened?

The lady who had conducted the interview was middle-aged, had blond hair and gold-rimmed glasses. Though he did not see any link or even realize what was happening, Robert had fallen prey to the emotional mechanism of the lower mind. In the course of the interview, he became once again the little five year-old boy he had been and lost all of his adult composure, caught as he was in his fear of ridicule, fear of this woman who, of course, had nothing in common with his aunt. Yet, as far as the unconscious is concerned, whether it's this woman or that aunt, it's all the same. The old wound was reopened and it reactivated a whole way of behaving that was in total contradiction with what Robert consciously wanted. **As long as these active memories have not been cleared away, our unconscious is more powerful than our conscious mind**. It makes us do the most inane things in accordance with its own logic, its own will, which often thwarts our conscious will.

Here again, the principles of Jungian analysis come to mind. Following is another quote from *Man in Search of His Soul*, by Carl G. Jung:

> *Any constellation of complexes leads to a disturbed state of consciousness: it precludes unity of consciousness, and* **wilful intention** *becomes impossible, if not* **seriously flawed**... *One must conclude that a complex, seen in terms of energy, is a psychic factor bearing* **a potentiality that sometimes overrides** *that of conscious intention: otherwise such intrusions into the orderly structure of consciousness would not be possible. In fact, an active complex throws us into a* **state of non-freedom,** *of obsessive thoughts and constricting actions.*

Two direct consequences of this distorted perception of reality:

◆ Inefficiency and inability to live in the present moment

No matter what behaviours may be activated by the computer's automatic response mechanism, it seems obvious that these reactions stand very little chance of being appropriate in the situation at hand, since the detail that generated the reactivation bears little resemblance to actual reality. Not only is this reaction a mere replay of old scenarios, but also we become deaf and blind to the present reality we are faced with. **We have no way of being in contact with the reality of the present moment.** Since we are unaware of what is really going on, **we lose any real sense of discernment, any power to act in an appropriate and efficient manner, and thus any kind of mastery or freedom.**

From this angle, it is easier to understand the problems we face when we try to practice spiritual teachings to the effect that we should "be here now". We may be willing and eager to put this into practice, but our unconscious may not necessarily cooperate. So there is more elaborate work involved than a simple act of good will.

◆ Inaccuracy of judgements concerning others

It is easy to see how this distorted perception of reality conditions any judgement we may pass on others. **We do not perceive others as they are, but rather as our distorting memories project them to be.** Some people, or certain types of behaviour in others, tend to rub us particularly the wrong way, as they activate certain memories within us. **Our judgements, especially when they are emo-**

> The way we perceive others tells us more about the content of our unconscious than about whom these people really are.

tionally charged, are often nothing but an unconscious reaction to a past situation, which has been reactivated. Knowing this, we can use our judgements to further our own self-knowledge, and leave others alone.

   One way to remember this fact is to note how, whenever we judge someone, we have one finger pointed at this person, and three fingers pointed in our direction.

A suggestion: Every time someone, or someone's behaviour, rubs us the wrong way, we could look in the mirror and try to see what part of us is being reactivated. This can lead to major development in our awareness of our own programming, and be a first step towards liberation. In addition, this will foster an attitude of minding our own business. We hardly know our self, so how can we presume to judge others as if we knew them?

These mechanisms whereby the past is projected onto the present do not just come into play occasionally in special circumstances. For as long as the memories are active, the unconscious is forever on the alert, to ensure our survival 24 hours a day. It is constantly on the lookout for clues that can be fed into its system of comparison and projection, so as to keep the situation under control as much as possible. Most of the time, we unconsciously make decisions that are based on these automatic mechanisms. When the time comes to choose a partner, a job, a purchase, an activity, be it of major or minor significance, our decisions are dictated by these unconscious reactions. Of course we find all kinds of rationalizations and "gut feelings" to justify our choices, while most often our preferences were determined by unconscious mechanisms. So it is not surprising, under the circumstances, that these choices eventually lead nowhere. **This unconscious mechanism will remain constantly active** as long as we do not pull our self free from the grip of these memories, either through specific consciousness work, or through multiple experiences over many lifetimes.

Our thoughts are quotations, our emotions are imitations,
our actions are caricatures.
—Swami Prajnanpad

The words of a spiritual master who taught Arnaud Desjardins may seem pessimistic. Yet their meaning becomes clear when we realize how accurately they describe the conscious space of ordinary people who are caught in the mechanisms of their personality.

Defence Systems

Robert's story was a relatively simple example. In fact there is more to it than that. When we have a non-integrated experience leading to the formation of an active memory, **the lower mind,** while it records the actual circumstances, **also makes generalizations and draws conclusions** so as to minimize risk further down the road. Some very basic general decisions are then recorded at the same time as the memories, for self protection purposes or to provide subsequent well-being, and for the sake of "survival" in future situations which **it will interpret** as being similar.

Thus a wide range of **automatic responses** are installed in the computer, in the form of fears, needs, desires, attractions, repulsions, etc., that are in fact just **defence systems** built up in past situations in order to avoid the recurrence of suffering. These are of course very basic primary systems, that are most often inappropriate and constricting, but without the wisdom of the Self, they are the best we could come up with. The computer thus builds a kind of false knowledge, or counterfeit wisdom, that in fact amount to **a system of defence mechanisms and ways of dealing with life**.

Going back to Mary Beth's story, some active memories were recorded when she was assaulted. From that moment on, and for the rest of her adult life, if nothing is done to defuse that memory, her attitude towards sex will be seriously affected. Without her realizing it, she will automatically associate any sexual experience with past trauma. She will unconsciously associate any male who gets too close to her to the cousin who assaulted her. The computer then builds a variety of defence systems in order to prevent the recurrence of past suffering. In some cases this may translate into a weight problem. The unconscious knows exactly what it is doing: "If I'm fat, I will be less attractive, and I am less likely to be assaulted." There is a defence system in place whose aim, in this case, is to use every means to try to curtail sexual activity, since deep-seated memories equate sex with pain. This system will use a whole arsenal of reactions, both physical and emotional, to provide a false sense of protection: frigidity, inability to sustain long-term relationships, mood swings, fear, or a whole assortment of behaviours and choices that will ensure that sex can never be experienced as a natural and spontaneous activity.

The sequel to Benny's story, after the crushing humiliation of reading his poem in class, is another example:

As an adult, Benny found an interesting job. A few years later, given his competence and the quality of his work, he was offered a position of major responsibility. Unfortunately, this position involved regularly speaking to groups of clients. Each of these meetings was an ordeal for Benny, who considered resigning even though this position suited him perfectly. His defence system was dead set against speaking in public, even if, from a rational standpoint, he had all the competence needed for this aspect of his job. As he worked on defusing this memory, he was able to recover his natural potential for self-expression.

These very simple stories reflect thousands of examples that have turned up in the course of my work. They come from perfectly normal people, who get by just like everybody else in their ordinary, day-to-day life. While it is true that, in some cases, these shocks can result in irrational or abnormal behaviours to the extent that the individual can no longer function, most often these inadequate behaviours are not sufficiently acute to prevent "normal" living. Nevertheless they result in endless difficulties at all levels: dysfunctional relationships, low energy, limited creativity, failure, disastrous choices, fears of all kinds, stress, anxiety, anger, depression, hyperactivity, burn-out, health problems, etc., all of which undermine our quality of life.

Do we not often say, I don't know what came over me, why I acted in this way, or I couldn't help myself? Such statements amount to a confession that one's unconscious simply took over. Most often, however, we do not even realize that we acted inadequately. We think we see things as they really are, and we rely on such perceptions, on our "feelings". Yet where do these perceptions and feelings come from? We don't even think to question them, though they are the reason we lose control of our life.

Let us note here how the Dictionary of Psychoanalysis defines a defence mechanism:[7]

In the light of psychoanalysis, a defence mechanism can be defined as:

*1) a **self-preserving or self-protecting operation** against the internal or external intrusion of forces, situations or representations that might threaten* *the integrity of the personality (in either physical or psychic terms): this oper-ation works by **reinforcing acquired mechanisms** and by dispelling elements that may be threatening or foreign;*

2) a mechanism which operates according to an economy of conservation: if the threat comes mostly in the form of external assaults (tendencies, represen-tations, etc.), the ego's defence mechanism will mainly tend to find ways of reducing tensions;

*3) an activity involving both the ego and the superego and which, by that very fact, **can be both conscious and unconscious:** each person, shall we say, has defence strategies that are uniquely personal and that function most often as partly conscious personal reactions (for example a person who regularly falls asleep in certain circumstances, or who finds a defensive escape in work or play, etc.).*

We have chosen examples going back to childhood, for that is the period when most of the psychic records that condition our adult life are (re)created.[8] Indeed, if we assume that the mind bears no trace of any memories at birth, then our early childhood is the starting point where we begin to experience physical life and relationships. This, obviously, sets the stage for recording a multitude of active memories. Each time the child feels frustrated, or loved too much or too little, or stifled, or not respected, or deprived of recognition, or obliged to perform or sim-ply to do things he/she does not feel like doing, whether these events are real or perceived as such, all of these occurrences can lead to active memories being installed in the unconscious. After a while, every new occurrence in life begins to bear a close resemblance, more or less, to something previously experienced. Beyond a certain age—4 or 5 years perhaps—the child, and eventually the adult, will do nothing but **unconsciously replay past scripts and activate defence systems for the purpose of self-protection,** unless he/she learns to control and defuse these mechanisms. In the second part of this book, we will take a closer look at some major defence systems that presently condition most people's consciousness.

Robot Man

The worst thing about this is that we fail to realize that the lower mind is project-ing a screen between reality and us, and we get caught unawares in these auto-matic reactions to a false reality. We honestly believe that our reaction to any given situa-tion is a reasonable one. Our consciousness is thus completely paralysed, and even the most brilliant intellect can be hung up in this type of mechanism: he/she will simply have more brilliant rationalizations to "logically" justify his/her actions, which will nevertheless continue to be condi-tioned by this unconscious mechanism.

> When our life is dominated by the lower mind, we behave as pre-programmed robots, having lost our creativity and our freedom.

Not only do these mechanisms make us blind, inefficient prisoners of automatic behaviours, but they also make us highly subject to **manipulation** by all kinds of outside forces. Indeed a robot has no power and no freedom, and can be easily manipulated once its operating systems are known. If someone is consciously or intuitively astute enough to perceive some of our automatic programmings, he/she can easily "press our buttons". We thus carry on in the world with a keyboard indicating all our automatic mechanisms. Anyone can use that keyboard to make us react any way they wish (consciously or not), especially since our programmings are far from unique.[9] The pervasive manipulative systems of our modern times use this robotic aspect of the human psyche to channel mass behaviour and get people to do just about anything. One can easily see how urgent it is to bring about some form of awakening if this is ever going to end.

> In short, when caught in the mechanism of the lower mind:
> - we identify the present situation with some other event (usually traumatic in nature) that we experienced in the past;
> - we are completely mistaken in the way we perceive the present situation; and
> - the personality reacts on the basis of this deceptive perception, by activating defence systems stemming from active memories.

The Cycle of Dissatisfaction Resulting from the Mechanisms of the Lower Mind

All these pre-programmed responses constitute an aggregate of automatic reactions that we see as typical attributes of our being, rather than as the ego mechanisms they actually are. To have our daily existence ruled by such mechanisms not only deprives us of our freedom, but it promotes a **constant feeling of emptiness** and dissatisfaction, which can never be assuaged. Indeed **a mechanism can never experience the beauty and fullness of life.** This explains why, at the personality level, we get caught in the cycle of dissatisfaction as described in Chapter 2. Prodded by this unpleasant feeling of inner emptiness, we continually, unconsciously seek to compensate for it through external physical or psychological means. We can see how satisfaction is impossible under these conditions, no matter what we get, and why we have this feeling that we will always need more.

> A mechanism can never be satisfied; it can only be reinforced or deactivated at its source.

Some Examples

Following are a few very simple examples of actual experiences, which illustrate how these mechanisms work.

Julie and the lifeguard: *Julie is 4 years old and is spending a wonderful family vacation by the sea. One day, her young cousin invites her to go with him on a sea excursion* *in their grandfather's boat. Julie gleefully accepts. The two kids start rowing out to sea, but the weather takes a turn for the worse and the sea become choppy. As they try to get back to shore, a big wave upsets the boat. The lifeguard on duty on the beach rushes to rescue Julie who is drowning, paralysed with fear. He brings the little girl back to safety, lays her down and resuscitates her. When she opens her eyes, feeling safe and sound, she sees this handsome, tanned, young man with blond hair and big blue eyes who smiles at her and keeps her snug in his arms, an image which is imprinted very deeply in her unconscious, due to her state of physical and emotional shock.*

Then Julie grows into an adult. The details of this event are long forgotten. But her unconscious does not forget, not in the least. Curiously, Julie just melts in the presence of blond men with big blue eyes and, preferably, a gorgeous tan. Whenever she encounters one of these specimens in the street, her heart starts pounding. She thinks this reflects her preferences, her taste in men. In fact, this is just an old memory being projected on the present. Being strongly attracted to men of this type, she inevitably ends up getting involved with one of them. One day, she makes a commitment and gets married. At first, she is in seventh heaven, feeling secure, protected, and totally fulfilled with this masculine presence. The mechanism is working full-time. But **this distorted perception of reality is bound to crash into reality itself.**

As time goes by, Julie finds that this handsome blond hunk wakes up in a bad mood every day, that he loves those western movies that she can't stand, that he leaves her alone to take care of their two kids, that he adamantly objects to her going out with her women friends, that he makes love with less and less feeling, that he is cheap, and that he expects her to go fishing with him though this bores her to tears! She finally realizes that they have no connection with each other. All of these details were covered up, for a while at least, because of an emotional reaction that was recorded long ago in her unconscious. This recorded event is what led to Julie's marriage to this gentleman. Her choice was determined by a mechanism created in the past, rather than by a clear perception of her real needs and of reality.

Of course, we all think we know our real needs, and that such a thing could never happen to us. But who knows.

Spaghetti: *James was six when his parents decided to separate, after months of arguing. Not knowing what to do about James, they decided to follow a friend's advice, and place him in a boarding school run by nuns, where he would be well taken care of and given a sound education. On a dismal Sunday afternoon in November, with rain pouring down outside, James is asked to gather his stuff and get ready to head out to the boarding school. Off he goes with his mother, who takes him out of town to an imposing large building where she stops. She gets out of the car, asks James to take his luggage, and they walk into a large hall. A smiling nun turns up to greet them. James' heart is aching. He wasn't able to see his father before leaving, and now he knows that his mother is about to go and that he is going to stay here, alone, in this place where he doesn't know anyone. Having taken care of a few formalities, his mother comes to him, gives him a kiss, and tells him that he is going to be just fine here, and that the lady is going to take him to supper, whereupon this lady takes him by the hand. James tries to turn to see his* *mother one last time, but all he gets is a glimpse of her going through the door. Despair and fear fill his heart at that moment. The nun gently takes him to a dining hall where supper is being served. James takes a seat and a big plate of spaghetti and tomato sauce is placed before him. He isn't hungry, though he eats a little because he is pressed to do so. This spaghetti turns his stomach, as he is far too tense to take in any food. Shortly thereafter he is taken to his room, where tears of fear well up in his eyes. What little spaghetti he has eaten is just not going down, and he ends up throwing up, feeling wretched and alone.*

Days and years go by, and his life changes. James grows up, goes to another school, and becomes an adult. All that is left of this sinister event is some vague set of memories. But his unconscious has recorded every minute detail.

James is now leading a "normal" life. His health, however, is curiously affected: James is allergic to spaghetti and tomato sauce. Any time he tries to eat some, he becomes violently ill, extremely irritable, depressed, and in a generally bad mood. Even the sight of a plate of spaghetti is too much for him, and makes him aggressive. Spaghetti just does not agree with him. Yet he wishes he could eat some just like everybody else. So he talks about it with doctors, who prescribe all kinds of pills and treatments to improve his digestion, but there is no change. James cannot eat spaghetti without getting ill. The cause of course, has nothing to do with spaghetti or the state of his digestive system. What is happening, quite simply, is that whenever James is faced with a plate of spaghetti, he is instantly brought back to when he was six years old. His unconscious remembers: spaghetti equals abandonment, fear, solitude, and deep suffering.

Besides spaghetti, James also loathes the month of November. Each year, at this time, he becomes terribly depressed and anxious. He has been told this is normal, since this is the beginning of winter and there is less sunshine. To counteract his depression, he has been given medication, which, of course, has not worked. He has tried to spend that time of the year travelling, but that didn't bring on any significant improvement. As far as his unconscious is concerned, November means solitude and abandonment. As long as that pain is not healed, as long as the memory has not been defused, James will be stuck with his limitations and his unpleasant reactions to life.

One might think that James' situation is not that bad. All he needs to do is eat something other than spaghetti, and go away on vacation in November. Yet when someone experiences this kind of shock, such violent negative reactions, both physical and emotional, will be triggered by a plate of spaghetti or the coming of November: any other detail recorded by the unconscious during this emotional shock will tend to be projected onto the present, at any given time.

This spaghetti story is an illustration of how trivial the sources of reactivation can be at the level of the lower mind. Yet this is what conditions our daily experience of life. How many dreams and aspirations end up never being turned into reality because some memory lodged somewhere in our unconscious has acted as an energy block, **has prevented us from thinking intelligently and clearly,** and led us to believe that these dreams were either unrealistic, dangerous, or uninteresting? Or, on the other hand, how many times have we enthusiastically plunged headlong into choices and actions, which, in the end, were totally inappropriate? How often are we burdened with psychological limitations and difficulties that can be traced to some event in our past? How many physical ailments originate from this type of experience rather than from some malfunction coming out of nowhere?

The stories we have presented here as illustrations of the mechanism of the lower mind are simple examples of how the mind interferes with our direct perception of reality, interprets this reality according to its own operating system, and determines our behaviour at any moment of our life. Here is another story that shows how an entire lifetime can be conditioned by some unresolved shock, in this case an emotional shock:

Amelia and the stars: *Amelia was a five-year-old girl who worshiped her mother, who was so gentle and considerate, and who gave her all the love and affection she needed. She would tell her wonderful stories and, as the summer was just beginning, the two of them had developed the habit of going out in the garden every evening to look at the stars. To Amelia, this was the most beautiful moment of the day, as her mother would tell her stories of people who lived on the stars. Amelia would then go to bed under the benevolent gaze of all these wonderful beings in their enchanted celestial world. One day her mother had gone shopping in the next town, and didn't come back for supper. Her father got an emergency call and a woman in their neighbourhood came over to look after Amelia, who was very disappointed. This evening there would be no story and no stars. She ended up sadly going to bed, wondering where her mother could possibly be. She usually called whenever she was held up somewhere. The next morning, her grandmother came to her home, and everyone looked thunderstruck. Mother was still absent and, when Amelia asked where she was, her grandmother told her that her mother had had a car accident and that she was being cared for at the hospital. Amelia could not understand why she couldn't be cared for at home, and started to cry. Grandma did her best to console her. That evening, Amelia went out by herself to look at the stars. Grandma came and sat next to her. Amelia talked a little about the star-filled world her mother had described. Grandma heaved a heavy sigh and, with heavy tears streaming down her face, told little Amelia that her mother had gone to join the other beings among the stars, for she would never come home from the hospital. Amelia didn't quite understand at first. In the end, her grandmother clearly explained that she would never again see her mother, that she was gone forever. Something froze in the little girl's heart at that moment.*

She looked at the stars one last time, then Grandma led her to her bedroom, for it was bed time. Amelia did not fall asleep right away; her sorrow was too great, it was too much for her, it seemed as if her heart was going to burst. For a long time she cried in her pillow, thinking about her mother up there in the stars, until she finally fell asleep.

All this was too painful for Amelia to remember consciously. Her loss and the pain of that loss were simply too much for her young heart.

Days passed, turning into months, then years, and Amelia completely forgot those gentle evenings with her mother. She had no conscious recollection of those moments spent in the garden with her mother, exploring the stars. Yet the deep scar left in her unconscious as a result of this experience ended up conditioning a large portion of her life afterwards.

Once she became a university student, Amelia opted for studies in science, and she did reasonably well. At one point, as part of her curriculum, an optional course in astronomy was offered, with a major in astrophysics. When she found out about this, she felt a very strong force emerging within her. She registered not only for this course but also two other related courses. Her career choice was made, as she had discovered her passion: astrophysics. She studied night and day, and passed all of her exams with high honours. She was accepted to take part in an advanced study group in a government research centre. She had a passion for her work. She was the first to enter the lab in the morning, and the last to leave, often coming back on weekends to complete a report or an experiment. She was fascinated with space, and wanted to know what was to be found on all those distant planets. She would spend entire days monitoring the movement of certain stars in space. Her colleagues were amazed at her patience and dedication to her work. She would have liked to be part of the space exploration team. She applied several times, but her precarious state of health and nervous condition were deemed unsuitable. Her disappointment was great, but she made up for it by plunging even deeper into her lab research work. Her intelligence and hard work led to some interesting discoveries in her chosen field. She quickly became well-known in the world of astrophysics, and took part in prestigious think tanks. She would often feel tired and near the end of her rope, but she would work ceaselessly in pursuing her research. Her whole life was centred around her work. She rarely went out on dates. She ended up marrying a colleague, and had two children. Yet this aspect of her life took second place to her research work.

Thus the years went by until the day came when Amelia found herself alone and burnt out. Her children, with whom she had only been marginally involved, had left home, and so had her husband who was tired of living with a wife who was constantly stressed out and tense as a result of her work, and who was scarcely available for the simple joys of life and was never really happy. Amelia was also becoming ill. Not only had she spent these long years without enough physical activity, but she had also had to cope with a state of inner tension that she could not explain. The work was interesting and non-stressful in itself. Yet Amelia wore a perpetual frown as if something was wrong somehow. All of this began to have a painful impact on her physical body. In her lonely and sickly state, Amelia began to wonder about things. She tried to change some aspects of her life. Everyone was telling her to work less, but she couldn't help it. Not working was like tearing her heart out.

It took some time before Amelia began the inner journey that led to her discovering the foundations on which her life had been built. In her work as an overzealous, well-known scientist, what was she doing unconsciously? She was trying to reconnect with her mother. The energy which had been blocked during her childhood needed an outlet, and had kept Amelia in a state of constant inner stress and tension, ruining her health, her family relationships, and ultimately her own fulfilment as a person. As long as the mechanism of her unconscious remained active, Amelia could never really find satisfaction in her work or anything else for that matter. For at the level of her unconscious, the intention was not really to excel in her chosen profession, but to get back together with Mom in order to gain release from this non-integrated experience. And even if she had been successful in this, it would not have been enough. **In order to be delivered from such a mechanism, one must heal the wound and defuse the emotional charge built up in that memory.**

In the course of her inner work, Amelia brought back the experience of that profoundly wounded child within her, and most importantly, she was able to heal that wound.[10] As soon as she was able to defuse that memory through appropriate means,[11] Amelia was liberated from the tyranny of her unconscious, and was able to continue making valuable contributions to the world of science. Only now she was able to do it in a balanced and graceful way, without compulsion, without tension, without undue stress, and especially with a great sense of satisfaction.

For Amelia, work had been an outlet for blocked energy, where her conscious will was intertwined with the will of her unconscious, which controlled and stifled her energy. The details may be different for others, in different situations, but the outcome is always the same: dissatisfaction, failure, stress, anxiety, physical and emotional tensions, fatigue or hyperactivity, burnout, in short every form of "ill being".

This particular example illustrates many similar cases I have observed in the course of my practice, and clearly shows the mechanism of the personality. No matter how positive our activities or gains may be, we are perpetually dissatisfied and feel as if something is missing. It is then easy to complain, to give in to depression, to lay blame on others or on circumstances, to waste one's energy, to fall ill, or to keep trying to force things. This is indeed a bottomless pit. Luckily, Amelia's compulsion translated into a positive activity...her work. Even though the quality of her life had been squandered, this compulsion had at least led her to valuable studies and research projects. The will of her soul was still active to a certain extent. For this reason, it was relatively easy for her to set things right.

In other cases, the mechanisms of the unconscious can lead to far less positive outcomes. Some people find themselves in a state of emotional dependency, spending their lives seeking love and approval; others endlessly resort to all the variations of physical stuffing (food, drugs, sex, alcohol, tobacco), act like victims, or remain paralysed with fear and insecurity; others are compulsive controllers, or their reactions take the form of withdrawal, violence, or abuse of power. These dynamics can be very destructive physically and psychologically. In fact they include all the behaviours described in Chapter 2.

To complete our basic account of the way our computer functions, we will now describe another dynamic. Indeed, not only does the lower mind project past experiences and decisions onto the present, but it must also protect this accumulation of memories, and it has a number of strategies for this purpose. They are an integral part of the mechanism of the lower mind: let us now examine a few of them.

Strategies of the Lower Mind to Protect the False Self

The quest for a perpetually elusive identity

When we as human beings lost our connection with the Self through the identification of consciousness with matter, we also lost any real sense of our true nature. Since then we have been seeking to experience once again our true identity, a full and deep sense of existence that now seems out of our reach. In the meantime, our only frame of reference remains the mechanism of **the lower mind, which can only define itself in terms of past-recorded memories**.

Thus we end up building an illusion of identity, a false self.

But when we identify with this false self, since our lower mind has no real connection with our inner life force, this creates a very unpleasant and stressful unconscious feeling of non-existence, a **feeling of non-identity**. To compensate for this feeling of non-existence, the computer generates an array of automatic behaviours and strategies designed to constantly redefine and reinforce its false-identity based on this accumulation of non-integrated memories. At this level, therefore, not only do we react automatically on the basis of these memories, but we must also protect and reinforce these memories at all cost: this is a matter of survival.

This, in particular, is the reason why the unconscious defends its memories as if they were its most precious belonging, and resists any attempt to change its mechanisms, as if this were its own death warrant. In fact this is indeed a kind of death; the death of its automatic will to make way for the resurrection of the true self. The process of changing one's memories generates a terrible fear in the unconscious, and this fear will have to be transmuted into love and intelligence.

Most of the usual behaviours that we encounter in our everyday life are based on psychological defence or attack systems to protect and reinforce the illusion of this false self.

The strategies

As we observe these strategies, we find many of the behaviours described in Chapter 2. Thus we can begin to identify the source of these behaviours. Following are a few examples of these strategies:

- **Hanging onto one's point of view** and discrediting or invalidating other people's viewpoints. Our viewpoints—our way of perceiving things from the perspective of the lower mind—are a direct outcome of our memories and defence systems. It is therefore hardly surprising that, at this level of awareness, we put so much dogged effort in defending our views and refusing to change them. Our very survival is at stake!

- **Hanging onto what is known, and resisting change.** We can easily understand how anything that is new can be seen as a threat, since the lower mind has no grip on this new element. All it has on which to base its illusion of control and security is what is known and stored in its memories. Routine is reassuring to the ego, for it can thus "live" in the past. To change, to create or to innovate requires a level of flexibility that is totally unfamiliar to the computer, and it will put up as much resistance as it possibly can.

- **Wanting to prove that our belief systems are valid by endlessly recreating similar situations.** As it projects its memory-based perception onto the present, the lower mind cannot perceive anything it does not already have in stock. Thus it manages to validate all of these memories by recreating situations, whether real or perceived as such, which are reminiscent of similar situations in the past. This is why we see so many people constantly repeating the same mistakes, and falling into the same destructive and painful dynamics.

*Janet, who was raised by a violent father and a submissive mother, has unconsciously registered the fact that men who are affectively significant are violent and dangerous. In her adult life, Janet constantly attracts violent men. She wonders why. And even if some men in her social environment are neither violent nor dangerous, she manages to perceive them as such, which feeds the deep sense of mistrust stemming from her past and reinforces her withdrawal behaviours. In order to remain in tune with her memories and reinforce them, she will tend to avoid quiet and generous men, and to feel attracted, without her realizing it, to more aggressive men. She thus **validates her inner mechanism**: men are violent, women are victims. Yet this is quite the opposite of what she consciously wants.*

When we are unaware of this inner mechanism, we are generally unable to do anything but blame other people or circumstances for what happens to us. Yet this is just our distorted perception and our recreation of reality. As long as the memory-based mechanism remains active, it will continue to condition our choices, our attractions or revulsions, in order to validate these unresolved memories. For this reason, **reality as it is can never prove that these memories are inadequate**, since we perceive this reality through a filter of memories that distorts it so as to make it fit with our past experiences. Thus life can never provide evidence that our memory-based perception of reality is inaccurate. Life at this level of awareness can only provide reinforcement for past memories, with corresponding limitations and suffering.[12]

- **Dominating, manipulating, "colonizing":** The quest for power and domination is one of the strategies the ego uses to protect its memories. By dominating other human beings who can be manipulated according to one's whim, one turns these people into a kind of extension of oneself. Thus by seeking not only to be right but also to impose his own point of view, an individual who functions in this manner also reinforces his false identity.

- One aspect of this attempted "annexation" of other people to oneself is often found in couple relationships or parent-child relationships. The ego defines its own identity through the other person. A parent who has not fulfilled his/her own potential will try to compensate for this emptiness through his/her children. The child thus ends up carrying the load of this constant energy pumping and this stifling affective projection. This is a case where the ego seeks to **reinforce its own false identity by pumping it up with other people's energy.**

- **Avoiding domination:** Resisting other people's domination or power, or what the ego perceives as such, is also a reaction designed to maintain the illusion of the false-self. While trying to invade other people's territory through a wide variety of strategies, the lower mind cannot see anything but the same intention in others.

- **Feeling separate** is another tactic used by our computer to reinforce its false identity. The ego needs this illusion of separation. Painful as it may be, the sense of being different and separate from others provides an illusory sense of existence.

- **Comparing oneself to others:** The computer activates the mechanism of comparison in a desperate attempt to find a frame of reference that it can use to define itself, which is impossible.

- **Needing to possess:** The feeling of possession gives the ego an illusion of existence and self-definition. In a materialistic society such as ours, many people identify with their material possessions (Chapter 2), which they protect not only for the sake of security, but because they serve as a basis for personal definition as the false self. Thus we see people identifying with their cars, their Persian rugs, or anything material. As we know, if these possessions are "threatened" in any way, such people can become quite aggressive, as if the threat involved their very existence. In fact it is their very existence, since this is what they identify with. Of course this is also applicable in the case of affective possession, which causes even greater difficulties and suffering. We all know the tragedies this leads to on a daily basis. It is helpful to remember that we are possessed by what we think we possess...be it on a material or affective level.[13]

- **Destroying anything one does not identify with,** protecting what one identifies with at any cost. This explains a whole array of destructive behaviours that we can observe in the world at large, from criticism to physical aggression.

All this in a desperate quest to define, protect, and reinforce an identity, which does not exist.

When we live as prisoners of this false self, we can never experience a genuine, nurturing and natural sense of our existence, no matter what we do. It is a hopeless quest, for **we can only find our self when we stop identifying with this mechanism, instead of throttling it up to its maximum performance.**

The Experience of Reality

When our consciousness identifies with the lower mind, we can see that, on the one hand, our perception of reality is distorted in a major way, and, on the other hand, we react to this false perception on the basis of automatic defence mechanisms that generally have little to do with what is actually happening around us. How can we possibly be happy under these conditions? How can we gain any kind of mastery over our life, and experience freedom? This is simply not possible in such a context. It may be the best we could do up until now, but when we realize the nature of this mechanism, and **the profound state of illusion in which it binds most people**, the pathetic conditions they create for themselves and for others on this planet come as no surprise. The situation can be summarized in the following diagram:

Diagram 3

The Perception of Reality Through the Lower Mind

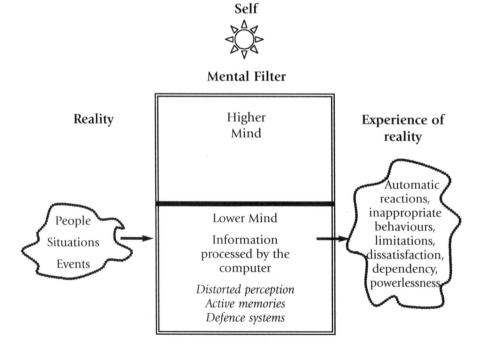

How Do We Sort This Out?

How can we become free again? Instead of living like a computer-controlled automatic device, we would like to be able to turn this computer into an instrument that we can use deliberately and consciously, on the basis of wisdom and genuine knowledge of the Self. Is this in fact possible?

The first thing to do is to become aware of the existence of this computer within us, and to recognize how it functions in our daily life. As long as we do not have a clear grasp of this fact, we will remain in a state of complete stupor at the mercy of these automatic mechanisms. Just knowing these mechanisms exist can help us become more of a witness to the dance of our personality. This neutral and compassionate **witness stance**, a first step towards unidentification, is an attitude that all spiritual traditions recommend.[14]

In this chapter, we have begun to discover the general workings of the lower mind, based on memories that generate a whole array of defence systems. In the Part Two of this book, we will take a closer look at five major types of defence systems, which will also be illustrated through living examples and will provide a more specific understanding of the mechanism of our lower nature.

In Part Three of this book, once this basic knowledge has been established, we will elaborate on the different stages involved in working on the conscious, unconscious and supraconscious levels, to allow us eventually to be free of the bonds of the lower mind, and to experience the emerging presence of the soul.

In the meantime, we shall continue our exploration of the human machine and observe in more precise detail how memories are installed over time, and how links develop between them.

> It is possible to stop being a machine, but in order for this to happen
> we must first get to know the machine.
> —*Gurdjieff*

[1] Alice Bailey, *A Treatise on White Magic,* page 85

[2] Obviously the following description is only intended as a model. Yet here again, this model is founded on reality. Not only is it consistent with the latest discoveries in transpersonal psychology, and with basic spiritual teachings, but also I have experienced it and found it to be effective in my professional activities as I worked with thousands of people on their way to personal transformation. It has proven to be a useful tool for genuine and practical consciousness development.

[3] This explains why, according to certain spiritual Masters, transformation is not something to be "worked" at. Indeed, divine qualities are not cultivated: they are simply there, permanently. To access these qualities, all that is needed is to make the personality receptive and ready, and to get rid of past hang-ups. When we say "all that is needed", this actually means quite a program! (This is what takes time.) So the past does not make us what we are: in fact, because of all its non-integrated aspects, the past is filled with limitations. However, once it has indeed been integrated and harmonized, the past is what allows us **to have a reliable instrument that is available to us so that we can express what we are in the three worlds.** This outlook flies in the face of any linear, rational principle of cause and effect. As we have often been told, "there is nothing to be learnt; we have only to go back to who we really are" (but this time with an instrument that can manifest this on the worldly plane).

[4] The term "unconscious" may lead to some misconceptions, bringing to mind a weak, almost inactive mechanism. In fact, that part of the computer can only be called unconscious in relation to our waking consciousness. In reality, it is very much awake and active, as it fastidiously takes note of everything that happens. It is consistent, very well organized and effective in the way it functions, working non-stop, 24 hours a day, on the performance of its tasks. And it never forgets. This is an extraordinarily well-designed and efficient mechanism.

[5] Yes, even joyful moments can generate active memories when they are experienced against a backdrop of anxiety or compensation for some form of deprivation or trauma.

[6] This is why some oriental traditions describe the world as an illusion. In fact the world is not an illusion: rather it is our perception of the world that is completely illusory, as long as our consciousness is bound by ego.

[7] Op. cit., page 101.

[8] Further on we shall see why we say that these records are "recreated" rather than "created". In fact, childhood is just an occasion to reactualize memories that go back much further. We will examine this point in greater detail in Chapter 5. For now, we will just focus on what happens during childhood as a way to illustrate how the lower mind works. Later on we can easily broaden this perspective.

[9] In Chapter 2, we saw how common personality-induced behaviours really are. In Volume 1, we examined in greater detail a number of character structures which are deeply rooted in the collective consciousness of our times, and which clearly illustrate how unoriginal the ego actually is.

[10] It is not necessary to know the whole story in order for the healing process to take place.

[11] This will be further developed in Chapter 10.

[12] This is an important point, which was developed, in greater detail in Chapter 2 of *The Power of Free Will,* op. cit. note 1, Chapter 1.

[13] A classic on this topic: *To Have or To Be*, Erich Fromm.

[14] This will be further developed in Chapter 11.

chapter 5

Where do Memories Originate?

When we described the workings of our computer (the lower conscious and unconscious mind) in terms of a reservoir of "memories", we generally referred to "past" experiences. These were the building blocks that went into the construction of the ego, whereby our consciousness was ushered into the physical world. But we have also seen how, as a result of certain unintegrated experiences, the lower mind became cluttered with residual debris and locked in self-programmed responses, thereby curtailing any direct expression of the Self. What is the specific content of these past experiences? Where do the memories come from?

The examples mentioned thus far all went back to early childhood. We can easily imagine how, in our present lifetimes, we have accumulated a sum of experiences, which have remained imprinted in our unconscious. On the other hand, when we work towards a deeper level of self-knowledge, we cannot help but notice that our unconscious seems to harbour a great deal of stuff—that is to say other sources of memories—which has nothing to do with our present life. In order to initiate a genuine and durable process of inner transformation, we must expand our perception of what constitutes our "past".

First of all, referring to the model presented in Chapter 3, the active and loose memories stored in our unconscious could have originated in all the experiences through which our soul has perfected its instrument, in the course of its evolution. From this perspective, we will examine memories that were created:

- **in our present lifetime** (beginning with yesterday and going back not just to **early childhood** but also including the experience of **birth** and of **intra-uterine life**); and

- **in "past lives",** or whatever we choose to refer to as such.

In addition, our observations have shown that the unconscious could carry an even broader spectrum of memories as a result of two other types of factors:

- **our ancestry:** the soul seems to also find material directly in the ancestry that it has chosen as part of a personality's experience within a given lifetime; and

- **the collective unconscious: as human beings,** even though we have gone through the process of individuation, we are not separate from each other in essence. This fact can also have a bearing on the content of our memories.

Our Present Life Experiences

These cover all of our past within this lifetime, starting with the last few minutes and going back to early childhood, birth, and intra-uterine life.

- **Early childhood**

It is a long-established fact, even in the most conventional approach to psychology, that early childhood circumstances have a bearing on individual behaviour. In the Western world, Freud was a pioneer in this field. Though it may seem rather sophisticated at first glance, his approach is somewhat limited and outdated in the light of all the discoveries made in the course of this century regarding the content of the unconscious. We can now go much deeper and be far more precise as we analyse the dynamics of our unconscious, though this does not have to be a complicated process.

Yet even though we recognize the impact of early childhood circumstances on an individual's adult behaviour, a more pointed observation shows that a human being is not a simple mechanism reacting to such circumstances in a predictable, automatic manner. Indeed, if our behaviour were conditioned solely by early childhood circumstances, at least two questions would arise:

- Why is it that two children growing up in the same circumstances can end up behaving in radically different ways? There are examples of this all around us.

- Why are some children born in very favourable circumstances, while others face very unfavourable circumstances? Pure chance? This is an easy but unsatisfactory answer, for it implies a lack of knowledge of some fundamental laws. Einstein himself said, "Chance is the path chosen by God when He wants to travel incognito."

Many other observations of human behaviour have also been made that cannot be explained simply as a result of external childhood circumstances. Mozart's father was a musician, yet not all children of musician parents end up being Mozarts. We must therefore expand our perspective and consider different aspects.

- **Birth and intra-uterine life**

Besides early childhood circumstances, which have been amply examined in the light of conventional psychology as well as many alternative approaches, one can easily detect and consider other factors. For instance, it is now generally recognized that conditions prevailing during birth and during intra-uterine life can impact an individual's behaviour in very specific ways. Otto Rank, a psychiatrist and dissident disciple of Freud, was one of the first to emphasize the importance of the birth trauma. Another psychiatrist, Stanislav Grof, took the matter further and developed a comprehensive approach focusing on the different stages of intra-uterine life and birth. Since the 70s, the popular Rebirthing movement has brought the subject into the public eye. Professionals from various sectors have conducted many studies in this field.

No matter what our individual viewpoint may be, or which philosophy underscores these various approaches, there is a point of convergence regarding the impact of prevailing conditions during birth and intra-uterine life on an individual's behaviour, on his difficulties or ease of coping with the world. In my own experience, I have seen clear evidence of this influence, and have developed my own debugging methods so that anyone can manifest his potential more freely.

Physical birth in particular, is an experience that leaves a very deep imprint at all levels. After nine months spent in the relative tranquillity of the mother's womb (though as we shall see, there can be many occasions for blockages to occur in utero), and in a state of consciousness that is still in touch with higher planes of existence, a highly sensitive being is suddenly expelled from the matrix. Now the unborn child is anything but unconscious, as our materialistic viewpoint might lead us to believe. On the contrary, this child is hypersensitive at all levels. The latest research on what goes on during intra-uterine life and during the process of birth has produced new and important data on the unborn child's state of consciousness, and on the psychological and spiritual aspects of this momentous event called birth. As we are beginning to realize that we need to rethink our approach to assisting people through the process of dying, we are also realizing how urgent it is to relearn how to welcome those who are going through the process of being born.[1]

In the meantime, the kind of birth available to us until recently as Westerners has been the source of all kinds of trauma. In Part Two of this book, we will go over some real life examples that illustrate this fact. However, our experience suggests that it is not enough to focus strictly on conditions at the time of birth and during intra-uterine life, no matter how crucial and determining these factors may be. One must dig a little deeper if one wishes to gain a better understanding of how complex the structure of the unconscious actually is, and to develop a more comprehensive approach that is also more consistent with the evidence of practical observation. We must then look for other sources.

• Looking beyond our present lifetime

In the course of my professional experience working with the unconscious, though I was not trying to prove anything, I could not help but notice that every individual carries a bundle of "stories" that seem unrelated to his present life experience or environment. We can look at the source of these stories from several viewpoints.

To suggest that these deeply embedded stories are merely figments of our imagination, without significance of any sort, or that they are the result of some external influence, is simply not consistent with the actual experience of countless individuals. To reject them offhand because we cannot find any explanation for them, or because they challenge rigid belief systems, is both simplistic and ineffective. Indeed **these stories are energetically charged**. When we happen to make contact with them, they trigger specific emotions and physical sensations. The depth, variety and resonance of these "stories" cannot be ignored. I am certainly not alone in this observation, which I have had ample opportunity to confirm through my studies and experiences with thousands of cases.

In addition, and this is the most interesting facet of this field of inquiry, when we take these memories into consideration and deactivate them, we can achieve clear and long-term healing of physical ailments, as well as psychological liberations that make a positive concrete difference in our everyday life. Is this not what we are looking for?

The source of these charged stories seems to spring from three levels: our "personal" past lives, our ancestry, and the collective unconscious. It is interesting to observe each of these categories.

Let us note that as far as healing is concerned—being liberated from the stranglehold of these memories—all of these experiences can be treated in a similar fashion. Whether these stories stem from actual personal past lives, or from a collective unconscious, is ultimately unimportant. What matters is to observe that these memories are active, regardless of their origin, and to find a way to deactivate them so as to be able to re-establish a connection with the soul.

Memories Stemming from "Past Lives"

To begin with, let us consider the perspective of past personal lifetimes. Going back to the esoteric model presented in Chapter 3, the accumulation not only of knowledge but also of psychic debris in the course of past lifetimes makes sense. There is no problem with treating the resulting stories as if they stemmed from an individual's past lives (except for the lower mind, which likes to hang onto its viewpoints). All that is needed is that we remain vigilant, as we mentioned previously, making sure that our ego does not appropriate this perspective to feed an illusion of continuity.

Following are two examples of healing among the thousands I have heard.

Martine is a beautiful woman in her thirties. Everything in her life is going well, except her love life. She tried three times to develop a serious relationship with a man, each time ending up in the same scenario: the minute she begins to feel committed to a significant other, she becomes worried, stressed out and riddled with fears. She would like her partner to be constantly at her side. Whenever he leaves, even for just a few hours, she feels sad, despondent, and anxious for his return. Each time, her partners wearied of her constant anxiety and incessant demands. She began a process of inner work in order to free herself from this dependency. Shortly thereafter, she developed a new relationship with a man who lived in England. They had met in Paris and regularly spent time together each time he travelled to France on business. Martine found the periods of separation more and more distressing. Once, when she had a few days off, she decided to go and visit her boyfriend at his home, in a beautiful place in the country, a couple of hours' drive away from London. He was very happy to see her.

The next day, he took her sightseeing in the surrounding area, stopping in particular at an old mill that was considered a landmark. When Martine entered the place, she suddenly felt very uncomfortable, for no apparent reason, to the point of almost fainting. Her boyfriend took her home in a hurry, and told her to lie down on the sofa while he started a fire. Martine's discomfort worsened. When she tried breathing to dispel this burden of gloom, she relived the following story: she was in a very similar setting to where she had been only a few hours before. She was the daughter of the lord of the county, young and beautiful, with several young men vying for her favour. But she had a secret love, the son of the wet nurse who had been in charge of her upbringing. She often went to see him secretly, at her father's mill. They took long walks together in the woods, and dreamed of being able to live together forever. Her father became aware of his daughter's excursions, and ordered her to stop seeing this man, who was beneath her station in life. This could be tolerated as long as she was a child, but now she had to honour her title. Martine continued to see her boyfriend nevertheless, until the day when her father had her followed, and found out that she secretly went to him every night. The father had a fit, and decided that this had to stop immediately.

One of his friends was a ship's captain who was looking for young men to be part of his crew on a journey to the South Seas. The father arranged to have his daughter's young lover aboard the ship until the latter set sail for the open sea. That night, Martine waited for her lover, who did not show up. She asked for him the next day, but no one had seen him. She became more and more worried, and searched for him everywhere. She went to her father's mill and eventually found out that her beloved had left aboard a ship. Her heart was broken; she could not understand how he could have let her down this way. She cried for a long time, and so deep was her grief that she lost her will to live. She only found out much later what had actually happened. But it was too late…the scar of abandonment was there for good.

As a result of this painful experience of abandonment, which "Martine" was not able to integrate at that time, a powerful active memory was imprinted which, during subsequent lives, conditioned everything that had to do with love relationships. Following this spontaneous jolt of awareness, Martine continued her inner work, focusing specifically on her unconscious. She was able to heal this scar that she had carried unknowingly for so long, and to defuse the memory. The permanent state of anxiety that had haunted her for so long disappeared. It was as if a great burden had been lifted from her shoulders. She was able to enjoy her new relationship without fear, feeling calm and relaxed, with a sense of freedom such as she had never known before.

Michelle, a young woman of twenty-eight, still lives with her parents. She refuses to live an independent adult life so as to remain close to her mother and take care of her. Yet the latter is in fine health and does not need any particular form of aid, leading a pleasant life with a wonderful husband. Though she has done very well as a student and is about to graduate with a degree in medicine, Michelle has a deep lack of self-

confidence. She always has to check how well she is doing, and is forever seeking to fulfil an unrequited need for approval. Though she has all the requisite qualifications, and she passed all her exams with the highest marks, she is not sure at all that she has what it takes to succeed in her chosen career. This totally irrational doubt is poisoning her life, and she knows it. While going through a process of inner work, she spontaneously came across a "story", deeply lodged in her unconscious. The story took place around the Eighteenth Century. She was travelling with her mother on a sailing ship, which eventually went down in a storm. She found herself in a lifeboat, fighting for her life along with a few other people, including her mother. The storm raged, with huge waves breaking all around them. Her mother fell overboard. "Michelle" reached out to her, but her mother was already beyond her reach, and all too quickly vanished under the waves. Horror stricken, Michelle felt a great shadowy form descending upon her, smothering her with guilt, saying, "It's your fault your mother has drowned." In this awful state of stress, panic and grief, an active memory is branded into her unconscious: "I am unworthy, unable to be of help; I will be judged and hated by others for having let my mother die."

Michelle came into this life carrying this memory, which never fails to be reactivated on any occasion, no matter how insignificant. Through an adequate process of inner work, she was able to get rid of this unconscious mechanism. Her permanent state of anxiety with regard to her mother vanished. She regained a natural self-confidence, which now allows her to practice her profession far more efficiently. She started to feel alive, free, and inwardly serene.

Thanks to the esoteric model presented in Chapter 3, we can better understand the process whereby these memories were stored, their purpose, and what we can eventually do with them. Yet to work on these energetically charged memories, it is not necessary to believe in reincarnation. All that is needed is to recognize their existence, even if we are not particularly interested in finding or exploring their source. We have been led to this perspective as a result of the practical work of inner healing and liberation, which this model makes possible, more than through the theory itself.[2] This model closely reflects the reality of the many experiences I was privileged to observe. As in any scientific research, experience is what validates the model, rather than the other way around.

As far as we are concerned, we shall therefore assume that, along with our present life experiences, we carry memories stemming from past lives, from past experiences undergone by the various personalities taken on by a developing ego…the whole process being orchestrated by the soul, which oversees the evolution of its instrument.

We can now expand our perspective even further, adding to these memories the memories of our ancestral lineage and of the collective unconscious, which were selected by the soul to speed up the process. Before we go into this aspect, we would like to draw a clearer picture of a specific dynamic, which brings all these memories together. Indeed it seems that these memories, and the conditions that foster their creation, do not occur independent of each other. A link seems to exist, which is often very strong, between unintegrated past life experiences (whether they stem from a personal, ancestral or collective source), and present life circumstances, especially initial circumstances (intra-uterine life, birth, and early childhood).

The Link Between Past Life and the Initial Circumstances of Our Present Lifetime
(or how material is selected to be worked on in each lifetime)

Based on what I have observed, even if the initial circumstances of one's present lifetime seem to have a bearing on one's behaviour, they do not appear to be the basic causes, but rather the **consequences of much heavier baggage stemming from past lives.** This is an important factor, for it allows for a far more flexible and thorough approach to inner work. In reference to this impact of past lives, we need to go beyond a general and often simplistic theory of karma, and to develop a more precise understanding of the dynamics whereby certain circumstances surrounding one's childhood or birth are recreated.

According to the esoteric model, with each journey into matter, each lifetime, the soul "chooses" certain life circumstances for its personality in order to foster the latter's construction and refinement on the way to becoming a better instrument. So in this sense there is no question of chance, as evolution is seen as a grand process of learning to gain mastery in the three worlds, a process orchestrated by the higher consciousness of the Self. This perspective, by the way, is a major incentive to take full responsibility for our fate and the circumstances of our present life, and it also gives us an opportunity to shed a very debilitating attitude, that of the victim.

Regarding this concept of selecting our present life circumstances, certain clarification is needed, as it may lead to some confusion. To better understand this selection process, we can look at the issue from an energy viewpoint. According to the model described in Chapter 3, whenever we descend into a new incarnation, we energetically attract all the appropriate materials to build a new personality. In particular, as the lower mind and the emotional body are being constructed, we attract a number of active memories that are part of our baggage and that we have the option to work on during the course of this incarnation. Once loaded with these memories (both the active and the loose memories), we attract life circumstances that are in tune with these memories. Despite appearances, this resonance is not there for nothing, or just to have us endlessly go through the same difficulties.

Indeed, our practical observations have revealed the following mechanism: we attract or "choose" our early childhood and general life circumstances and events in order, first of all, to allow us to express previously acquired qualities, and second of all, to **revive certain memories that remain fixed in our unconscious so as to have an opportunity to defuse them by bringing them to the forefront once again,** in some form or other. So the circumstances surrounding our birth or early childhood are not the primary cause of subsequent behaviours. They are merely occasions for reactivating much stronger memories recorded over a series of past lives, and which have yet to be resolved. On the personality level, we then have the choice, as human beings, to do whatever we like with these conditions.[3]

An interesting fact worth noting and considering is that the entire process of evolution occurs in a non-linear fashion, in a kind of spiral dynamic. This explains why we notice certain apparently recurring situations within a given lifetime or in a series of lifetimes. This process can be observed at all levels and in all natural phenomena. It stems from a resonance, an echo, a repetition of "lessons" which must be consciously integrated in order to further the process of evolution. If we compare this to a school, we review what has been learnt so as to better integrate it, and so as to be able to follow it up with new knowledge. Each lifetime is a review as well as a program for further learning.

Specifically, my observations have shown that we often reconstruct birth circumstances that reactivate the experience of an earlier traumatic death (though not necessarily from the immediately preceding lifetime, as time does not exist at the level of the soul). A classic example is that of a person born with the umbilical cord wrapped around his neck. In a case such as this, what often emerges is a "story" of death by hanging. The average human being has not yet reached a level of development that would allow one to accept such a death in total serenity and with total detachment. So at that moment a very strong charge is created, both at the physical level (the survival mechanism of maximum resistance) and at the emotional level (there must have been some rather unpleasant occurrences leading to the hanging). At the moment of hanging, the entire personality tenses up in resistance, and the stress registers as an active memory, which will be reactivated in the course of another lifetime, at a time deemed appropriate by the soul, so as to give the personality a chance to integrate the experience.

During a traumatic death experience, the imprint goes very deep since it is a matter of physical survival, and since there is no possibility to defuse the stress because the body disappears. For this reason, along with all our life experiences, we carry with us all our violent death traumas, and we have all had such experiences. These will have to be re-enacted either at birth or at some point in a physical lifetime, so that we have a chance to let them go.

Birth, in particular, is an especially potent occasion for memory reactivation, since at that moment the child is undergoing some rather difficult circumstances while in a state of great physical and psychic vulnerability. The following are just a few examples: going through the birth canal can reactivate memories of suffocation, of being buried alive, of powerlessness; a forceps birth may conjure up memories of physical aggression; being immediately taken to the nursery (a common practice in North America) will trigger memories of abandonment, etc. Many specific birth conditions, which were common for the last several decades, may have reactivated all kinds of traumas, especially traumas relating to physical survival and death.[4]

We are talking about events surrounding birth and the first few years of life, for this is when the personality is most malleable and can be reconstructed in a specific manner. But obviously, beyond early childhood, one's entire life history is full of circumstances having the potential to reactivate old memories (whether personal, ancestral or collective), and to allow a process of integration to take place according to whatever level of consciousness the individual has reached.

The following story gives a specific example of how past life conditions are reactivated during childhood, and how they can have an impact on adult life.

Lewis is a woodworker. His life might have been a pleasant one, if it weren't for a state of stress and fatigue making life very difficult for him as well as for those close to him. Yet he loves his work, for he really likes using his hands to create things. But each piece of furniture, each object he creates quickly becomes a source of tension. He cannot help creating under stress, which obviously leaves him quickly exhausted, and he doesn't understand why. True, he sometimes gets urgent commissions. But generally speaking, there is no specific tension involved in his line of work. Or sometimes, without any apparent reason, his energy disappears, and he becomes incapable of working. He can thus spend weeks without taking any orders, feeling discouraged and lifeless. He has seen doctors who have alternately prescribed sedatives to reduce the stress, and stimulants to counter fatigue. Yet nothing seems to work. What is going on?

In that instance, we were able to retrace the memory stemming from a past life, and how it was reactivated during childhood.

This happened in Italy around the Thirteenth Century. Lewis was an armourer working for the king. He was in charge of designing and manufacturing weapons for the royal army. One day he got an urgent message from the king asking him to make a unique weapon, one designed especially for His Majesty, which the king would bear on the occasion of a great feast honouring a visit from a neighbouring Lord. Lewis got to work, approaching the project with utmost care and creativity. He knew the king was a very demanding customer, and that one had better not trifle with His Majesty's despotic nature. He came up with something that he found very beautiful, and certainly very original. Nowhere would anyone find another weapon like it. He proudly delivered his handiwork, fully expecting to be showered with praise. A few days later, an emissary of the king turned up at his home, bringing back the weapon along with a note letting him know that the king did not appreciate such jokes, and was very angry. Lewis was stripped of his title as armourer, and his belongings were confiscated. He was expected to leave the city at once, failing which he would be sent to prison for daring to make fun of His Royal Majesty. He was devastated. His son had just married, and his wife was expecting a baby. When his son heard the news, he disowned his father for he did not want to be smeared with such a disgrace. Lewis had to drop everything and leave in a hurry. So he fled, alone, overcome with a profound sense of injustice, treason, seething anger, and feeling deeply wounded inside with regard to his creative ability. Whereas his had been a noble and wealthy life, he now found himself destitute, with barely enough to eat. He thus lived out the rest of his life in poverty and disgrace.

In his present lifetime, during his childhood, Lewis always wanted to make things with his hands. Yet each time he was ready to act, it was as if the desire vanished. So in the end, he did not accomplish much. He was sad. Sometimes he might take the chance of creating something for the fun of it, but then it always had to be very beautiful and absolutely perfect. He never stopped fixing whatever little thing he had made, as if it were never good enough, and he would end up dropping the project, with always a sense of unfinished work. He would have liked his father to encourage him with a positive comment; maybe that would have helped. But the latter was cold and distant, and hardly took notice of what his son was doing. He never even gave it a glance.

One day, when he was eight years old, Lewis took a chance and built a lovely little blue and white boat. He had made a nice, little paddlewheel, and had placed an elastic band in the stern so that it could move under its own power. It was a brilliant piece of work, and he was very proud of it. He was so pleased with it that he decided this time to go and see his father and show it to him. So he went to see him one morning while he was having breakfast. Feeling a little nervous, he placed the boat on the table close to his cup of coffee, ready to show him how it worked. Before he had a chance to open his mouth, his father pushed the little boat to the other end of the table, telling him not to bother him with trifles, and at once turned towards the television set, turning up the volume as he did so. Lewis tried to bring back the boat and give some explanations, but the TV was too loud, and it was obvious that his father was not about to take a look at his work. He left with his little boat, feeling very sad. He cried all day, put his boat in a closet and left it there. Old unconscious memories had been reactivated (the father, the king, the original creation, the boat, the weapon, his father's non-recognition, rejection, etc.). Then everything was repressed deep in his unconscious. The boat remained unused in the closet until the moment when, four years later, Lewis's parents moved. His mother found the boat and gave it to the neighbour's son.

Lewis's difficulties in his present work have nothing to do with a lack of vitamins, or competence, or other external circumstances. The dynamic is very simple: the minute Lewis wants to get down to work, his unconscious either shuts down the energy supply or generates an intense state of stress since producing original creations has had very painful consequences in the past (during childhood and in a past life). The active memory is there, the defence system is in place, simply trying to minimize the risk of suffering.

But Lewis did not choose this father and this trade in this lifetime for no reason. This is an opportunity for him to reactivate and to heal the wound, and thus to free himself from the constricting mechanism embedded in the memory. He in fact did manage to liberate himself from this memory through inner work and a change in consciousness. He thus recovered his capacity for unfettered, totally original and joyful creativity.

I have witnessed a multitude of similar stories. Evidently one may experience many limitations even though one may not have had a terribly traumatic childhood or birth. The slightest little event can become the subject of a genuine trauma, if this event reactivates a traumatic experience from a past lifetime.

On the other hand, for some individuals, even very difficult circumstances may not turn into a major handicap, providing these circumstances are not meant to reactivate some deeper memories, but rather to foster the development or the manifestation of certain qualities. This partly explains why children who were raised in similar conditions can end up behaving in very different ways. This depends on the baggage carried within each being, which will lead to specific ways of reacting to external circumstances.

> One's reaction to childhood circumstances depends on each person's level of evolution (the proportion of active and loose memories).

There are well-known cases of children raised in dreadful conditions who later turn out to be generous adults serving their community. There are also cases of children raised in the best possible conditions, who collapse at the first sign of difficulty. Genetics do not provide a satisfactory explanation for everything. From my perspective, a child comes into this world with some evolutionary baggage and psychic programmings that will determine how he or she copes with life and with circumstances chosen by his or her soul (including genetic conditions).

The following account accurately describes this apparent "contradiction" between specific childhood circumstances and subsequent behaviours. Dr. E. James Anthony is a psychiatrist, head of the Department of Child Psychotherapy at Chestnut Lodge, and professor at Washington University in St. Louis, Missouri. During an interview,[5] he described two cases that he feels clearly illustrate two types of behaviours encountered in his work. He mentioned the following case of a little girl who was one of his patients.

She was cute, intelligent, well-mannered, pampered by her parents (well-educated and affluent people) and very popular with her peers and teachers. Here was the perfect child, always coming out first in her class, the one student set up as an example to others. One day, this little girl was goaded by a classmate into throwing a snowball through a school window. The young rascal thereupon was quick to squeal on her to the principal. With some surprise, the latter sent for the girl and very gently asked her why she did this. The child began to tremble and cry. Then she lay down and rolled on the floor. The principal tried to soothe her, unsuccessfully, and then sent her home, where she continued her fit. The girl literally lost contact with reality. The parents took her to the hospital, where she was sent to my department. I went to see her the next day. Her behaviour was weird. I approached her nicely, jokingly. She became aggressive, threatening, refusing to talk about herself. She told me: "Your hospital is unsafe. There is no emergency exit here!" I explained that this department had no need for emergency exits. Little by little, as the days went by, she found her balance again. Two years later, she had a relapse, this time over a common pimple on her cheek. Her feeling was that this pimple was a symptom of some deadly disease. Once again, she managed to overcome her fitful state. In the following months, she had another relapse. I finally had to explain to the parents that their daughter was seriously ill and needed to be placed in an institution. In spite of growing up with loving parents, who were obviously attentive to the point of doing whatever they could to shelter her from life's inevitable trials, here was a child who could not withstand the slightest little shock.

Evidently this child did not need dramatic circumstances to bring up powerful active memories. From our perspective, we do not see this person as being "sick"; she is merely reacting to conditions that reactivate powerfully traumatic circumstances from past lives. To "heal" this type of seemingly abnormal behaviour, one needs only to work on the unconscious in order to release the previously installed memory which is replayed according to the dynamic described earlier. It is interesting to note that, in the doctor's own words, this little girl "lost contact with reality". Obviously, she was reliving a memory from another time. Based on my observation of similar cases, it is possible that, when the girl was summoned to the principal's office, this reactivated a memory such as being summoned before a court and being sentenced to torture, or to incarceration in terrible conditions, or to a violent death. In addition, if she saw the hospital as a dangerous place because it did not have an emergency exit, this is not just unsubstantiated madness. She knows very well what she is talking about, on the basis of a past reality that she is projecting onto the present. Most likely, in some past circumstances, she was caught in a terrifying place from which there was no exit to save herself. All this may seem unreasonable from a narrow, rational viewpoint, but it is perfectly coherent when viewed in the light of active memories.

This is an extreme example, but we all carry these types of memories within us, perhaps not so heavily charged, or so poorly integrated, yet nevertheless capable of generating aberrant behaviours, which translate into a variety of pain-inducing limitations. It may be less spectacular, but the dynamic is the same. The induced behaviours are simply more socially acceptable, to the extent that the behaviours described in Chapter 2 are considered acceptable.

On the other hand, Dr. Anthony states:

It was striking to note the absence of disorders among some children who are going through horrifying experiences in appalling environments. And, like most researchers who have taken an interest in this issue, I tried to find out what traits these invulnerable children have in common. They are very comfortable in group situations, and are able to make everybody else comfortable. They are kind and well-liked by their peers. Socially, they act in appropriate ways. They work well, play well, love well, and are very optimistic. They constantly try to control their environment, and have a sense of their own empowerment. They also know how to make good use of the help they get from adults, and are able to spot those who can give them such assistance. They are self-supporting at a very early age—they have no choice! They are not affected by whatever ails their mothers or fathers. Nevertheless they distance themselves, psychologically and physically, from the sick parent, yet this does not stop them from understanding that the latter is suffering and is not responsible for whatever he or she is doing. They build themselves a little private territory where they seek shelter whenever things turn too ugly. They are often very creative and original in the way they play, and later in their work.

Dr. Anthony gives an example:

One day a little 9-year-old girl was referred to him. She lived in an overcrowded and unsanitary neighbourhood. Her father was frequently in jail for drunkenness and family violence. Her mother was chronically depressed. In addition, the child had a malformation of the hip and limped as she walked. "What immediately struck me was how nice she was. She went through the interview with a forthright, cordial manner that I found completely disarming. In fact I was expecting some form of aggressive behaviour. She made me so comfortable with her that I was soon talking to her with far less reserve than I usually do! This little girl, who was surprisingly well-balanced, and well-liked by her teachers—she had excellent marks in school—told me she wanted to become a nurse and take care of poor children! There is another characteristic trait of these invulnerable children: they have such a sense of inner strength that they are prepared to help those whom they consider to be even less fortunate than themselves."

These examples are interesting as they demonstrate how, even in circumstances that are tailor-made to reactivate memories, the determining factor in an individual's reaction is not the circumstances themselves, but the quantity and intensity of the active or loose memories that the individual carries within, his level of evolution. Specifically, the qualities this doctor describes as typical of these "unbreakable" children are some of the qualities manifested by the Self, which we shall describe further on. These children, who are still a minority at this point, are highly evolved beings. They probably carry relatively few active and heavily charged memories, and a great deal more "loose" memories. They have chosen difficult conditions for reasons of evolution, just as any other, but for them the presence of the Self is stronger than the mechanism of the lower mind. They are able to use these conditions to develop specific qualities, and thus to be able to make a positive contribution in the world.

Yet it is important to recognize that the soul is consistent in its intention, and that it chooses living conditions, particularly initial conditions (intra-uterine life, birth and early childhood) that will, on the one hand, foster the maturation of qualities already present, at least potentially, and on the other hand, reactivate past life experiences which were not integrated so as to create a setting for potential release.

• Must we know all of our past stories?

Further on we shall see that working on self-liberation **does not mean that we have to know the entire history of our past lives.** Thank goodness, for that would take an enormous amount of time, and what we are concerned with is not the history itself but our own release from its constricting legacy. This release process varies, of course, depending on what method we use. But whatever that is, we shall see that there is one aspect to these memories that can allow us to gain relatively quick release and integration of many experiences at once, without having to research every one of these stories.

Indeed, all of the "memories" linked to a particular type of energy blockage, whether they stem from our own history (our present and past lives), or, as we shall see further on, from our ancestral lineage or the collective unconscious, all of these memories are energetically linked and constitute specific aggregates. At the level of the unconscious, there is no passage of time and our experiences are not catalogued in chronological order. Rather they are classified, so to speak, into blockage categories, i.e. groups bearing similar forms of energy. **As far as the unconscious is concerned, all of the memories linked to a specific defence mechanism are identical.** For example, every event classified under the heading "abandonment" is the same and is energetically linked, no matter what moment in time this event was experienced or re-experienced. Consequently, if we work on releasing a specific memory, from our childhood for example, or from a particular past life, we will energetically contact a whole chain of memories. It is as if we were pulling on the energetic thread running through all of them, so that the entire lot can be unravelled relatively quickly.

For this reason, an effective release process can be initiated by working on traumas or blockages going back to our childhood, and especially our birth, a highly charged event. Conversely, a release from some past life trauma can undo many blockages that were recreated at birth or during our present lifetime. A chain of memories can be deactivated without specifically recalling all of our stories and working on each one of them, providing of course that the deactivation process is genuine and properly accomplished.

Even if Lewis had not retraced his past life history, he could have unravelled the knot by working on this aspect as it showed up during his childhood, without necessarily recalling past life experiences. And vice versa: a past life experience that is integrated in the course of one's inner work can resolve hang-ups from one's childhood. What is important is not the particular story that happens to be contacted, but the flexibility of the method used to approach the unconscious, which *will open the door at the most appropriate moment* so that liberation can take place. This will be examined in greater detail in the third part of this book.

• Memories do not fade over time

The fact that the unconscious does not register memories on a time line also explains why, whenever someone contacts a memory, he or she can experience all the emotions and sensations connected to that memory, often in great detail, as if it were happening now. If we do not consciously recall these "stories", or if we just get a vague recollection, it is not because the memory has "faded" with the passage of time, it is simply because we are not yet able to have clear enough access to the unconscious.

In our ordinary state of awareness, where we use only a small part of the mind, we are incapable of recalling every little event, even from this present lifetime. This is why we think memories fade over time. In fact, they are merely **transferred from the conscious to the unconscious level.** Let us remember that the computer, as described in Chapter 4, records everything and keeps everything scrupulously stored in memory, in minute detail, in order to ensure its own survival. Once recorded, **each of these memories remains as is and time is of no consequence.** All of the potential, whether positive or constricting, that was built up through past experiences is thus permanently available for recall at any given moment, except that our waking consciousness is very limited, and thus cannot perceive the total content of our consciousness as a whole. The process of transformation could be defined as the process whereby the content of the unconscious and the supraconscious can be brought to the conscious level.

> The process of transformation can be defined as the process whereby the content of the unconscious and the supraconscious can be brought to the conscious level.

When a person reaches a high level of development, he or she then becomes aware of the entire history of his or her evolutionary past. To get there, one must reach a level of awareness that makes it easy to remain unidentified with this history, and to perceive it as only one aspect of the overall development of one's soul and of the collective soul.

We might wonder why it is that we cannot recall everything in our normal state of awareness. One of the reasons is that the emotional charge of these memories is simply too strong and it would be impossible to recreate these experiences in a new way. This is why there is no guarantee whatsoever that some external input describing these past "lives" will trigger a genuine release at a deeper level. If some clairvoyant tells us that we have experienced a certain traumatic death, or certain forms of abuse in the course of a past lifetime, this input does nothing to reduce the emotional charge of the memory. It can be reclaimed in many ways by the ego, which may even reinforce this emotional charge. At best, this information can motivate us to work more diligently towards our own liberation. Certain techniques are now available to enable us to reach these memories, not on a verbal level, which elicits very little response from the unconscious, but directly on the level of energy, which is far more effective.

Memories Related to Ancestry

Researchers are now paying more and more attention to memories of another type, memories of an "ancestral" nature. Certain coincidences have been noted that are simply too amazing to be merely a matter of "chance". These observations lead to the conclusion that an individual not only carries memories from his own sequence of past lives, but also bears the imprint of his ancestry. There have been a number of studies along these lines, and some good material has been published for anyone wishing to delve deeper into this subject.[6]

The fact that our ancestors' history might be incorporated in our stock of memories is not hard to conceptualise if we look at the transmission of information as a holographic event. The scientific principle of the hologram is now well-known;

within a given system, any part of the system, no matter how minute, contains all the information regarding the entire system. Now at the point of conception, there is a union of two cells: the ovum, which carries all the information connected to the mother's memories, and the sperm cell, which carries all the information connected to the father's memories. It is easy to see how we might be saddled with memories that are not necessarily linked to events that we have actually "lived through" or experienced directly. They are nevertheless present as part of our system, and they can also be very active. Thus we see that the Self does not program everything on a strictly individual basis, but can also call upon one's ancestral lineage, which it may choose as part of the context of a given lifetime, in order to have a broader range of material to work with and thus accelerate the process of evolution.

Yet the same parents do not necessarily produce similar children. What is the driving force behind the impact and the level of activity of these memories transmitted by our parents? When choosing the parents, the soul knows, and thus simultaneously chooses, the memories that will be attached to this being about to incarnate, according to this being's personal plan. If one incarnates in order to manifest certain qualities, one will choose an ancestral lineage that will facilitate this expression. If one must work on certain traumas, one will choose an ancestral lineage that is already attuned to this type of trauma. From this viewpoint, we can see that, rather than being subjected to our ancestors' history, we choose to work with some material taken from the history of the family in which we choose to incarnate, in order to further enrich our own experience. On the other hand:

- we will use this material so that it resonates with our own history;
- these memories will be processed according to the individual's level of awareness.

They will be:

- either instantly transformed, if this is a highly evolved person; in this case, thanks to the energetic link, the individual's liberation becomes available to the entire ancestral lineage and the memory will no longer be transmitted to other descendants;
- or worked upon and eventually transformed, if the person is conscious enough to do so;
- or replayed unconsciously, if the person has reached a relatively low level of development.

In the first instance, it will be an occasion for service to humanity; in the second, it will be an opportunity to work on mastering the mechanisms of the ego, as well as an occasion for service if one succeeds in this work; and in the third case, it will be an opportunity for experience which will, at first, reinforce the memories, and then later on lead to new levels of awareness that will allow the individual to defuse these memories. This is why we see widely varied reactions, depending on the child, to these ancestral memories that are passed on at the out-set of any given lifetime.

In this we can see once again the process whereby personal past lives are linked to childhood circumstances. One's reactions to these circumstances are a function of material stemming not only from whatever positive or negative experiences we have accumulated over past personal lifetimes, but also from the experiences of the ancestral lineage which the soul has chosen to re-enact, and possibly to liber-ate within this present lifetime.

At this point, we already realise that we are linked to other human beings and, though each of us must take full responsibility for his or her own evolution, there is no such thing as a strictly personal process of evolution. The process is there-fore broader in scope than a simple, personal and separate process of evolution for, as much as we can use the experience of our ancestors and benefit from what they have learned, our own evolution will benefit those who will come after us. But obviously we can only benefit from this learning if we are ready for it. Nothing comes "free" in this universe: everything is based on energy exchange.

Memories Related to the Collective Unconscious

Based on my experience, I have had to broaden my model once again. Indeed, when doing advanced release work, I have experienced this link with the collec-tive unconscious. This can be understood from different viewpoints, which, in the end, complement each other, if we look at them all from a broad enough perspec-tive.

We may consider that when an active memory has not been integrated in the course of a given lifetime, it becomes imprinted in the collective unconscious and thus becomes accessible to all. When the Self selects a new incarnation, it can incorporate certain aspects of this collective unconscious, either for the purpose of experiencing a memory that is in tune with what its instrument (this personal-ity) needs to work on specifically (considering the possibility for personal evolu-tion), or (if personal evolution is not a consideration) to work on liberation and healing of the collective unconscious in order to further advance humanity's glob-al state of awareness. In fact, there is a close link between both of these aspects.[7]

To illustrate these viewpoints, which are in fact complementary, we could broaden the previously mentioned analogy of the house. Our situation as part of all humanity is comparable to that of a group of people living in the same house, which is still under construction. Each person is responsible for his/her own room, which must be finished, cleaned up, improved and beautified. We can choose to be concerned only with our own room, especially if we have relatively limited means and little energy (a less advanced level of evolution). If we have already done an excellent job in our own room, we can go and help others who are less advanced, so that they can benefit from our experience. We can even do a little housecleaning for them to provide some incentive, but we cannot do all of the work for them; the way their room is set up must be an opportunity for expressing their own original contribution to the general beauty of the house. Furthermore, besides individual rooms, there are also some collectively shared spaces (kitchen, living room, bathroom) that belong to everyone. It does not matter who did what or who messed up. We build, clean up, and beautify according to our energy level, our areas of competence, and our love (a function of our level of evolution). This could also apply in the case of the great house of the general consciousness of humanity.[8]

Our own observation is that, when "personal" memories are sufficiently defused, we find the entire history of humanity deep within our unconscious. We can then access and work on memories that are not part of our individual lot, but that resonate deep within our being, because we are part of the great human family. The healing work that can be done at that point has to do with the collective unconscious, and in this we can be of great service to humanity. This brings us to a point where we can access a transcendent aspect of our being, one that goes far beyond the boundaries of our present personality.

This will come as no surprise if we once again look at the model described in Chapter 3. At the outset, each of us is a spark of the divine, so our consciousness contains far more than the consciousness of some small separate individuality. This can indeed be experienced in the course of advanced consciousness work. When one reaches certain states of transcendence that are well known to ancient traditions, it is possible to experience oneself as a part of humanity in a much larger sense than our limited personality. For example, we may touch the consciousness of a whole segment of humanity (all the mothers, the warriors, a whole race), or the consciousness of part of the plant kingdom (flowers, trees), or the mineral world, or the planet, the galaxy, an atom, in fact anything that exists in this universe.

These states, which are often referred to as altered states of awareness, are becoming more and more common, and are just an expression of an ever-expanding consciousness.[9] They are not always easy to handle, but they are part of the consciousness expansion that we will need to integrate in times to come, in order to gain access to a broader and more direct source of knowledge, and thus to regain full potency in our concrete worldly manifestations. This is not about being disconnected from ordinary reality, through drugs or as a result of some form of psychic imbalance. This is about controlled expansion, that fosters a broader, more concrete and more intelligent perception of reality, and thus leads to far more effective, practical and positive action in the world.

The more evolved an individual is, the more liberated, and the more he can consciously tune into the collective unconscious and spread a healing influence, because the individual is less and less dependant on this collective unconscious. There is also an interesting paradox: **the more an individual is individualized** (i.e., advanced in terms of evolution) **the less he feels like a separate entity**, the more he is connected to the soul of all humanity, and the less he is bound by personal memories which have been transcended in the course of his personal spiritual development.[10] The following story of the vision experienced by a disciple of a great spiritual master of ancient India will illustrate this point.

The Master was a fully "realized" being—as such people are called in oriental traditions—and he and his disciples lived in peace in an ashram, until their land was invaded by Barbarians, who arrived at the gates of the ashram, broke them down, and massacred every member of the community, including the spiritual Master. Only one disciple, who was able to hide just in time, survived and witnessed the massacre. Because of his ability to perceive higher forms of energy, he could see the different subtle bodies of each of his co-disciples leaving their physical bodies and ascending towards the light. This made him very sad. Then his attention was drawn towards a very special vision. His beloved Master had just been killed, and was just leaving his body. But instead of seeing the latter's subtle bodies ascending towards the light, as the others had, he saw a stream of light directly emanating from the Master's body and spreading into space. The soul of the Master that was apparently free of karma and had no further lessons to learn, was on its way to merging with the universal Self. His consciousness no longer had any need of a separate form. Having left his physical form, which he had taken out of love in order to serve mankind, his consciousness was regaining its universal dimension. His "individuality" was expanding to the point of encompassing all other individualities and the entire universe.

This little story is here to remind us that ultimately we are the entire universe. We are all of divine essence, we are separate from nothing and from nobody, and we are not this little personality. Separation is the illusion in which we are bound by our ego, for a while, until we reach the point where we have achieved complete mastery over matter, both personally and collectively.

In this sense, our own inner work is not separate from the work done by others. It brings us closer and closer together and dispels the illusion of a separate identity. We then realize how, through conscious inner work, we can greatly accelerate not just our own process of evolution but also the evolution of others, especially that of all our descendants, and ultimately the evolutionary process of all humanity. Indeed, beyond simple transmission through the physical link of each cell, we are all energetically linked through the universal energy field. According to the principle of morphogenetic fields of information, which we will delve into in greater detail in Chapter 10, any individual evolution in consciousness has repercussions on all of humanity.

> When one of us reaches the state of enlightenment, all of us share in it.
> —*A Buddhist teaching*

At this point, we realize even more the extent to which the quest for strictly personal liberation is an illusion. At a certain level, humanity is one, and we can no longer be ignorant of the fact that we are part of the whole. If we do ignore it, it is because our ego has reclaimed our inner quest for its own advantage. We then find our self moving away from the light of the Self, rather than coming closer to it. Complete liberation can only occur when the ego has ceased to try to define itself, when the soul is in complete possession of its vehicle. At that moment, there is no longer any sense of a separate identity. What naturally emerges is an immense love for humanity, and a desire to serve not from an individual stance, but out of a profound sense of belonging or, more accurately, a sense of identification with all mankind. We then have an expanded awareness that encompasses the consciousness of the entire human race and the entire universe.

As the book unfolds, whenever we mention "past" experiences, these can be viewed either as stemming from personal experiences (childhood or past lives), from our ancestry, or from the collective unconscious. Knowing the precise "historical" source of these memories is not the main issue, as these may be just hypotheses. However the crucial point, for our purposes, is to find ways of freeing our self from their grip. And **whatever their source may be**, these memories generate the same type of behaviors and limitations, and we will see that **we can use the same approach to loosen their hold on our life.**

Active Memories Generating Five Major Structures of the Unconscious

These incomplete experiences, these memories that we are burdened with and that strongly condition our way of being according to the principles we described earlier, can be boiled down to five major types of stressful experiences, five specific sets of active memories leading to five major ways of functioning at the personality level. These ways of functioning are actually just defense mechanisms developed by the ego over time in order to avoid suffering, and ultimately survive, based on its own logic, of course.

These mechanisms are not just stored away in our unconscious in a haphazard, obscure or complicated manner. **They are constantly being manifested in our daily life.** They condition nearly all of our thoughts, actions, choices, and decisions, from the most basic to the most inconsequential. For instance the way we choose a mate, a job, professional associates, friends, the types of love or sexual relationships we have, and that have a long term impact on our life, as well as how we choose a piece of clothing, a holiday location, a certain brand of car, our recreational activities, or the way we react to the slightest of life's little setbacks. If we are unaware of our mechanisms, all of these choices are automatically conditioned by these structures that are orchestrated by our unconscious. Getting to know them is a huge step forward in terms of fostering expanded self-knowledge as well as gaining mastery over our life. This knowledge becomes a naturally liberating force in our day-to-day existence, on the level of our relationships, our creative endeavors, indeed every aspect of our life. It allows us to clarify the direction of our inner quest, no matter what psychological or spiritual approach we use. And above all, it allows us to **consciously transform these hardened structures**

into specific qualities whereby we can express our essence in a free, rich and supple manner.

The first volume of *Free Your True Self—Releasing Your Unconscious Defense Patterns*, focuses on a detailed description of these structures. Numerous examples and real-life experiences make this content very tangible and in tune with our day-to-day life. For the reader who is not familiar with Volume 1, we will now provide an extremely succinct summary of these five major structures. This very brief overview may already bring to mind certain familiar patterns in the way we function.

First of all, we must remember that, although the names of these structures (some of which are abbreviated) have been borrowed from Wilhelm Reich, a well-known psychiatrist of the last century, **we have greatly extended and deepened their meaning** in the course of these two volumes. We are describing our behaviors as "normal" human beings, which allow us to somehow function in today's world. But functioning does not necessarily mean being fulfilled, serene, happy, and in complete possession of our full potential for creation and contribution. Although they do not necessarily make us totally dysfunctional, these unconscious structures nevertheless severely limit our access to our full potential.

Schizoid structure:

Basic fear: fear of physical existence.

Emotional charge: stress, anxiety, distress, insecurity, depression.

Source experiences *(active memories)*: great physical suffering and stress (difficult birth or past life experiences).

Energy level: tired, very little energy available

Defence system: withdrawal, escapism from active life any way possible, absence, refusal of implication at all levels (in relationships, at work), refusal to be part of this world, tiredness, depression to justify withdrawal from the physical world.

Relationships: little activity

Sexuality: little activity

Needed work: renew one's contact with earth energies, ground oneself in these energies in order to become free of fear, stress and anxiety; develop a willingness to be in this world, to be aware of one's body and happy to create and play the game of life.

Qualities of the structure, once transformed: lightness of being, refined intuition, creativity, originality, natural detachment, genuine contact with subtle energies, free, light and joyful relationships.

Oral structure:

Basic fear: fear of deprivation, of solitude, of abandonment; fear of loss, of not having enough.

Emotional charge: sense of emptiness, insecurity (mostly in relationships), depression.

Source experiences in the past *(active memories)*: deprivation, loss, abandonment.

Energy level: always needy, tries to take energy from others.

Defence system: stuffing, emotional dependency or substance dependency, attachment, parasitic behaviour, excess.

Relationships: dependency, attachment, need

Sexuality: used to fill oneself up, but satisfaction is never fully reached

Needed work: reconnect with one's inner source in order to experiment plenitude and satisfaction, whatever the circumstances. To heal the past to find one's affective independence.

Qualities of the structure, once transformed: generosity, kindness, relaxed state of being; nurturing attitude, will be able to take care of others while letting them be free, a cheerful and balanced person.

Masochist structure:

Basic fear: fear of being taken in, fear of the power of others, fear of losing one's own power.

Source experiences *(active memories)*: victim of abuse of power, oppression, annihilation, loss of freedom, exploitation; very painful experience of powerlessness and of loss of one's power. Or experience as a perpetrator filled with guilt, which also leads to the refusal of one's own power.

Energy level: compacted, very low energy, being strongly suppressed. May explode occasionally if the structure is reactivated, which then yields great endurance.

Defence system: submission-rebellion, criticism, blame, irresponsibility, and the whole arsenal of the active or passive victim; illness, suffering to make the others feel guilty.

Sexuality: difficult, frustrating.

Needed work: Take full responsibility for one's life, reconnect with one's creative power and let go of every mechanism of victimhood or of the role of saviour. (A must: read *The Power of Free-Will*, by the same author, to heal this structure.)

Qualities of the structure: compassion, courage, toughness, reliability (trustworthiness), excellent support, high qualities of service and self-sacrifice in a state of joy, creativity and freedom.

Psychopath structure:

Basic fear: fear of not being loved or acknowledged, fear of betrayal.

Emotional charge: pride, arrogance, selfishness, need to be loved, need for popularity.

Source experiences *(active memories)*: position of power followed by betrayal, trauma related to the loss of power followed by betrayal, loss of fundamental sense of identity.

Source experiences *(active memories)*: position of power and influence followed by betrayal, trauma of loss of power through betrayal, loss of a genuine sense of identity.

Energy level: very high, overflowing.

Defence system: performance, seduction, manipulation, quest for influence and power at all costs, identification to one's image, selfishness.

Sexuality: to perform

Work to be done: learn to love oneself as we are and love others without expectations. Rediscover the true meaning of love, of simplicity and of one's true nature.

Qualities of the structure: genuine love, human warmth, compassion, respect, humour, intelligence, inner wealth, originality

Rigid structure:

Basic fear of the structure: fear of feeling and being vulnerable, fear of suffering emotionally, fear of losing control.

Source experiences *(active memories)*: intense emotional shock leading to loss of sensitivity and a closing up of the personality.

Energy level: high and balanced.

Defence system: closing up emotionally, control, arrogance, intellectualisation, coldness, pride, development of the intellect.

Sexuality: cold, solely physical.

Work to be done: open one's heart again, recover one's sensitivity.

Qualities of the structure: centeredness, purity in sentiment, intelligent and kindly willpower, emotional self-control, courage, heroism.

---·-·-·-·-·-·-·-·-·-·-·-

[1] There is a wonderful book on this subject: *"L'accompagnement de la naissance"*, by Bernard Montaud, éd. Édit'as.

[2] A good reference on this topic: *Other Lives, Other Selves,* op.cit., Chapter 3.

[3] This is a broader and far less guilt-ridden perspective than the simplistic karma-retribution-punishment perspective, which doesn't make much sense at the level of the soul and of our inner learning process.

[4] We described in detail in Volume 1 the direct consequences in our daily life of five major structures of the unconscious. It is easy to see how the same holds true of intra-uterine life.

[5] Chatelaine magazine, March 1987.

[6] Anne Ancelin Schützenberger, *Aïe mes aïeux*, éd. Épi, La méridienne; Michel Larroche, *Mes cellules se souviennent,* éd. Guy Trédaniel.

[7] What happens on the unconscious level could also be applied at the "supraconscious" level. The acquired knowledge of certain human beings can be considered to be available to the rest of humanity. Nevertheless, there has to be a certain unity of consciousness in order to be able to tune into this acquired knowledge, which presupposes a certain level of "personal" evolution.

[8] It is also possible that, when everything is finished, and everyone has contributed to everything, these "roommates" may drop the notion of individual space. The entire house would then be available to all, according to the just needs of each person.

[9] In oriental spiritual traditions, one seeks to attain such states of expanded awareness in order to reach the final stage of expansion called "samadhi", a state of merging with all of creation. In fact these states of awareness are just an expression of one's liberation from the fetters of our human condition.

[10] In this sense, we can appreciate certain oriental spiritual approaches, which reject the idea of a "personal" karma or history, as well as certain psychological approaches. When we look at our situation as human beings not as a static condition, but as a process of evolution, we can thus establish links between approaches which may seem contradictory at first glance. What may appear as paradoxes on the path to self-knowledge should not hinder our progress, but rather motivate us to find an ever-broadening perspective wherein apparent contradictions are in harmony. By combining these various approaches into a more coherent whole, each of them takes on new meaning. We thus create the potential for gaining greater mastery over our personal and collective destinies.

PART TWO

The Future of Humanity

✦

The Manifestation of the Self

"Let us not seek God anywhere but everywhere..."
—**André Gide**

chapter 6

The Two Components of the Mind: The Lower and the Higher

OR

HOW TO LIVE IN FREEDOM AND PEACE IN ANY CIRCUMSTANCE

We shall now examine another way for us to function, one that generates a far better quality of life than what we are generally used to. For though we may be very limited by the mechanisms of the lower mind, we are also endowed with a higher mind which makes it possible for us to experience life in a totally different way.

Before we go into a detailed comparison of how the lower mind and the higher mind function, let us go back to the automobile analogy, a variation on the horse and carriage analogy (Chapter 1). This will provide a more precise illustration of the automatic aspect of the lower mind, and the creative, efficient aspect of the higher mind. We will then follow up with a more specific description of the two dynamics in order to get a better grasp of their fundamental differences, to be able to recognise their features within our self, and to use them for our greater benefit.

Let us compare a human being to an automobile with a driver and passenger travelling in it:

- the passenger represents the Self;
- the driver represents the higher mind;
- an on-board computer, with an automatic pilot function, represents the lower mind;
- the fuel represents emotional energy; and
- the mechanical components (engine, brakes, steering) and the body of the car represent the physical body.

As we saw in the horse and carriage analogy, the passenger (the Self) is the one endowed with genuine knowledge of the road. He conveys his instructions to the driver, the higher mind, who hears them, as long as he is active and awake. Thanks to his intelligence, he controls the on-board computer as well as the car's mechanisms (mastery over the lower mind, the emotional body and the physical body). He is thus able to drive the vehicle at any given moment in an accurate and appropriate manner according to the wisdom of the Master. The journey is both rewarding and pleasant.

In our present state of consciousness, the higher mind is more or less active and tends to be somewhat asleep. It only occasionally hears the Master's voice and is not always in driving mode. To make up for the driver's absence as the vehicle was being assembled, a computer-activated robot, loaded with programs based on past journeys, was built into the steering wheel. When the driver falls asleep at the wheel, the computer takes over. The problem is that the computer is unable to see the road as it actually is. It can only spot certain aspects, which it then cross-references with a similar past itinerary stored in its memory. We thus proceed along the road leaving the driving to the computerised robot, according to operating principles described in Chapter 4. Any road that looks somewhat like one we have previously travelled is automatically considered to be the same; the steering wheel, the accelerator pedal, and all of the vehicle's mechanisms are activated according to the blueprint of a past journey.

But previously travelled roads are rarely the same as those we are faced with at any given moment in our life. The programming is therefore not really appropriate. If the vehicle is controlled by this programming and our consciousness identifies with the lower mind, we often end up in the ditch. We then find the journey unpleasant and experience life as a chore. Not knowing how we got there, we curse the road in anger, and resist reality instead of considering the possibility of learning to see the road as it is and adjusting our driving accordingly. In this state of resistance and frustration, we may want to change the road instantly. We pull out a shovel and immediately set out to build a new road, our kind of road, one that matches past itineraries: we try to change things or people around us in order to make them meet our expectations based on past experiences. And since we get poor results, we have even more reasons to feel frustrated in the face of so many difficulties and problems; we want to blame the whole world and to hate this life that forces us to put up with such outrageous fortune.

During this journey, which seems so unsafe and unpleasant, we may experience rare moments of satisfaction when the road closely matches our past programmings. At those times, all is well, we feel we are making headway and we can enjoy the scenery. It is easy to see how fragile this kind of satisfaction actually is, since sooner or later the road will no longer correspond to our old memories, and once again we will lose control of our life. But since these are the only moments of satisfaction we know, we spend our time wishing the road would match the landscape of our memories. We want the road to match our programmings because, according to our experience, this seems to be the only way to have a pleasant journey. This generates so-called pre-programmed desires and expectations, attachments, fears, demands, and permanent inner stress. Depending on the content of our memories, our desires, expectations and ways of reacting to the curves of the journey will vary greatly. The five major structures of the unconscious described in Volume 1, which are related to different types of "programming", can be approached from this perspective.

Martin is in charge of presenting a project for his company. His conscious desire and need are to gain recognition as the best presenter the company has ever had. If life meets his expectations and he gets a lot of compliments (if the road unfolds according to predetermined expectations based on past programmings), Martin is happy, and the journey is pleasant. If he gets criticisms and mixed results, he is very unhappy, and it's a bad day at the office. He becomes impatient, anxious, and tries to manipulate and perform even more in order to restore his image (Martin is in the ditch and tries to manipulate the road so as to make it match his expectations).

Since everyone seems to function this way in everyday life, we tend to think that such is life. Yet we notice that the masters of wisdom do not end up in the ditch, and that some individuals are less often likely to end up in that position. How do they do it?

Instead of trying to make the road correspond to pre-established programmings, instead of resisting life's unexpected twists and turns, they have chosen to awaken the driver (the higher mind), who then takes charge of the vehicle using the computer (the lower mind) according to the will of the Master. They stop analysing the road on the basis of memories, and see it as it really is, thanks to the higher mind's clear and free awareness. They are then able to respond in perfectly appropriate ways to the reality of the road. They have no emotionally charged memories, therefore no expectations, no attachments, and no desires with regard to whatever comes up. In this instance, one is able to adjust effectively to any new twist in the road. One does not resist reality. The journey becomes pleasant and totally safe, since the vehicle is under control. Life is beautiful. Yet in both cases, one is dealing with the same path of life.

At this point, most of us are at an in-between stage. Sometimes the driver is awake (the higher mind is active), and we are in charge of our inner and outer life. At other times, we get caught in the computer's mechanism. In order to gain better control of this computer, we are going to examine some of its aspects in greater detail, so that we can compare its dynamic to that of the higher mind. This corresponds to very specific inner states, and as soon as we understand the extent to which the quality of our everyday life depends on how the lower and higher minds function, we become really motivated to gain a higher level of mastery of this extraordinary instrument.

Perceiving Reality Through the Two Levels of the Mental Filter

Our experience of reality

Any information coming from external reality reaches our brain through our physical senses. It is then processed by the mental system. The accuracy of what we perceive depends on what part of the mental system we use, the higher or the lower, or what our consciousness identifies with.

> Reality and our perception of reality are two different things.

One of the great illusions that keep us mired in our own mechanisms is the belief that we perceive reality as it is.[1] We saw what this illusion is about when we described the workings of the mental computer in Chapter 4.

To illustrate this fact, let us take another look at the diagram presented in Chapter 4, adding to it the presence of the higher mind:

Diagram 1
The Perception of Reality through the Mental Filter

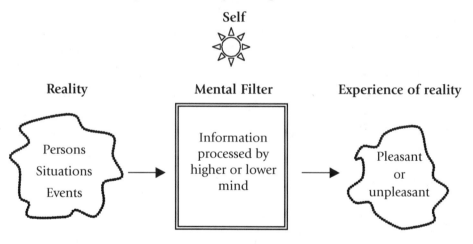

According to this diagram, we have the following:

- **Reality** as it is, composed of everything around us: physical or psychological situations, persons, events, and circumstances of all kinds.

- **The mental filter,** which receives and processes this information on the basis of either of two systems: the lower mind or the higher mind.

- **The experience of reality,** in which the result of the process determines what our experience of reality will be. This generates a response that can be positive or negative, pleasant or unpleasant, and that consequently leads to certain kinds of behaviour.

One spring morning, the outdoor thermometer registers 20 degrees Celsius; my mind records and processes this information. My response may be positive, as it pleases me to know that the weather is good, and my experience of reality is therefore pleasant.

If, some time later, I get an electricity bill for twice the amount I was expecting, my mind records and processes this information. The result of this process is probably that this does not match my expectations. This information therefore leads to an unpleasant feeling.

This is a very simple example, but the mechanism is the same no matter what major or minor events turn up in our life.

We are strongly conditioned to believe that our experience of reality, our satisfaction or dissatisfaction, depend solely on external circumstances, yet if this were the case, everyone would react in the same way to situations, and we would be in a state of total dependency on external stimuli. Such is not the case, which leads to the following questions: Could there be a way to be happy regardless of circumstances? Could there be a way to be free with regard to the people and things around us? To put it another way: **how do we have a pleasant experience of reality,** how do we remain free and at peace regardless of the circumstances that may confront us?

According to the diagram, we can see that our experience of reality is dependent on two factors:

- reality as it is; and
- the outcome of how the information was processed through the mental filter, on the other hand, depending on how the latter perceives reality.

If we want to consciously generate a pleasant experience of reality at all times, we will need to work on these two factors.

- **Can we change reality?**

Unless we have a direct line to God Almighty that allows us to instantly change the world according to our wishes (which may happen in due time), there are some things we can change in an instant, others we cannot. This is especially true with regard to the people around us: trying to change someone so that he/she matches our needs and desires is a hopeless endeavour. We have all experienced that, especially with our spouses, our children, or our parents.

Furthermore, we are now well aware that our perception is limited and that we are not really in touch with reality. How can we change something we do not clearly perceive? How can we be happy with this state of affairs? If we find certain circumstances distasteful, must we suffer, become frustrated, aggressive, or violent? Must we try to force things, fight to impose our will and crush any opposition from others, or resist and have a fit of "acute victimitis",[2] which is no fun for anyone? How can we maintain our power without dispersing our energy in vain activity or resistance?

If we cannot instantly change reality, might we perhaps change the way we process the information we get from reality? This brings us to a more precise analysis of our response to reality, on the basis of the two aspects of the mental filter. Thus we have the following diagram:

Diagram 2
Two Possible Paths of Consciousness

Self

| Reality | Mental filter | Experience of reality |

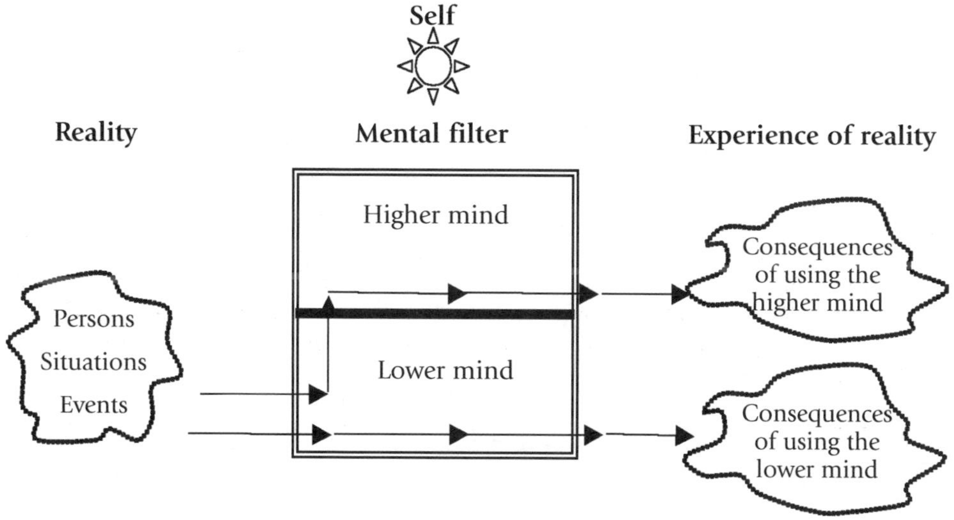

This diagram demonstrates the potential for grasping reality either through the higher mind (the lower mind is silent and merely forwards the information without distorting it), or directly and solely through the lower mind, which short-circuits the higher mind as a result of emotionally charged memories.

Human consciousness is presently alternating between these two ways of functioning. By becoming aware of the respective dynamics of these two paths of consciousness, we can observe their consequences and consciously strive to use the part of the mind that carries the greatest potential for personal and collective growth.

Using the Lower Automatic Mind

or what happens when we use the lower mind
as an instrument to perceive reality

We know how using the lower mind distorts our perception of reality. Let us now take a closer look at the phenomenon of desire, one of its major mechanisms, for it is this aspect that will need to be worked on in order to access the higher mind.

The mechanism of desire and artificial needs: a by-product of the development of our defence systems.

*Once we get to see things as they are, instead of how we would like them to be,
then we will no longer fall prey to disappointments and we will rarely experience grief.*
—**The Initiate**

We have seen how the lower mind, when faced with a non-integrated experience, will build a series of automatic defence responses in order to avoid suffering in future somewhat similar situations. In Volume 1, we described five major unconscious defence patterns that we carry within us. These systems all function in basically the same primary way.

Let us go back to a simple example:

In a past life, Betty was the son of a Lord sometime in the Middle Ages. Despite his youth, he is taught horseback riding, which is a great thrill for him. One day, while his instructor is not around, he decides to take a ride on his own. He leaves the stable, and everything is fine. He ventures a little further into the countryside, and in the thrill of the moment, he decides to pick up the pace a little. He spurs the horse, which begins to gallop faster and faster. It is great fun at first, but the child soon realises that he does not know what to do to slow down. He is now riding at full speed on his horse and becoming afraid. Fear turns into panic when he gets to a bridge blocked by a large cart. He is unable to control his mount, which rears up and throws him violently over the bridge. The child lands hard on boulders several meters down, terribly injured. People arrive on the scene to help, and he is brought back to the castle, where he eventually dies in great pain.

In her present life, Betty has a panic fear of bridges. She tries to stay away from them as much as possible, to the point of making great detours to avoid them. Every time she has to cross a bridge, she feels extremely ill at ease and anxious, and very eager to get to the other side.

Diagram 3

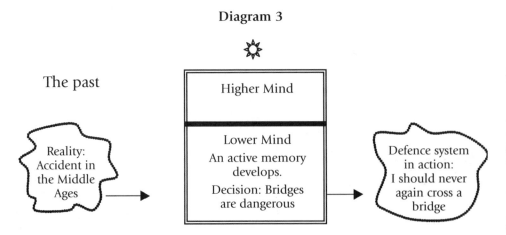

diagram 3, continued

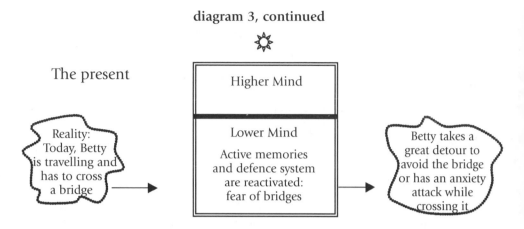

The present

Reality: Today, Betty is travelling and has to cross a bridge

Higher Mind

Lower Mind

Active memories and defence system are reactivated: fear of bridges

Betty takes a great detour to avoid the bridge or has an anxiety attack while crossing it

The bridge is recorded in the active memory. In addition, a conclusion has been drawn: bridges are dangerous. A very primary conclusion, of course, but that is the way the unconscious works.

• The dynamic of desire

These defence systems generate artificial needs and the **desire phenomenon, which is just our attachment to the pleasure of having these "needs" met.** The term "desire" includes both conscious and unconscious desires (the strongest and most active desires), direct desires as well as repulsions, aversions or resistances, and of course, fears; in fact it covers all the mental-emotional tensions that drive us to behave in certain ways. Let us not forget that the emotional body[3] is the one that gives us the energy to act (the horse is used to move ahead). The mental body gives direction to our desire.

The examples mentioned in Chapter 4 illustrate this dynamic: Julie "desires" to get involved with handsome blond-haired, blue eyed hunks, but the desire is based on a memory rather than on the objective reality of the present moment. Benny abhors speaking to an audience, James hates spaghetti, Amelia is an astronomy freak, Michelle always needs to be reassured regarding her value as a person, and Janet doesn't like men.[4]

Obviously we all have real needs: the need for food, security, supportive relationships, etc. But when we are caught in the mechanism of the lower mind, these real needs become distorted and reclaimed by the structure to the point where the desires generated by these needs end up going against the real original needs. A wholesome desire to surpass oneself is reclaimed by a need to perform to feed the ego; a genuine contact with spiritual energies is reclaimed as a pretext to withdraw from this world's reality; the natural physical need for food is reclaimed for the sake of stuffing, and so on.

Often what we fear is far less dangerous than what we desire.
—Anonymous

When we perceive reality through the lower mind, all of our preferences, aversions, attractions, all the choices we make, are merely expressions of our computer's mechanism. We desire certain things, we loathe others, simply on the basis of accumulated emotionally charged memories, not on the basis of what is in synch with our true nature.

This is why any skilled manipulator can motivate masses of people of low awareness and make them do almost anything. There is an obviously urgent need to bring a higher level of awareness in this field if humanity is ever to recover a genuine state of freedom.

• Expectations

This constant emotionally charged tension generates a malaise, which creates **the illusion that we will feel good when our desires are eventually satisfied.** As long as we remain caught in this illusion, we live in the hope and expectation that life and other people will meet these needs and satisfy these desires. Now, as we know, a memory can never be fulfilled, it can only be defused. The ego's false needs can never be met in any durable way. This is the reason for the constant re-emergence of these expectations.[5]

Each of the five unconscious defence patterns presented in Volume 1 has its own style of automatic desires and expectations that generate characteristic behaviours.[6] Trying to fulfil these memory-generated expectations in order to feel good is one of the major illusions affecting us all. This will never defuse the emotional charge carried by the memories and we will never get what we are seeking: quite the opposite, in fact.

> When we try to fulfil ego desires, we activate a desire-generating machine that is self-reinforcing and that binds us more and more.

Yet, generally speaking, we are not aware of this illusion. Unless we have attained a great deal of mastery over our computer, we really feel that our desires are well-founded, that our needs are genuine, and we are deeply attached to them. We stick to our impression that letting go of our desires would be tantamount to self-denial, and that this would be very painful. This is the point where we become prisoners of the machine, and lose whatever freedom we have.

We always try to bridge the gap between what is and what should be; and by that very fact we give rise to a state of contradiction and conflict wherein we waste all our energies.
—Krishnamurti

• No more desires?

The ego balks at such a notion. Indeed, what is wrong with having desires? Isn't that what drives us to action, makes us alive, and makes us want to relate to others?

For thousands of years, the great masters of wisdom have been telling us that to find the path to enlightenment, we must liberate our self from desire. Most of the time, we do not understand what they mean; we think that this is the exclusive domain of a few saints who are disconnected from the realities of life, who are practically no longer of this world, and who are generally rather eccentric exceptions in the human race. We feel that we would become insensitive without desire, and that life would be terribly boring. In fact, there is a great deal of confusion regarding this subject, which we may be able to clear up to some extent.

• Automatic ego desires and the will of the soul

The confusion stems from the fact that the soul also has desires, which we prefer to call its "will" or "intentions". The soul is totally interested in using the energy potential of the emotional body to express its will in the phenomenal world. So it generates "desires" in the emotional body (the Master wants to be able to use the power of the horse).

In fact the emotional body starts out being little more than a reservoir of neutral energy. The directions it gets from the lower or higher mind are what activates it in one direction or another. As we have seen, when these directions come from the lower mind, the outcome tends to be rather disappointing. On the other hand, these directions can also come from the soul, through the higher mind. This will of the soul is expressed in the form of a desire for action, a desire to create beauty and goodness, to grow in awareness, to know and to discover, to love and to serve, etc. These are other types of desires that express the soul's intention.

> The problem does not stem from our desires, but from the fact that automatic desires, emanating from active memories, stifle our true desires, the desires of our soul.

So the work we need to do is not about killing desire, it is about **differentiating between computer-generated desires and soul-generated desires.**[7] How can we tell the difference? Soul desires do not generate stress or any excess tension. They leave us free, centred, happy, and they generate a constant flow of energy. On the other hand, ego desires, though they may appear just as strong and pressing as soul desires, or even more so, turn us into pre-programmed robots and sooner or later leave us feeling unhappy, dissatisfied, tired and disappointed. As we become aware of the specific dynamic of the higher mind, which we are about to describe and compare with that of the lower mind, we will be able to see the difference more clearly.

For the majority, physical and emotional purity are the objectives, and are therefore primarily liberation from emotional control and desire. Hence the constant, e'en though badly worded injunction in many of the esoteric books, "Kill our desire". Perhaps a more just rendering for the immediate present would be "reorient desire" or "re-direct desire", for a constant process of re-orientation of the entire desire nature so that it eventually becomes a habitual state of mind is the clue to all the transmutation processes, and to effective magical work.[8]

Saints and great sages know what they are doing. They have found the way to be profoundly happy and free, not by killing desire but by elevating it so that it serves the purpose of their soul. This has so far appeared totally incomprehensible and uninteresting in the eyes of average people, and it is simply because our consciousness was not sufficiently developed to be able to see where true happiness is to be found. Recognising the source of the mechanism of desire will enable us to proceed with our inner work far more efficiently. Otherwise, asking anyone to stop seeking to satisfy his/her desires without explaining why, would be like asking a one-legged person to run a marathon. The individual will either refuse to do it, or will make an attempt, fail, and then feel guilty about it. Some religious teachings—either crudely stated or poorly explained—have condemned desire and nurtured this confusion, leading to guilt, repression, and ultimately a number of perversions that are painfully obvious in today's world.

There is nothing wrong with having automatic desires. It simply generates a great deal of suffering and it deprives us of our freedom. Just as there is nothing wrong with owning an automobile equipped with an engine dating back to 1910. It is simply inefficient, works poorly, and prevents us from moving along at a satisfactory pace. It is very important to look at our desires from this perspective, so as not to see ourselves as monsters in the light of teachings extolling unconditional love, light, detachment, and angelic behaviour such as we find in New Age philosophies.[9]

Now that this mechanism of desire has been clarified, it will be easier for us to understand the dynamic underscoring behaviours that stem from the lower mind, and to compare them with those of the higher mind.

The illusion of the quest for pleasure

When something or someone turns up in our daily reality, the mechanism of perception works as follows:

- We compare the present situation with a past situation and we project a past reality onto the present situation. This generally translates into a false perception of reality (Chapter 4).

- Based on this false perception, the lower mind activates its defence systems, which are loaded with desires, false needs and expectations.

We then have two possibilities.

- **First possibility**

The "perceived" reality meets our expectations as defined by our active memories stemming from past experiences; we are therefore content. If everyone behaves as we want them to, if the weather is exactly right, if our boss (or our employees) behave according to our wishes, if our love partner fulfils our wildest fantasies, and if everyone agrees with us, then we are happy. This can happen, of course, but for how long? This is what we have so far equated with "happiness" or "satisfaction".

> At the ego level, the only possible pleasure is the momentary satisfaction of automatic desires stemming from our memories.

• The quest for pleasure

Even if these moments of pleasure are short-lived and subject to chance, they are enough to maintain the illusion that we will find happiness whenever our expectations are met. So we will try to relive these moments of contentment, which lead to our all too familiar pleasure-seeking behaviour. Yet what kind of pleasure is this exactly?

The quest for pleasure at the ego level is doomed to failure since, on the one hand, it is very difficult to meet expectations and, on the other hand, even if we manage to do so momentarily, external circumstances keep on changing. Our life circumstances change (work, finances, behaviour of people around us, unexpected events); our expectations, false needs and computer-generated rigid demands do not change. This is why, after a blessed time when life met our expectations (and we have often worked very hard to make it happen), there comes a time when our desires are no longer satisfied.

Nothing is constant, except change.
—Buddha

Nevertheless, this quest has some positive aspects: it motivates us to action and makes us want to experience life. We need to confront the illusion day after day, year after year, life after life, until we finally become aware of it and are able to liberate our self from its grip. And we cannot let go of an illusion unless we have experienced it (often at great personal cost).

On the other hand, this quest for pleasure springs from a quest for something far greater and far more beautiful…a quest that is felt at the soul level—something that is aptly referred to as ecstasy—that we miss and try to recover through our ego mechanisms. The quest for pleasure therefore originates from a perfectly justified source. It is the quest for a state of bliss such as only the soul can provide, and which far surpasses all the pleasures of the personality in quality and intensity. If we really want to reach that state some day, we need to start looking in the right direction.

In the meantime, as long as our life is directed by the mechanisms of the lower mind, we cannot help but find our self, sooner or later, in the second scenario:

• Second possibility

People or things, as we perceive them to be, are not exactly the way we would want them to be. We then react emotionally or mentally according to our memories and unconscious defence patterns that are activated in that situation: frustration, anger, impatience, stress, depression, violence, closed-mindedness, withdrawal, and the entire victim's arsenal. Each of these unconscious patterns has its (illusory) desires, its expectations and its demands, its "alienating demands", as Ken Keyes calls them.[10] Why alienating? Because they make us unhappy if they are not met.

Looking for happiness beyond the ego's desires and false needs is most often an attitude that is totally foreign to the average person. Caught as we are in automatic responses developed over thousands of years, we habitually try to manipulate and change things and people through a variety of means, so that they meet our expectations, thus hoping to find happiness, instead of questioning these expectations. The very idea that we might change them does not even enter our mind since, at the ego level, they stem from active memories with which we totally identify.

Thus, this particular characteristic of the lower mind, which generates expectations and demands, leads to brief periods of contentment as well as major moments of dissatisfaction. It constantly projects our consciousness into an unreal future and prevents us from being here, at any given moment, to enjoy the present as it is.

One direct consequence of automatic desires is a resistance to life as it is, another mechanism that is deeply rooted in the collective unconscious.

Resistance

Whenever reality does not conform to our expectations (whether they be conscious or unconscious), our computer generates a general reaction in the form of resistance. This state of resistance is the driving force behind our desire for things and people around us to be different, a desire strengthened by all our emotionally charged memories. **We resist what is** and we want things or people to change.

It must be noted that, in this case, the desire to change our surroundings stems from false needs that clamour for satisfaction. It does not spring from the will of the soul, which may also wish to change things, but from a totally different perspective. **The soul's "desires"** are processed by the higher mind in an altogether different manner, as we shall see further on in this book and, for one thing, they do not generate any resistance.

Each of the five major unconscious defence patterns presented in Volume 1 stems from specific active memories and thus generates automatic desires, expectations and a way of dealing with disappointments whenever these expectations are not met. Each of these patterns therefore has its own style of resistance:

- Schizoid structure-withdrawal
- Oral structure-excess stuffing, manipulation, depression
- Masochist structure-frustration, blame, aggression, sabotage and the entire arsenal of the victim

- Psychopath structure-stress, anxiety, hyperactivity
- Rigid structure-stiffening and activation of power in order to gain more control.

To find out what form our resistance takes, all we need to do is look at our actions whenever we are unhappy about something.

This resistance mechanism is also deeply entrenched in the collective unconscious. We have been taught this way of functioning since early childhood. This is such a familiar mechanism that we don't even notice it anymore. Everybody does it. Based on our computer's operating system, we believe that we can change things or people around us by putting up a resistance to what is. In fact, it is the other way around, as we have previously seen: "Whatever we resist persists!"

Furthermore, when we resist what is, our energy is consumed by negative emotions, so that there is very little energy left for us to take action and eventually change what does not suit our needs. Resisting is very tiring and highly inefficient.

Each of us has surely had the opportunity to verify this principle in the context of relationships. In particular, we think that in order to have a healthy couple relationship, we need to find the right person. Yet, in this context, what do we mean by the "right" person? According to the logic of the lower mind, we are talking about a person who will satisfy our old memory-driven expectations and demands. And should that person fail to satisfy these "needs", we are annoyed, frustrated, and unhappy. So we

> Our inner resistance to what is only serves to amplify what is.

hope that he/she will eventually change and, in the meantime, we resist. It is easy to see, therefore, why harmony is so hard to come by in the context of couple relationships. The more we want people to change, the more we resist what they are, and the less they change.

Diagram 4, on the next page, is an illustration and summary of how the lower mind perceives reality.

Reality

Lower Mind: *Comparing perceived reality with the expectations, desires, fears, and emotional charges embedded in one's memories.*

Reaction: • *if reality matches the expectations and desires springing from one's emotional charges, one is satisfied, usually for a brief period of time;*

• *if the perceived reality does not meet our expectations and desires, the **emotional charge is reactivated**: frustration, anger, impatience, disappointment, depression, victimitis, shutting out the world, withdrawal, manipulation, stress, anxiety, inner tensions.*

✦ ✦ ✦

Diagram 4

How the Lower Mind Perceives Reality

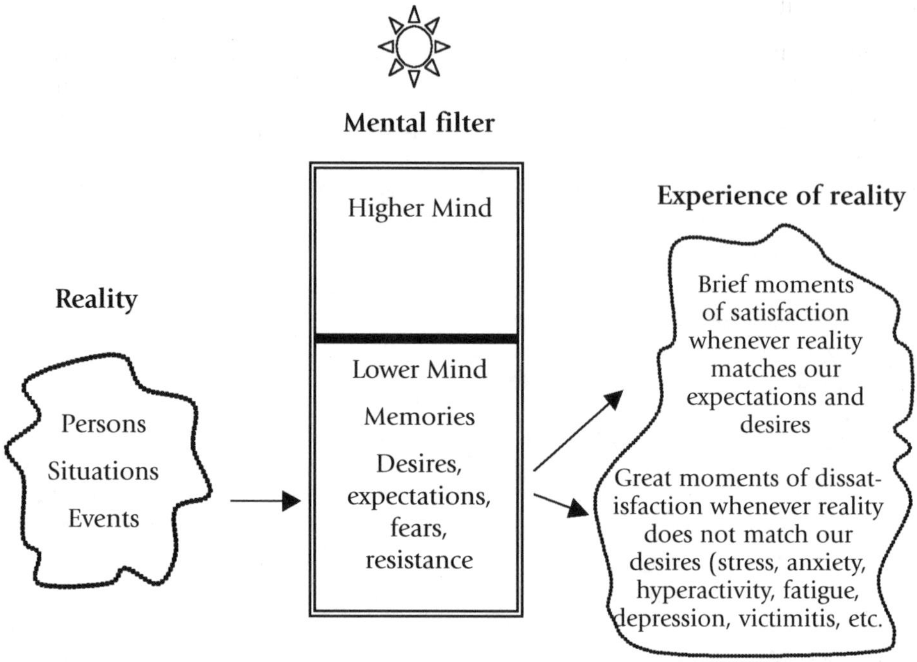

Mental filter

Reality

Experience of reality

Persons

Situations

Events

Higher Mind

Lower Mind

Memories

Desires,
expectations,
fears,
resistance

Brief moments
of satisfaction
whenever reality
matches our
expectations and
desires

Great moments of dissat-
isfaction whenever reality
does not match our
desires (stress, anxiety,
hyperactivity, fatigue,
depression, victimitis, etc.)

The quest for ego pleasure leaves us constantly dissatisfied; and resistance is ineffective. In order to change things around us, and to recover the peace and freedom that are part of our nature, we need to use a different approach. Let us now look into this alternative way of dealing with reality by observing another potential dynamic, a different positioning of consciousness, at the level of the higher mind.

Perceiving Reality from the Perspective of the Higher Mind

A definition of the higher mind and its function

The higher mind is an aggregate of thought mechanisms, which are directly connected to the will of the Self through what is commonly referred to as genuine intuition. These include higher intelligence, inspiration, creativity, direct knowledge, and all the higher mental processes. Its function is twofold:

1. Accurate Perception

The higher mind is the instrument that allows us to have a direct, accurate, intelligent, objective and undistorted perception of reality. It is fresh and new at all times. This mental dynamic is not pre-programmed, and it does not carry any emotional charge from past memories. Emotionally charged memories are only found in the lower mental computer, and the higher mind can function perfectly well without them.

Going back to our previous analogy, an active higher mind would be represented as the wakeful driver of the car, who no longer allows the computer to run the vehicle on the basis of programs which he knows are only a rough and inadequate approximation of reality. He has replaced the content of memories originating from the past with conscious, appropriate programs that make it possible for the computer to respond instantly to any of his commands. Having a direct, accurate view of the road, he is able to drive with just the right reflexes at every turn. His knowledge and mastery of the computer will still serve him well with regard to certain automatic functions, but he will no longer allow it to overstep its intended functions. This means that **one has dispelled the mists of illusion and is in contact with reality.**

2. Right Action – The Expression of the Will of the Self

Once our perception of reality is accurate and forwarded without distortion to the soul, the higher mind becomes a vehicle for the will of the soul, tuning into its wisdom and knowledge through the mechanism of intuition. This will translate into right action at all times.[11] This is where the second function of the higher mind kicks in, as its response to reality will simply be a manifestation of the creative will of the soul. The Master lets the driver organise the concrete details of the journey, as this is his function.

This twofold function of the higher mind—accurate perception and concrete expression of the will of the soul—has already emerged in Chapter 4, when we described how consciousness should ideally function in a context where the lower mind is quiet while the higher mind is active. Diagram 1, illustrates this ideal state of affairs. We shall restate this dynamic here, in contrast with that of the lower mind, using the double chart on the following pages.

When the higher mind is in charge, it transmits the soul's energy directly to the personality, which then behaves very differently, as it finds its sustenance and source of energy within. This will be developed in the course of Chapter 9.

Let us note that the lower mind has its place, and that its function is the same in either case…to generate thought forms. In the first case, these thought forms emanate from the absolute wisdom and knowledge of the soul. They are clear, creative, orderly, silent and efficient. In the second case, thoughts have their source in the previously described mechanism of memories, with all the limitations and illusions this entails.

Higher Level Functioning

Expressing the will of the soul
"The Will to Good"[12]

Reality of the Physical World To the Awareness of the Self

The sense organs transmit information to the silent lower mind, which forwards it without distortion to the higher mind, which, in turn, forwards it to the Self.

Reality of the Self Towards the Physical World

- The **Will of the soul** (the "will to good"), the response to the information received, and accurate knowledge are forwarded, by way of intuition, to the higher mind.
- The **higher mind** transforms these into ideas (inspiration, creativity, abstract intelligence) and passes them on to the lower mind.
- The **lower mind** (to the extent that it is receptive and silent) transforms this impulse into right thought forms[13] that activate the emotional body.
- The **emotional body** reacts by creating a desire that is transmitted to the physical body.
- The **physical body** takes action based on the will of the soul (rather than on old, inadequate memories).

CONSEQUENCES: right action, manifesting mastery, freedom, and all that is "good".

Lower Level Functioning

Expressing the will of the ego
The memories' will to survive

Reality of the Physical World Towards the Ego

The sense organs transmit information to the lower mind, which interprets this information on the basis of its memories, bringing very limited or inaccurate knowledge (Chapter 4).

Reaction of the Ego Towards the Physical World

- The **Will of the ego,** the impulse towards survival and self-protection of the memories is expressed by the lower mind as it is activated in its defence systems.
- The **lower mind** activates its own thought forms stemming from the ego's defence systems and transmits them to the emotional body.

- The **emotional body** reacts by creating a desire that is transmitted to the physical body.

- The **physical body** acts accordingly in the physical world.

CONSEQUENCES: inappropriate action, limitations, suffering, ignorance.

The following is a simple example illustrating this dynamic:

> It is late in the evening, and I am alone in my house, resting in silence. I have turned off the lights so as to better relax. Suddenly, I hear a strange noise. I look out the window and see an unknown male prowling around the house. My senses send the message to my lower mind. If the latter is able to remain silent, I can contact my higher mind, which, after forwarding this information to my Self, gets an immediate response through my intuition. The latter tells me to go and lock the back door to the kitchen, which had remained open, and to turn on the lights in several of the upstairs rooms, indicating that this would be sufficient. I do this without losing my inner state of tranquillity. After a few minutes, I see a car start on the other side of the road. I know that my unexpected visitor is gone, and will not return.

> In the same situation, if my lower mind, loaded with memories of fear, short-circuits the information, it is quite possible that emotion will take over and that I will panic. Being inwardly totally destabilised, I will probably act in a far less appropriate way: for example, I might forget the kitchen door (fear paralyses one's intelligence), I would keep the lights off so as not to be seen huddled up in a corner of my room, I will call my mother in the dark, who will panic along with me on the phone, while the prowler comes into the kitchen, etc. all inappropriate actions that will generate confusion and unpleasant outcomes.

Let us now describe the dynamic of the higher mind in greater detail, so that we can use it more consciously in our day-to-day existence, and highlight how different this dynamic is from the mechanisms of the lower mind. First of all, we mentioned that the transmission of the will and knowledge of the soul to the higher mind occurs through intuition. Let us take a closer look at this mechanism.

The Higher Mind—The Seat of Intuition

Following are a few quotations from the Tibetan Master regarding intuition:

> That which is the opposite of illusion is, as you well know, the intuition. The intuition is that recognition of reality, which becomes possible as glamour and illusion disappear. An intuitive reaction to truth will take place when... the

disciple has succeeded in quieting the thought form—making propensities of the mind, so that light can flow directly, and without any deviation, from the higher spiritual worlds.[14]

Intuition is also a function of the mind; when used correctly, it allows man to have a clear grasp of reality and to see this reality without the deceptions and illusions of the three worlds. Any man, when it is active within him, becomes capable of acting directly and correctly, for he is in contact with pure, unadulterated facts, and with totally undistorted ideas. Facts and ideas are free of any illusion and come directly from the Universal Mind. One is then able to see life and all its forms in their proper perspective; a just sense of values and of time then becomes manifest.[15]

The spiritual seeker "finally learns to substitute intuition, with its quickness and infallibility, to the slow, painstaking work of the mind, with its convoluted ways, its illusions, its errors, its dogmatism, its thought, and its separative culture."[16]

• Intuition

The term 'intuition' can lead to confusion, and its meaning needs to be clarified, since we often confuse genuine intuition with certain automatic unconscious reactions. Many good people, though they think they are relying on their intuition, are in fact merely succumbing to unconscious emotional reactivation. Many people who are steeped in New Age philosophies, where everyone tries as best they can to go off the beaten path of ordinary consciousness and "follow their intuition", will fall into this trap because they are unaware of their internal dynamics. The confusion stems from the fact that both experiences outwardly have some points in common. Yet they lead to very different outcomes because their source is not the same. Let us examine the similarities that lead to confusion, while also noting the fundamental differences.

Intuition is a direct (and accurate) perception of events that does not need to be justified by any rational explanation. It springs from the exact knowledge of the soul. It is experienced as an idea, a "sense" of the way things are, one might even say a "certainty", which comes to us spontaneously, unemotionally, often in totally unexpected ways. It is as if something were evident yet unexplainable. One has the impression of knowing, without being able to rationally justify this knowledge. This can apply equally to ordinary everyday situations and to more specific circumstances, where the intellect is intensely involved. Great scientists often have an intuition as to how to solve a problem they are working on, which they then set out to prove through a logical demonstration. Most of the great scientific discoveries follow this pattern. A great artist's talent is linked to inspiration, which is one form of intuition, and is beyond rational justification. Confusion tends to affect our day-to-day life, where the will of the Self and that of our ego is most often mixed up.

Indeed, the reactivation of a computer program can appear to share some similarities with the emergence of intuition. In our daily existence, when we are reactivated by a memory, most often unconsciously, we do in fact have a direct sense of things, a very spontaneous sense that is not rational and is often unexpected. The resemblance stops there, yet it is sufficient to create confusion. In the instance where active memories are reactivated, our perception is spontaneous in the sense of being automatic. This reactivation does not come from an accurate sense of the way things are, springing from the wisdom of the soul, but from automatic responses built into the computer, which projects its own distorted perception onto reality. It is "unexpected" because we are not aware of our mechanisms, and they turn up at the most unexpected moments. It is felt, or sensed, because it is emotionally driven. Indeed it is not rational. But the fact that it is not rational does not make it intuition. In effect, when old memories are being reactivated, it would be better to have an intelligent rational mind come into play to bring some objectivity into the picture and limit the extent of the damage.

This confusion has generated a lot of suspicion towards intuition among people who are more mind-oriented. Intuition has been confused with something vague, definitely unreliable, based on chance, a trait belonging to rather emotional people. And yet genuine intuition is the source that feeds the greatest scientists and the greatest artists, as well as all those who have opened new doorways to exploration in all fields of knowledge since the advent of humanity. It is time we restored genuine intuition to its proper place, and tried to foster its development, especially among our children—who are the creators of tomorrow—through a more varied and open educational system that would specifically promote right-brain development as being the seat of intuition.

In order for an unobstructed contact between the mind and the soul to occur, the lower mind must be liberated enough not to interfere with the little voice of intuition, for this voice is indeed a "little voice". It does not impose. And this may be a sign that will allow us to tell the difference between a simple reactivation and an accurate intuitive perception of things.

• How does one tell the difference between an accurate intuitive perception and an unconscious automatic reactivation?

The difference is not always easily perceivable, and we learn through experience and self-scrutiny. In particular, we will observe that intuitive perception is not emotionally "charged"; it is present, makes clear suggestions yet without imposing anything. It usually comes with a sense of lightness, of subtle wonder, and of freedom. It comes to mind like a butterfly alighting on a flower.

On the other hand, an automatic perception is highly charged. There always seems to be a sense of heaviness, of necessity, of strong "feelings", even of urgency or discomfort connected to this type of perception. This is due to the fact that the perceived vibrations occur at a much lower rate. **Instead of hearing the subtle voice of the soul, we hear the din of the computer.** For people who are aware of this mechanism, the computer will attempt to muffle the din with a buzzing that simulates the little voice of the soul. But this buzzing is always heavier that the subtle breath of intuition.

In a "past life", Nicole died in a mid-ocean shipwreck, and she carries unconsciously within her an unintegrated memory in relation to sea travel. Being a city dweller, she has never had any occasion to contact this memory. One day, some friends invite her to take part in a South Seas vacation on a cruise ship, a golden opportunity. The price is very affordable, and the trip includes a most interesting educational program. Her friends hand her pictures of the large ship on which they will be travelling. Nicole immediately starts to feel very uneasy, and a few hours later develops a high fever. Even though the educational program is a perfect extension of her present research interests, and she would have the opportunity to meet some very interesting people, she really does not want to go on this trip. Something tells her that it would not be good for her, and she feels irritated every time someone mentions it. She is unaware, of course, of the memory that has just been reactivated. It may well be that the weather will turn nasty, or that people will be boring, or that other circumstances may make this trip unpleasant. Or maybe the trip will be marvellous. She has no idea. There is no reality in these "feelings", just an unconscious negative reaction due to an old memory. Nicole will thus perhaps needlessly deny herself the pleasure of a wonderful journey.

If Nicole had not had this memory buried within her psyche, or if this memory had been *integrated* (had she reached a high enough level of evolution), the flow of intuition could have gone unfettered through her consciousness. She would have known the truth: the trip was perhaps perfectly safe and highly rewarding; she would have known this, and could have enjoyed its benefits. If it were not, she would also have known, and would have turned down the invitation. In either case, she could have acted appropriately.

As long as there are active memories, the computer goes berserk at every opportunity, and it is very difficult to tune into genuine intuition. One does not develop "intuition". Intuition is always available, and we can simply regain access to it. To this end, it will be necessary to free the lower mind as much as possible from these memories.

This very simple example can be adapted to any life situation, from the most simple to the most complex. Whether we are talking about minor or major life choices, physical conditions or human interactions, when genuine intuition is active, we have an accurate perception of things, and we can say that we know the "truth" at any given moment. In this state of awareness, there is neither past nor future, just an understanding of the reality of the present moment. This knowledge is serene, light, silent, flexible and it is not emotionally charged.

At present, this kind of intuition is not yet readily accessible to the average human being. Yet every one of us is equipped with this aspect of the mind, at least in potential form. Its activity depends on the level of evolution of each individual, as well as all the unresolved experiences with which the lower mind is loaded. As we cultivate the qualities of the higher mind and defuse the emotional charges of the lower mind, each of us can focus more and more on this aspect, and thus develop knowledge, mastery, and eventually freedom.

To support this process, we will now describe an essential inner dynamic that is a great step towards opening the doors to higher consciousness.

The Higher Mind—Mastery of the Emotional Body through Dynamic Acceptance, Letting Go and Non-Resistance

The higher mind can function only when the lower mind is quiet; this "silence" requires acceptance, non-resistance, letting go.

When reality strikes the mental filter and is processed directly by the higher mind, it is not compared to any past experience. There is no conscious or unconscious evaluation, no emotional reaction based on the past. There are no expectations, no emotional or mental demands. What we have is simply undistorted recognition and perception of what is there. Emotions are not involved at the level of perception (the horse, being totally under control, awaits the orders of the coachman before making a move, and does not disperse its energy in useless bucking). All that emotional power remains available solely to execute the master's intentions.

Because this objective and clear recognition of what is there does not have any repercussions on any unconscious mental-emotional mechanism, and because there is no reaction linked to desires that were either met or not met, or linked to preconceived viewpoints, the use of the lower mind does not generate any form of resistance. There is a conscious, intelligent, clear and serene observation and evaluation of the situation, leading to quiet acceptance of what is there at any given moment.

> Letting go of the ego's demands, expectations and false needs allows one to use the higher mind and be in contact with one's soul.

In order for this to happen, our computer must be quiet and it must no longer function on the basis of old memories; this means that we have let go of all ego-generated demands, expectations and false needs.

But how can this make us happy? In fact the quietness and receptivity inherent in the way the higher mind functions make it possible for us to be in direct contact with all the richness buried in our soul. We then feel nurtured, filled by this presence; we naturally experience fulfilment, a sense of identity, peace, power, joy, and love. We do not need to wait to get this from some external source. We already have it.

A great Zen master lived close to a fishing village. Every evening, sitting by the door of his modest dwelling, he would share his teachings with whoever was interested. Among his most regular disciples, there was a young girl who was full of admiration for the great Master. This girl had a boyfriend, a young fisherman, and one day she became pregnant. Her boyfriend, who loved her, promised to marry her as soon as he came back from his next fishing trip, which would bring in enough money for him to ask for her hand in marriage and start his own household. So off he went. The girl tried to conceal her state as best she could, but the wait for her boyfriend dragged on. In her village, it was quite unacceptable for a girl to have a child without being officially married. She dreaded having to break the news to her parents. Since the Zen master was revered by all, the girl, in a vain attempt at damage control, said that the Master was the father of her child. This did not help matters in any way. The villagers were furious, as they felt betrayed by the Master, and they cursed him and vowed not to come to him any more. The Master, remaining calm and serene, said, "Very well". When the baby was born, the villagers brought it to the Master, with the understanding that since he was the father, it was up to him to care for it. The Master, still calm and serene, said, "Very well". He took the infant and raised it for a whole year with tender love and care. When the young fisherman returned several months later, having made his money, the girl ended up confessing that the father of her child was her boyfriend. The villagers then went to the Master, berated him for misleading them, and took back the child. The Master handed him over and, with the same unfaltering serenity, said, "Very well". Nothing could disturb his serenity or his love.

We can easily imagine how a less evolved person would have reacted in a similar situation to that of the Zen master. This depends on the content of each individual's unconscious. For example, if we go back to the five unconscious structures presented in Volume 1:

- a schizoid person would have taken the child to the nearest orphanage, would have resumed his meditation and thought no more of it;

- an oral person would have become attached to the child, turned him into a possession, and refused to hand him back;

- a masochist would have felt victimised by an unjust fate, and very angry. He would have played the martyr and suffered a great deal. He would have kept the child, perhaps taking out his frustration on him;

- a person in the psychopath structure would have placed the child under his mother's care, and would have managed to regain his lost popularity with the villagers with all kinds of expert moves (although being a psychopath, he might very well have truly been the father). He would have willingly handed the child back, as long as this made him look like a hero;

- a rigid person would have given precise instructions to a wet nurse and started planning a very strict education for this child from a very young age, so that he wouldn't become like his mother. Or, especially if this happened in North America, he would have sued the girl and her family.

This is not the way the Zen master reacted, for he was in touch with the love, the wisdom and the impersonal detachment of his soul. This state of acceptance, detachment, and serenity may seem out of our reach, and actually, is this really the way we would like to be? In fact, this is a dynamic that, for now, is quite foreign to average human beings. We wonder how this can be achieved, and even whether this might go against our very nature. Indeed, in accepting, do we not risk becoming submissive or losing our sensitivity? And if we accept everything, do we not risk becoming insensitive as well as passive, idle, manipulated and tossed around this way and that by people and circumstances?

In fact, the contrary is true. We need to clarify what we mean by "acceptance", as the description of this unfamiliar dynamic requires caution. We are so used to perceiving everything as a function of our pre-programmed, unconscious desires that we can hardly imagine another way to function. Indeed we have seen how the mechanism of desire has been deeply ingrained for a long time in our mental computer, and how it is not easy to stop identifying with it.

• Dynamic Acceptance

Our vocabulary was designed to describe ordinary levels of consciousness. For this reason, the word "acceptance" may lead to some confusion and suggest things like submission, inaction, carelessness, insensitivity or indifference. From the viewpoint of the higher mind, acceptance is the polar opposite of all that. To emphasise the difference, let us refer to it as "dynamic acceptance".

At the level of the higher mind, accepting simply means being free of the mechanisms of our inner computer, i.e. letting go of the personality's desires and false needs. This process of letting go makes it possible for us to shift our consciousness from the ego to the Self. It is the

> Dynamic acceptance means letting go of the personality's desires and false needs.

indispensable starting point of the process of unidentification of consciousness, the fundamental process involved in self-transformation.

• Letting go

In most spiritual teachings, we are invited to let go. We now understand why this is no easy task. As long as the lower mind is loaded with active memories, our energy will be held hostage by these memories, which will thus continue to control our life. The process of letting go, which opens the door to dynamic acceptance, can occur only when we are free from the grip of active memories. The lower mind then becomes quiet and the higher mind becomes active.

As the higher mind brings us into contact with the richness of the soul, it is not hard for us to accept what is there and to let go, because we no longer expect circumstances or other people to provide us with reasons to be happy. Gone is the need for stuffing and for approval; gone are the fears, the existential angst, the quest for pleasure and power, the need to be loved, and all the

> Letting go means being free of the grip of active memories.

desires that tug at us in all kinds of ways. We are free and at peace.

Since happiness springs from the consonance between what I want and what is, if, instead of insisting on getting the world to meet my expectations, I am willing to make peace with it, the result will be exactly the same; there will be harmony instead of conflict and frustration. [17]

Easier said than done! Human consciousness has been operating on the basis of the personality's impulses for thousands of years. Yet this is the only way to function if we want to access guaranteed action power, genuine happiness and real freedom. This is why it is important to really understand what exactly is involved here. As we get a clearer grasp of what is at stake, we will also, by the same token, be able to describe some of the very positive outcomes we can bring into our daily life by using our higher mind.

Dynamic Acceptance Does Not Mean Submission

On the contrary, letting go and practising dynamic acceptance are the keys to freedom.

Submission is only a way to repress active memories that retain their full emotional charge (and in fact add to this charge as a result of repression), and which will inevitably reappear in full force at the drop of a hat. This is unexpressed resistance, which generates a lot of frustration and anger. It resides in the lower mind. Dynamic acceptance occurs when active memories are no longer involved, thanks to a higher level of mastery resulting from the development of the higher mind. We are then able to be objective, as we recognise what is there, no more, no less, without emotional connotations.

Real life situations remain the same. Reality may at times suit us and be in synch with our wishes, and then all is well. On the other hand, if we are confronted with something that does not suit us, we are able to let go of our expectations at any given moment, and take action while remaining centred on inner peace, intelligence and love, to change things if need be. So there is no question of submission here.

However, if action does turn out to be necessary, it will be taken in a totally different context from the one created by the mechanisms of the lower mind. We will act, but in a calm and centred manner (one might even say "impersonal"), without any of the emotional turmoil that consumes our energy and stokes up resistance. The mere fact of staying centred allows us to remain in possession of all our energy. We stop resisting difficulties. We perceive them no longer as obstructions, but rather as opportunities to enhance our creativity, and contribute to the development of something better, or meet challenges that are part of our human condition. We are not taking about a philosophy. Actually, dynamic acceptance stems from the fact that we maintain a constant connection with an inner sense of our own power. We maintain a state of freedom and centeredness generated by our soul connection, that nothing external can disturb. We live in a state of inner peace, no matter what the circumstances may be, whether they are favourable or not.

My birthday is in July, and I intend to use this opportunity to throw a party at my place. During the days leading up to the event, I regularly check the weather forecasts, which keep calling for sunny skies. So I make plans for a garden party. That morning, I get everything ready with the help of a few friends: garlands, buffet tables, armchairs for relaxed conversations; everything is perfect. As the day wears on, the sky becomes over-cast. My guests arrive, just as the first raindrops begin to fall, soon turning into a major downpour. I have a choice: either I resist, or I let go. In this case, letting go means that, without losing my cool or my good spirits, I accept what the sky is handing me today (in any case, whether I accept it or not, it's raining), and I invite my friends to rearrange the living room furniture so that we can move the party indoors. They, on the other hand, while a little taken aback at first, are soon swept into action by my energy and high spir-its, and everyone gets into it, finding creative solutions so that everything fits. Some are singing while others carry armchairs, move tables, reposition the garlands, improvise a buffet around the fireplace, etc. My father-in-law, who usually has such a stern look on his face, is laughing like a child. We carry on like a bunch of crazy fools, and spend the rest of the evening having a happy, wonderful time.

I could have slipped down into my lower mind, become stressed out and resis-ted, feeling victimised by the weather and by the slings and arrows of outrageous fortune (why did God do this to me, and on my birthday of all days?). My guests would have picked up on my low-level energy. We might have tried to move to the living room (but we would have been crowded in by the furniture), hoping for the rain to stop; I would have nursed my frustration through the entire evening, and it would have been a dreary scene for everyone.

While submission, a resistance-related state, will generate constant inner ten-sion, genuine dynamic acceptance and the ability to let go will bring peace, poise, energy and creativity. This fosters an inner state of lightness that takes the drama out of the various situations we may encounter in our life, and makes way for the full expression of humour and joy, which is a far cry from what happens in the case of submission.

If experiencing reality through the higher mind generates inner peace to such an extent that it leaves us always in a state of well-being, no matter what the cir-cumstances may be, does this mean that we float through life in a state of bliss-ful serenity, without desires, totally unmotivated, enlightened and inactive? Quite the contrary.

Letting go and Accepting Do Not Mean Inaction

On the contrary, dynamic acceptance increases our power to act, to create, while it enhances the effectiveness of our action

There are several reasons for this:

A Clear and Powerful Motivation

When we are caught up in lower-level consciousness, we have no other source of motivation than our conscious or unconscious will to satisfy personal desires stemming from old memories. In this state of consciousness, we are active only when prodded by desires. Otherwise, we become dispirited and inactive. Our ability to let go of automatic desires, this "acceptance" of what is, effectively defuses the mechanism of desire and its motivations. We might then worry that, once our desires are gone, our motivation would go as well. In fact, the opposite is true.

Indeed, when the mechanism of desires is transcended, it is replaced with a renewed connection to the will of the soul. Now the soul has no intention of staying inactive. Its intention is to become more and more active in this world; our bodily vehicle was built precisely for that purpose. So instead of sending us desires with matching expectations (the soul expects nothing and needs nothing in order to be), it imparts a clear and strong motivation to accomplish its purpose, which is simple to define: it is to foster happiness and fulfilment for all humanity. This intent is what permeates our being when we function at the level of the higher mind, rather than being impelled by automatic personal desires, with their string of attendant difficulties. The soul's motivation is very powerful, and it is also very stable and constantly energised. Contrary to the motivations of our ego, which momentarily stimulate us, only to leave us exhausted, disappointed and discouraged, the soul's intent generates constant, joyful motivation, propels us towards action, nurtures creativity and intense activity. As its intent is to create a world of peace and love on this planet, there is a lot of work to do, and no time to be bored!

> When the desires of the personality are transcended, they are replaced with the will of the soul.

Energy

When we experience the state of acceptance of the higher mind, all the creative energy of the mind and all the desire-related energy of the emotional body are available to us to be translated into action. Indeed, in this state, we do not waste energy in resisting; we remain in harmony with the flow of life. The supple operation of the higher mind, without expectations and therefore without resistance, allows us to access a seemingly infinite store of energy. So this actually enhances our capacity for action.

Accuracy of Perception

Our perception of reality through the higher mind is not clouded by memories. It is a much closer reflection of that reality than what we get through the lower mind. This means that our decisions, our choices, our actions stemming from that part of the mind are far more closely adapted to reality as it is, and therefore far more effective.

Flexibility and a Great Capacity to Adapt

Letting go means the ability to let go of our viewpoints and leads inevitably to open-mindedness. At any given moment, we are able to question our action and to improve on it according to whatever reality we happen to be faced with. We thus develop a high degree of flexibility with regard to change, and a capacity for intelligent adaptation, which stands in sharp contrast to the rigidity of the lower mind that clings to its systems like an oyster to a reef. This translates into a high level of efficiency in action.

Creativity

When we function at the level of the higher mind—since our consciousness is no longer compelled to constantly replay old tapes and is in contact with the power of the soul—we can access a whole other level of creative power leading to new and original avenues of exploration. This can only reinforce our power to act and to create in the real world.

Intuition

This creativity comes with an accurate intuition stemming from the soul's boundless store of knowledge, which allows us to act and to create always in appropriate ways. Our actions then become that much more appropriate, effective and constructive.

Stability, Reliability, Centeredness

The level of emotional mastery attained as a result of letting go will give us a high degree of stability, consistency and centeredness, which will allow us to act in a coherent, single-minded manner. Our actions therefore become that much more effective.

Rather than turning us away from action, these aspects, all of which are direct outcomes of the higher mind's capacity for dynamic acceptance and letting go, will make us infinitely more active, efficient and creative.

Letting Go and Accepting Does Not Mean Insensitivity

On the contrary, as we practice the disciplines of letting go and dynamic acceptance, we can express genuine sensitivity.

As long as we remain ego bound, what we call "sensitivity" is nothing but an emotional dynamic of memory-induced reactions. At the ego level, being sensitive usually means being *"susceptible, selfish, and perpetually defensive"*,[18] in other words always ready to be reactivated emotionally. This is a kind of mechanical sensitivity that only serves to express the automatic responses of our inner computer. **We equate sensitivity with being emotional.** It is easy to imagine all the things that can activate this pseudo-sensitivity in each of the five major structures of the unconscious.

Genuine sensitivity can only flourish when we are in a state of openness, of unclouded intuition and genuine love, when we are present in the here and now without expectations. It can only emerge when we are free of alienating demands, of fears, of false needs and of desires. Genuine sensitivity is ours only through dynamic acceptance, which allows us to let go of all our ego mechanisms.

> When we say practice desirelessness, this does not mean, "be insensitive". It means, "Replace desire with the irresistible will of pure thought." Through this will, you call upon all the powers of light and you get them **to align their input with the purity of your effort.**[19]

Letting Go and Accepting Does Not Mean Indifference

Letting go leads to genuine love.

Dynamic acceptance involves the conscious act of letting go of our expectations, the practice of detachment. This brings shivers to our ego, since at that level we are attached to all kinds of people and things, and we hope that others will remain attached to us. It seems to us that detachment, in the sense of the kind of absence of automatic desires we described earlier, might make us insensitive, cold, and indifferent. We think that we will no longer be able to love. We have trouble grasping the fact that letting go of our desires, and experiencing detachment as a result, might open the doors not only to genuine sensitivity but also to a greater capacity to love.

And yet it is through the practice of detachment and letting go that we will be able to create the most beautiful relationships with others; relationships based on unconditional love, self-reliance, respect, joy, and freedom. No more passionate melodramas fuelled by ego mechanisms.

> Letting go leads to the natural and blissful practice of unconditional love.

"Emotional love" as experienced at the ego level is in fact just an aggregate of demands, expectations and emotional reactivations. As we practice letting go, we are able to experience the power of love as it springs from the soul, without any personal investment, and without any useless and painful attachment. It allows us to love in the truest sense. We are free, and we allow others to be free.[20]

If we want to function at the level of the higher mind, we will have to learn to live in this state of non-resistance, of dynamic acceptance, and with this willingness to let go of our unconscious demand of what we mistakenly believe we "need" most in life. We shall see further on how we can get around to letting go, as this is no easy task.

In addition, this liberation from the lower mechanisms of the mind has a major impact in terms of how well we function at the level of our intelligence.

The Higher Mind: The Seat of Genuine Intelligence

As long as we remain caught in the automatic responses of the lower mind, we cannot be truly intelligent. Real objective intelligence, of the kind that enables us to deal with reality as it is, ceases to be accessible when such automatic responses kick in. This is why, in Volume 1, we found Josie who systematically bought shoes that were one size too small for her, in order to satisfy her unconscious pattern to the effect that

> Freedom and mastery are ours when we have recovered our capacity to think, unfettered by the automatic responses of the lower mind.

life is hard and we must suffer to be right. It may seem stupid, and we might think that we would never do anything of the sort. Yet we do indeed act in such irrational ways, though we are not aware of what is actually going on, because they reflect our own particular issues. They may have nothing to do with shoes, but they may surface in many other types of circumstances or situations, and some may have a major impact on the quality of our life, undermining our well-being and fulfilment without our being aware of them. Each of us, depending on our particular combination of active memories, has unintelligent ways of organising our life.

And this is not a question of intellectual development. Even people who are intellectually brilliant are not immune to this type of mechanism. In fact, on the contrary, the power of their intellect can be enlisted to serve old memories. These people can very easily use their intellect to nurture and justify automatic, deeply set behaviours. The trap, here, has to do not only with unconscious, emotionally charged memories, but also with the very mechanism of their highly developed rational lower mind, which is bent on hanging onto their viewpoints, remaining impervious to any kind of change, wanting to be right at any cost, etc. This is frequently the case with rigid or psychopath structures, which are often sustained by brilliant intellects. Intellectual development is desirable, as long as it occurs in conjunction with growing flexibility and open-mindedness.

Intelligence has little to do with the mechanism of the lower mind. Real intelligence can function only when we have learned to let go and be free of this mechanism.

The higher mind is the seat of genuine intelligence springing from the soul. It fosters sane and objective reasoning, flexibility, openness, inspiration, and intuition. It is the part of the mind that is brilliant and receptive to expanded, original and unfettered creativity. It is constantly questioning, passionately on the lookout for any discovery, contrary to the lower mind that clings to what is known and is afraid of anything that is new. It allows access to the universal mind, a source of infinite creative intelligence.

It is therefore very important not to fall into wholesale denigration of the mind. Our capacity to think is a precious tool that was given to human beings so that they can build their own freedom. But this requires that we be able to think freely, without being bogged down by inadequate automatic mechanisms. If we want to gain mastery in the three worlds and recover our freedom, we must develop our full capacity to think freely and intelligently, by overthrowing the tyranny of the emotionally linked mechanisms of our lower mind.

◆ Thinking and Silencing the Mind

Many spiritual masters emphasise the necessity for silencing the mind, and it is important to understand what this truly means in order to avoid unnecessary confusion. The fact that we possess a mental system is a great privilege for us as human beings. We need to master it, rather than get rid of it as being the source of so many problems. Silencing the mind does not mean stifling the process of thought.

In fact, what we are talking about is silencing the lower mind; this means calming the chaotic turmoil of our thoughts, stopping the constant building of thought forms activated by memories and unbridled emotional energy. It is a fact that when we master this part of the mind, we experience inner silence. And in this silence, the voice of our soul can be heard and expressed in the form of creative ideas and thoughts that are intelligent, impersonal, appropriate and useful. These are the "thoughts", the expression of the voice of the soul, that emerge once we have mastered the practice of silencing the mind.

Yet mental silence does not in any way imply that we stop thinking, in the sense of becoming a zombie who drifts through life on the basis of "feelings", mistaken for intuition. When we do this, we actually regress: we are guided by emotions, mistaking once again emotional feelings for intuition. It is true that when we function intuitively, the usual thought mechanism is absent, in the sense that it is no longer active…it is no longer in charge of operations. Yet it has to remain present in the sense of providing intelligent receptivity and a faithful conversion of ideas into creative thoughts. Our intuition needs a well-trained mental system in order to express itself. Developing and mastering the mind are essential steps towards spiritual fulfilment. The qualities of concentration, attention, reflection, focus, and higher understanding remain to be developed. Intelligence—the "intuitive" intelligence of the heart and mind—is a quality of the soul.

◆ When we use the higher mind, must we trash our inner computer?

Nature has endowed human beings with this computer, and it has taken thousands of years to perfect it. It has a purpose. We have seen this in the chain of command from the will of the soul down to the physical plane. It must therefore be maintained, but we will turn it into a completely silent, clear and receptive instrument that is not pre-programmed and that is ready at any given moment to take instructions from the Self. Thanks to this instrument, we will no longer need to focus our consciousness on certain aspects of life that have been totally mastered. We have already covered a lot of ground in this direction. For instance, it is not necessary for us to spend mental energy on digestion, or on walking for that matter. Both of these activities make it possible for us to function and be active in the physical world, and to use our creative energy to bring about concrete manifestations of the more elaborate aspects of the will of the soul into this world.

While it is good to know how the higher mind functions, it is even more important to put all this knowledge into practice, as this is where the reality of life comes in. For this reason, we can now try to find out what facilitates this higher mental functioning while minimising the chances of losing our freedom by falling prey to the lower mind. Specific work on the level of the memories will certainly have to be undertaken. This subject will be broached in the fourth part of this book. The precise knowledge of the five major character structures of the unconscious presented in Volume 1 is also an important tool to facilitate the task of defusing the memories. In the meantime, we will attempt to grasp certain principles that might shed light on the practical work we can do for the purpose of gaining mastery over our personality.

---

[1] This was developed in Chapter 2 of *The Power of Free Will*.

[2] See *The Power of Free Will*, page 47.

[3] Also called the "body of desires", with good reason, in certain esoteric traditions.

[4] The examples of character structures presented in Volume 1 illustrate a similar way of functioning: Peter (2nd structure) loves chocolate candy, Mark (2nd structure) needs job security, Sophie (3rd structure) always needs someone to take care of her, Paul (1st and 3rd structures) hates authority and dreams of owning a tiny house where no one will ever come to disturb him, Victor (4th structure) wants glory, Marianne (4th structure) has such a great need to be loved.

[5] See "The Cycle of Dissatisfaction" in Chapter 2.

[6] Here's a brief summary of these behaviours:
> 1st structure: We want to withdraw from the world as often as possible. We expect others never to ask us to get involved in anything.
> 2nd structure: We want as much stuffing as possible. We expect others to nurture us emotionally.
> 3rd structure: We want to prove that life is cruel and people are bad. We expect others to commiserate with us and save us (unless we choose to play the saviour ourself).
> 4th structure: We want to prove that he is perfect and, if possible, the best. He expects love, recognition, approval and unconditional admiration from others.
> 5th structure: We want to stay in control and to dominate. We demand that others conform to our way of seeing things.

[7] This confusion feeds many illusions on the spiritual path, especially in New Age philosophies. We talk about daring to be ourselves, daring to speak "our truth", finding our "personal myth", all worthy endeavours. And everyone gets to work with a great deal of good will. Yet it is very easy for the ego to reclaim all this to its own ends and to use these teachings to justify its own way of seeking happiness, to try to fulfil unconscious mechanisms such as lack of self-esteem, powerlessness, or any other automatic mechanism generated by active memories. **Vigilance is essential if we want to avoid feeding our ego with fine ideas.**

[8] Alice Bailey, *A Treatise on White Magic*, page 258.

9 Desires, such as we know them from the viewpoint of our present human nature, are part of the evolutionary plan. At the start, when there was no mind, life was directed by instinct. When the soul eventually takes charge, it will direct our life by manifesting its will through the higher mind. Until then, during the time it takes to develop the personality and the mind in both of its aspects, we have to go through these types of mechanisms, and eventually discard them. For many of us, that moment has come.

10 Ken Keyes Jr., *A Manual for Higher Consciousness.*

11 The higher mind can eventually make use of the rational mind's stock of knowledge accumulated over past centuries, but it will enrich this knowledge with new ideas. This is the part of the mind that generates innovations, discoveries, and creations that are off the beaten path.

12 The expression "will to good" is not used here in the sense of the opposite of evil, according to moral criteria that are subject to discussion, but in the general sense of beauty, harmony, peace, love, respect, and freedom.

13 The primary function of the lower mind is to create thought forms, regardless of their source.

14 Alice Bailey, *Glamour, A World Problem*, page 67.

15 Id., *Discipleship in the New Age,* Vol. 1, page 48.

16 Id., *Discipleship in the New Age,* Vol. 2, page 396.

17 Translation of *"En relisant les Évangiles",* Arnaud Desjardins, page 221.

18 Alice Bailey, *Discipleship in the New Age,* Vol 1.

19 Translation of an excerpt from *Hiérarchie, Enseignement de l'Agni yoga,* Éd. Le courrier du livre.

20 The ego panics at the very idea of letting others be free. Indeed, its interest is to hold others hostage in order to be able to feed on their energy. That is what attachment is really all about, and that is what we call "love" at the personality level.

chapter 7

Conditions that Facilitate the use of the Higher Mind

OR

HOW TO MAKE THE MOST OF TWO POWER MOMENTS

It is not easy to avoid falling into the trap of the lower mind, in view of the habits we've acquired over thousands of years, and of the gravitational charge of our memories. Yet some of us are now prepared to go through this transformation. As we deepen our understanding of the mechanisms of consciousness, it gets a lot easier to do the inner work required, no matter what approach we use.

Ideally, we would like to perceive reality through the higher mind at all times. But our automatic responses are so deeply anchored in our personal and collective consciousness that often, though we may not realize it, we still react to situations from the vantage point of our lower mind. Are we doomed to remain stuck at this level, or is there a way to regain a state of higher consciousness? Let us take a look at the possibilities for accessing the higher mind.

In the diagram representing our perception of reality through the double structure of our mental filter, we can observe two possibilities for accessing the higher mind, two "power moments".

The Two Power Moments When We Perceive Reality Through Our Mental Filter

• The First Power Moment

The first power moment occurs at the very instant when information enters our consciousness. Indeed, when reality is picked up by a quiet lower mind, it is forwarded directly and without distortion to the higher mind: our perception of reality is thus accurate. All is well, as we then function in the way we described earlier, with the result that our response will manifest the qualities of the soul. This is the ideal way to function, the most direct path, which also happens to be the least familiar to human nature, at least for now. Yet this is the path we will have to learn to use more and more habitually if we want to become masters of our life.

Diagram 1
The First Power Moment
Reality is perceived directly by the higher mind;
the lower mind is inactive and silent.

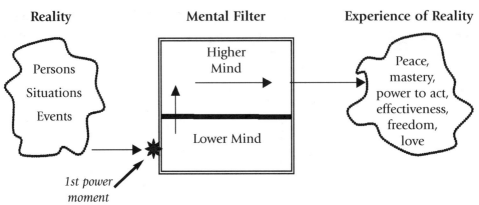

How to promote direct access to the higher mind

Is it possible to ensure that incoming information is not instantly grabbed by the lower mind, and that it naturally registers at the level of the higher mind?

Yes, and for this to happen, two things must be done simultaneously, for they are mutually interactive and are not effective one without the other:

Develop the higher mind; make it more active by cultivating our intelligence, our capacity to think objectively, to reflect, to concentrate, to observe, to be open and creative, and develop our understanding and knowledge, that is, our higher mental capacities and our mastery at the level of our general power to think.

At the same time, clear the lower mind of emotionally charged memories from past experiences in order to make it more and more silent and receptive. Indeed, if our mental computer is highly charged with memories, it will be very easily and violently reactivated by any number of aspects of life around us. Our capacity to think intelligently is then flooded with automatic mental responses (wanting to be right, imposing one's point of view), or emotional responses (fear, pleasure, power). Our consciousness is highjacked by our lower mind, and the wisdom of our higher mind is thus short-circuited. The less our lower mind is charged, the less pronounced our automatic mental/emotional responses will be, the less skittish the "horse" will be, and the less likely we are to be lured into the trap of the lower mind. It is then easier to use the higher mind directly.

This means that there is a lot of work to be done on the level of inner healing and liberation from old memories. Luckily, as human awareness gradually expands, we see more and more effec-

> The process of transformation implies that we free our self from the grip of memories stemming from the past.

tive instruments for personal healing and transformation becoming available to us. We will take a closer look at these in the last part of this book. In all spiritual paths of learning, this is what is meant by ego liberation. It is easy to see why this liberation is of primary importance if we want to find our way back to the wisdom and power of the soul.

Most of us have not yet gained enough mastery to function directly through the higher mind in all circumstances. Our unconscious is often quicker to react than our conscious will. Memory reactivation is so fast and unconscious that, before we know it, we find our self caught in emotional resistance or mental closure in all its various forms depending on the active memories we carry within us. If we have any kind of self-awareness, if we have developed the habit of being honest with our self, we can easily know when we are caught in a mechanism. We quickly recognize the signs, which, depending on the individual, can take the form of inner tension, unbalanced energy (either low or excessive energy), stress, discomfort, anxiety. It is a general loss of well-being, joyfulness and stability leading to many difficulties in all areas of our life. The more we have progressed in our awareness, the quicker we "see our self" caught in a mechanism. Less developed people can remain caught for years or even lifetimes in unconscious automatic behaviours and responses without having the faintest idea of what is actually going on. There is no cause for alarm: everyone learns at his or her own rate. However, if we happen to be further ahead in our progress and we begin to know our self fairly well (in this sense, the thorough knowledge of the functioning of the five character structures described in Volume 1 is a great help), we can fairly quickly recognize the mechanism at work within us at any given moment. Recognizing it does not mean being free of it, but it is an essential first step towards liberation and healing. *If our car malfunctions on a regular basis, we need first of all to be able to recognize that fact. If we are unaware of the malfunctions and of the fact that a car can run much better, then we remain dependent on a defective vehicle, and we complain that life is difficult, without knowing why. Or, if we know that our car is in bad shape, yet refuse to recognize the malfunctions because we are unwilling to put in the effort required for genuine repairs (we can polish the outside of the car or adjust the rear view mirror and pretend we are working on our self), this is not helpful either and we are no further ahead. The first thing to do is to acknowledge the fact that we are dysfunctional.*

> When something is "not right" for some reason or other, in the course of our daily life, it is because we have used the lower mind as our instrument for perceiving reality.

If we see that we have missed the first power moment that would have allowed us to function with the kind of serenity and well-being that higher consciousness brings, is it too late or is there a way to salvage the situation?

• The Second Power Moment

In order to regain a higher level of mastery, we will need to move our consciousness to the level of the higher mind; in concrete terms, that means letting go of these old mechanisms and changing our perception of reality.[1]

Diagram 2

The Second Power Moment

Reality is perceived by the lower mind, and its memories are activated.

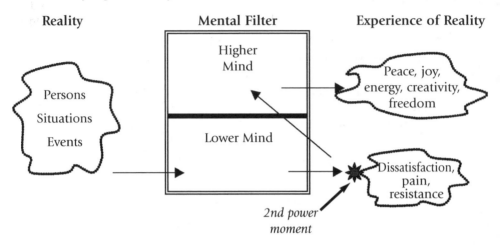

Changing our perception of reality, letting go, these are easier said than done. Our ego will use every means to resist this; it is very attached to its old way of per-

> Being able to change one's perception of reality is the key to any genuine spiritual progress.

ceiving things, with which it totally identifies. For the ego, letting go and changing its viewpoint means death. Even when we appear to be interested in "spiritual" growth, we may unwit-

tingly seek to avoid this process and nurture dreams of spirituality that remain disconnected from reality and, in the end, remain caught up in our old viewpoints. Yet being able to change one's perception of reality is a major consciousness-developing process in any form of genuine spiritual progress. The capacity to change our viewpoints just about guarantees our evolution in terms of consciousness.[2]

One secret to letting go is to be able to see things from a different perspective: if not from the soul's perspective, at least to be able to consider things from a broader, more objective viewpoint. Otherwise, trying to confront our emotions head-on without a change in context is a hopeless and repeated endeavour. *(It is as if we tried to calm the horse without giving the coachman the means to control it. As soon as our backs are turned, the horse will buck once again and the coachman will be unable to control it in any effective manner.)*

If we cannot manage to let go, it is not because we are right or because reality should be different, or because we are no good; it is because our perception of reality is warped by a mental/emotional charge emanating from the lower mind. Letting go is a natural and spontaneous process once the mental filter has been expanded.

Recognizing this reality does not mean that the work is done, but it is the key that opens the door to effective and lasting inner work. Once we have recognized the fact that we are dysfunctional, we can see, for example, that the electronic connection activating the throttle may be defective. We have not yet solved the problem, but at least we know where it comes from.

> If we have trouble letting go, it is because our perception of reality is distorted by a mental-emotional charge emanating from the lower mind

We then have two possible courses of action to change our perception of reality and function at the level of the higher mind: one involves using the power of our conscious will (expanding the mental filter), the other is geared towards addressing the content of the unconscious (cleaning up the mental filter). Both approaches are necessary and, if used simultaneously, they complement each other and make it possible for us to achieve mental/emotional mastery. We are now making serious repairs.

- **The First Step: a Consciousness Development Process**

When a situation reactivates our mental/emotional mechanisms and we find our self caught in their gears, we can begin by stepping out of the situation, or at least limiting the extent of the damage, by going through the following consciousness development process:

- *Recognize the fact that we are being reactivated*

This means being able to adopt a witness stance,[3] which means that we have attained a minimum level of self-awareness and authenticity in terms of self-perception. Adopting a witness stance means observing our inner mechanism from an objective, detached standpoint. It is important to observe our self with love, or even with humour, and not to blame our self, or blame others, for the fact that we have fallen once again into the trap of lower consciousness. We simply observe our emotional mechanism at work, just as we would observe the motor of a malfunctioning washing machine. It may be unpleasant, as we would have preferred to have things going well, but we know that it is a mechanism and that there is something we can do to fix it.

- *Become aware of automatic thought patterns*

These can underscore our emotional reactions. All we need to do is to listen to the chatter inside our heads, being always convinced, of course, that we are right. All those judgements: we judge others (people are mean, stupid, selfish, incompetent, ungrateful, bad); we judge our self (I am incapable, powerless, no good, I should be different); and we judge life in general (life is tough, meaningless, you always have to fight to survive, it's the law of the jungle). Add to these judgements all the automatic thought patterns stemming from our active memories and unconscious defence patterns. **All this mental chatter does is to reflect our perception of reality.**

- *Change the way we perceive things*

Through a conscious act of will (using our intelligence), we check to see if we can let go of our expectations and perceive the situation in another way, from another viewpoint. To this end, we can meditate, think, write, study, talk to someone who might help us see things more objectively...do something that will allow us to see the situation differently.

For example, we could ask our self the following questions:

- In this situation, what are my expectations?
- What are my demands in relation to others?
- What is it that I expect from life, that I am not getting?
- What is the issue on which I need to prove I am right?
- What am I resisting?
- Is it really important or can I let go of these inner expectations and restore my inner sense of joy and freedom?

In and of itself, this attitude of good will and openness in order to be able to let go of our way of seeing things is already highly beneficial, for it taps into the energies of the soul, though we may not be aware of it. With this attitude, we can tap into all the helpful conscious knowledge we have in order to clarify our thoughts, change our perception of reality, and transform the thought context that is confining our experience of life.

We do this already, intuitively. Whenever things aren't going well, we might say, "I'm going to go for a walk to take my mind off things." This is exactly what we need to do. Even if we do not necessarily use the best means to go about this (often, all we do is trade one kind of delusion for another, or one mechanism for another), this can give us just enough of a break so that we have time to get centred. Certainly if the source of reactivation is not worked on, the problem will inevitably resurface at some point. However, if we learn to take our mind off things in a more conscious manner, using effective tools, we can regain a more permanent state of peace and serenity. This is the goal of any gain in conscious knowledge leading to a deeper understanding of our self, of others, and of the universe.

In particular, knowing our personal character structures makes it possible for us to become more aware of the way our perception of things is biased. So instead of trying to force things, and demand that others behave differently in order to meet our expectations, or blame them if they do not, **we take responsibility for our actions.** We use our intelligence, our knowledge and our understanding of our self to try to perceive reality in a more expanded way and thus recover our inner freedom.

> Any gain in genuine knowledge will enable us to expand our perception of reality and make it easier for us to let go.

The principle of responsibility/attraction/creation, as presented in *The Power of Free Will,* is one example of a conscious tool we can use to expand our perception of reality. It enables us to perceive life, people, things and situations all around us from a broader concrete perspective, and by that very fact it makes it easier to let go in major ways.

If we manage to change our perception of any given situation, if we can let go of our expectations and look at things with the eyes of the soul, we can soon recover our inner peace and freedom.

Sometimes, this first conscious step is enough, when our connection with the soul is already relatively well-established (the higher mind is already awakened), and when the situation does not reactivate heavily charged active memories. This is what happens in many situations in our daily life, where we poison our experience of life through perpetual reactivations based on what are actually somewhat minor events. The mere fact of being aware, of being a witness to the mechanism, and of doing a few centering exercises, will allow us to regain our inner peace and freedom, a certain lightness of being (humour is very helpful), and thus reclaim our actual power.

The more we develop the habit of doing this inner work in the little things of our daily life, the more we expand the channel that links us directly with our higher consciousness. Daily living then becomes a genuine spiritual workout that brings us ever closer to the will of our soul.

• **The trap**

Let us note, however, that we must be very vigilant when we try to let go strictly through an act of conscious will, for it is easy to fall into the trap of repression. When we repress and deny our emotions, we get to a point where we no longer feel anything, and we can fool our self into believing that we have actually let go. But all we are doing is reinforcing the mechanism that has been reactivated, and which will surge again all the more powerfully the next time around. Some spiritual approaches that place a great deal of emphasis on willpower can lead people to fall into this trap. We do not let go through a simple act of will; we let go through an act of consciousness and, if need be, through a process of healing and defusing memories, which is quite different.

If we find our self unable to accept, or to let go of a desire or "need", it is better to be truthful with our self, and to have the courage to face the reality of our own emotional mechanism and recognize that there is work to be done. This will not solve the problem right away, but it paves the way towards more effective work, which will have to reach the depths of the unconscious.

Indeed, in some more heavily charged cases, despite our best intentions, our knowledge and our broader conscious perception of things, we remain caught emotionally or mentally, unwilling to let go, convinced that we are right, that our pained or troubled state is perfectly justified, and that, if things are not going well, it is because of others or because of circumstances. Even if we know that our reaction comes from our active memories that are reactivated, we may well remain unable to control our emotions and our minds, which go on spinning together out of control, or else we shut our self off and become insensitive. We don't feel well; we don't know how to regain a state of joyfulness, openness, creativity and peace. It seems as if what is needed is a change in our situation, yet it just will not change. All we can do is suffer, or else take another step to try to let go, and thus facilitate a change of perception of reality.

• The Second Step: Working on the Unconscious

If, despite our best intentions and conscious efforts, something in us remains dead-set against letting go, it is because the will of our unconscious is stronger that our conscious will. It is then obvious that we are dealing with a memory that is too heavily charged for us to be able to neutralize it through a mere act of will. We must then acknowledge the fact that we are prisoners of an unconscious mechanism that is embedded somewhere in our inner computer, conditioning our perception of things and thus our reactions to the reality thus perceived.

> Whenever we feel mentally or emotionally "overpowered" by something, and thus feel robbed of our sense of joy and serenity, it is a safe bet that an active memory has just been struck.

What prevents us from letting go is the strength of the memories recorded within us. Thus, the more our inner computer is free of memories of the past, the easier it will be for us to accept reality as it is, and to function at the level of the higher mind. We therefore need to get to work on debugging our unconscious. This work will result in our ability to actually integrate the dynamics of the higher mind as a constant practice in our daily existence.

Obviously we will not be able to do this work right away, at the time of reactivation. The only thing we can do at that moment is:

- put our self in "neutral", as much as possible, and refrain from acting on the basis of this reactivation (the coachman holds the horse in check and prevents it from running helter skelter); and

- find a means or a method for inner work that will allow us to liberate our unconscious from this emotional charge. This is when we must dare to confront our "shadow", the unconscious components of the automatic mind that controls our life.

Having examined the mechanism of the unconscious in the preceding chapters, we are in a better position to understand why it is so difficult for us to let go. This is not a matter of bad faith. We are being confronted with centuries of past history and suffering that must be healed and set free. This healing will open the door to liberating the ego, which will make it possible for us to let go naturally, without any need to force the process.

In the end, whether it is to foster our direct access to higher consciousness or to regain our lost sense of well-being, we will need to help the process along with specific work on the unconscious. Each of us will choose the method that works for him or her. There are now a number of spiritual approaches and methods of inner work to choose from. But this work of in-depth transformation is complex, as it involves both conscious and unconscious aspects. Building on what we learned in the first chapters, we will describe some of these aspects in Part Three.

On the other hand, any approach that would focus only on the unconscious would also be incomplete, as it would give the impression that we will never see the end of these emotional charges.[4] These approaches lack the broad and intelligent conscious context that is inseparable from our experience of life. In order for this inner work to be effective, **we must combine consciousness expansion through changes in thought contexts with work that focuses on debugging the unconscious, so that it becomes possible for us to integrate this change in practical terms in our everyday life.** We were once told, "In order for a bird to be able to fly, it must have wings, and so it is with human beings: in order to be able to evolve, they must have both the wing of knowledge and the wing of practice." Practice means mastering the ego in our day-to-day existence, which is another way to describe concrete mastery over the unconscious.

These different paths to consciousness could be illustrated with the following story:

A large company decides to transfer its offices from the capital to a regional location, and in order to do this, it must lay off a number of its employees. How will they respond to this information and react to this reality?

Through the lower mind:

Dennis has been working for five years as an employee in this company, where he enjoys many benefits. He feels comfortable with his work and has proven his worth. Thinking he had a long-term, steady job, he has just left a neighbourhood that he loved and bought a house close to his work, so as to be more readily available. He also wanted to have a more pleasant residence in which to entertain his new girlfriend, with whom he wanted to develop a deep and lasting relationship.

One morning, when he reports to work, he gets the bad news: his contract is being terminated this year. This reality is at odds with what he wants, and he perceives it through his lower mind; he is very upset. How dare they do this to him after five years of loyal service to the company? His employers are a bunch of selfish, ungrateful boars. For the remaining three months of his contract, he is very moody at work and unpleasant with everybody around him. His anger is coupled with a strong sense of insecurity. How is he going to make the payments on his house? He can't sleep at night, brooding over his bitterness towards everyone. He is convinced that it will not be easy for him to find another job, given how bad the economic situation is. He feels caught in a dreadful situation. His girlfriend, who has just moved in with him, does not appreciate his foul mood, and she lets him know it. His response is to accuse her of being a heartless bitch; how could she not understand what he was going through? The world is really in sad shape. At the end of the three months' notice, Dennis still has not found a new job, and his girlfriend got fed up with his behaviour and left him. He finds himself alone, jobless, and suffering from stomach pains. Life is tough. Dennis was caught in a mechanism of the lower mind, and so he remained. He resists, suffers, having lost all sense of his own power.

Through the higher mind:

Andrew was laid off, just like Dennis, but his reaction is completely different. Though his situation is just as uncomfortable as Dennis', if not more so (he has children), once the initial moment of disappointment has passed, he is able to use the first power moment. He accepts what is there and begins to take action with a cool yet firm attitude. He requests an interview with his employer in order to get more information. The latter explains the situation, and Andrew understands that there is indeed no immediate job prospect for him under these conditions. Yet he remains calm and centred. This is not what he would have wanted, of course, but he has gained some wisdom over the years. Although his present position is an excellent one and he would have preferred to remain there, he chooses to accept reality as it is; in his case, we are talking about active acceptance such as we described earlier. He lets go of his desires, knowing that each event happens for a reason. He is well aware that jobs are scarce in his field. But he does not let his horse go crazy. Instead, he chooses to remain confident and begins to make contacts with other firms. He meets a lot of people, and eventually begins to find this quest for a new job stimulating; he finds the prospect of change rather pleasant (this, for sure, is not the lower mind operating). He remains cheerful and continues to provide excellent service during the three months remaining until the end of his contract.

One day his supervisor asks him to look after an important client for him, as he has another engagement. Andrew is fully up to the task. In his conversation with this person, he finds that they share a passion for sailing. They share a few experiences on this topic, and agree to meet for supper the following week so as to explore the subject further. A friendly relationship has thus developed between Andrew and this person, who happens to be the president of a large company specializing in construction materials. When, in the course of a conversation, Andrew lets him know that he is looking for another job, the man immediately points him to one of his business acquaintances who is sure to need his services. Thus Andrew ends up finding a new job, one that is more interesting in every respect than the previous one, without having wasted a minute making his life miserable. When we stop resisting, and we let go of our expectations, life responds in kind and showers us with gifts.

> *"Acceptance becomes the most expedient and practical way of extricating oneself from a difficult situation, while resistance inexorably tightens the noose."*[5]

• Using the Second Power Moment

Dennis is obviously caught in an unconscious mechanism of resistance and powerlessness. Should he remain unaware of it, his life will continue to be chaotic for a long while. If he happens to be more aware, then after being depressed and discouraged for a few days, he may adopt a witness stance and choose to change his perception of things. He might, for example, visit a friend, not to complain but to seek counsel and inspiration. He may consciously choose not to panic and to look for solutions that allow the mechanism of powerlessness to begin to slow down. He may choose to act even though he feels inwardly insecure. That is the moment when one needs to use flexible, intelligent willpower. Having missed the first power moment (the mechanism of the victim momentarily overcame him), he still has another recourse: he can choose to use his second power moment, calling upon his knowledge of himself, his intelligence and his will.

If, despite his conscious efforts, he continues to have unbearable fits of anxiety, this would mean that a past memory has been reactivated, adding a powerful emotional charge to his present experience. In this case, Dennis will need to work more specifically on debugging his unconscious. But he can fully understand that this situation is not a matter of chance. He can look at it as an experience being presented to him by his soul in order to reactivate old energy blocks, so that he can undo them, develop other qualities, and thus have a much more liberated life experience afterwards.

All of life's situations can be seen from this perspective, which has the advantage of allowing us to stop resisting, and watching solutions emerge very quickly. Indeed, when we resist, our vibrational rate is lowered, and we attract more and more difficult circumstances. When we let go of our expectations, our vibrational rate rises, and we attract far more harmonious circumstances. This is not philosophy; it is an energetic law of the world of consciousness.

> When we resist life, it resists us; when we smile at it, it smiles back.

The ability to function through the higher mind opens the door to the full blooming splendour of the soul spreading its light in the world of matter that is in our day-to-day existence. What happens in our daily experience when we use our power moments and deal with reality with the awareness of the soul through the higher mind?

---

1 Let us not forget that if we are faced with difficulties, it is not because other people are no good or because life is difficult! (Just a little reminder, in case we might have lost sight of this fact as we read the last few pages.)

2 This topic was explored in greater depth in Chapter 2 of *The Power of Free Will*.

3 See the "Focusing" technique described by Eugene T. Gendlin.

4 This is what happens in certain therapeutic approaches involving a strictly materialistic perspective.

5 Piero Ferrucci, *What We May Be: the Vision and Techniques of Psychosynthesis*.

chapter 8

Clarifications Regarding the Manifestation of the Self

The ability to function through the higher mind opens the door to all the wonderful splendour of the soul, which must then manifest itself in our daily life. Indeed genuine spiritual exploration is not removed from the world. For a long time, human beings have confined their spiritual quest to the more or less conscious practice of a religion. Things are changing now, and many of us have embarked on an inner journey of inquiry with or without the framework of a religion. The pitfalls that await the spiritual seeker are considerable nevertheless, and for this reason, before we go on to describe the characteristics of daily manifestations of the Self, we would like to clarify a few basic points so as to get a clear definition of what is meant by "spiritual growth", since there is a lot of confusion in this respect.

Instant Transformation

Even though it may seem that we can progressively move towards a more and more complete manifestation of the Self, the fact is that the transition from our ego experience to the experience of the Self is not a gradual process. The manifestation of the Self is not an improved expression of the ego. On the contrary, in order for the manifestation of the Self to

> Each time we manifest a quality of the soul, it is because our ego has let go.

occur, we have to let go of the mechanisms of the ego. These are two opposite dynamics. It could be compared to parachute jumping: either you are in the airplane, or you are falling through the air. You cannot have the relative security of the airplane and at the same time have the marvellous experience of floating in thin air. It is in this sense that Krishnamurti, one of our great masters, said that transformation, rather than being a gradual process, is actually an instantaneous event.

> No preparation is required in order to perceive the truth; preparation means time, and time is not a path to truth. Time is a continuum, while truth is timeless and discontinuous. Understanding is discontinuous: it simply is, from moment to moment, without any residue.[1]

What appears to take "time" is, on the one hand, acquiring enough experience at the ego level in order to build it up, and on the other hand, once it is sufficiently built up, becoming aware of its limits and choosing to become liberated from it. It takes time and a great deal of suffering before we reach the point where we are ready to make that choice *(just as it takes time to go through training, get into the airplane, fold and strap the parachute onto our back, get to a high enough altitude and...make up our minds to jump)*. But when the moment of choice has come, it can only happen in an instant. In this sense, the transformation of consciousness is nothing short of instantaneous.[2]

> *(Regarding Zen), one must let the beans mature, mill them, and let them steep in a coffee pot. At the same time, when the situation is ripe (here Albert Low snaps his fingers), presto! It's over! If it is anything but sudden, it is anything but real awakening. Because there is no progression from ignorance to wisdom. It is not a stairway that we must climb. It is a leap! There is an abyss that needs to be crossed, and this is why it is said to be a steep path.*[3]

It is important to really understand this apparent paradox. We are told that transformation is instantaneous (so we do nothing? We just wait?), and at the same time we are told that we should work on our self, through whatever method we choose (what is the point of practice?). We must mill the beans (prepare the ego), and this takes time, but the coffee (the Self) is savoured in an instant. In order to be able to enjoy the coffee, we must prepare it. Understanding this apparent paradox allows us not only to reconcile many approaches that may appear to be contradictory, but also to have the right attitude as we do our work on the level of our personality.

The Indescribable Experience of the Self

We will need to take several precautions as we use words to describe the manifestation of the Self, for the words we use come from the mind and are laden with centuries of meaning defined by the lower mind. The reality of the Self is beyond the scope of the ordinary mind, and we must remain vigilant so that our ego does not reclaim the information and turn it into yet another belief system, another sterile philosophy. In our attempt to put the experience of the Self into words, we are often confronted with an irrefutable fact that may seem paradoxical to us. Yet intuitively, we do indeed understand. The paradox is only there because our ordinary rational consciousness, with its habitual mechanisms, is unable to comprehend a higher reality.[4]

The inner experience of the Self cannot be described; it can only be experienced, through direct sensation and intuitive perception, ever renewed each moment, in a state of awakened higher intelligence.[5] An intelligent understanding of the mechanisms of the soul is not to be equated with the experience of being in contact with the soul. However, it opens the door to this experience, which is beyond description, and it can inspire and encourage us to seek it.

> *To understand the mind, you must observe how your own mind functions as a whole. When you fully understand its mechanism—how it reasons, its desires, motivations, ambitions, areas of interest, envies, acquisitiveness, fears—then the*

mind can reach beyond itself, and it is when it thus transcends itself that we discover something entirely new. This quality of newness elicits a formidable passion within our being, a formidable enthusiasm that triggers a profound inner revolution; and this inner revolution is the only thing that can transform the world—which no political or economic system can achieve.[6]

On the other hand, a well-established connection with our soul naturally leads to new attitudes and behaviours in our daily existence. These can be described, and they foster an intelligent inner certainty with regard to the potential for happiness and freedom that dwells within each human being.

Manifestations of the Soul

Certainly, higher consciousness can manifest itself in many ways. Yet there is a great deal of confusion and a number of myths regarding "spiritual" realisation, spirituality in general, "enlightenment", and the "great liberation". The "spiritual" aspect of life has often been confused with some minor, incidental aspects, or even things that are completely off-track, distracting us from what is most important and yet most difficult: developing mastery over the three worlds, so that the soul can fully express its will within each of them.

Transcendental Experiences

We have often heard of these states of mystical ecstasy that seem to translate into indescribable bliss. Yet it is not our purpose to go into this aspect here, as these states cannot be analysed. They occur as a form of grace, often when we least expect it, and especially when we stop seeking it. For if we seek it for the personal pleasure or power it gives, then we have wandered off the true path, we are still caught in our ego mechanisms, and this blissful experience will never be ours. The trap of pleasure-seeking, pride and personal satisfaction is permanently set, whether we are on the spiritual path or navigating through the twists and turns of our ordinary lives.[7]

Such mystical or transcendental experiences are perfectly legitimate to the extent that they lead an individual to higher levels of love and service, and a more intelligent, loving and effective participation in this world. But they are not essential. They are in fact the expression of a sudden surge of the soul, which seeks to penetrate the personality. They often signal a beginning, rather than the fact that one has arrived. When our personality is not ready for such experiences, they can either be reclaimed by our ego, or sometimes they may throw us off balance. This loss of balance is not a negative thing, since it is only momentary and can lead to greater mastery if it is handled well.[8] Sometimes, this can be a doorway opening up to a more expanded consciousness, and as the spiritual energies permeating the planet become more and more active in these times of major change, a growing number of people may have this type of experience. This only emphasises the necessity to develop our conscious mastery of our personality so that, in the event that this should happen to us, we will be able to deal with this sudden flow of energy in a balanced, serene manner. But once again, we tend to place far too much emphasis on such experiences, due to the fact that our emotional aspect loves such spectacular events, though they are not really necessary. They are just passing experiences—events that may occur along the path—but they are not the path itself.

Salvation as Withdrawal from the World

These often misinterpreted, transcendental experiences have fostered the belief, among others, that spiritual realisation is out of this world. This is a second area of confusion that requires clarification. Indeed many people, being aware of the necessity for change, launch into a "spiritual quest" and withdraw from the world instead of integrating it in a harmonious and creative fashion. They place too much emphasis on transcendental experiences, visions, and unusual or spectacular practices, without seeing that, although all of this may indeed emerge in the course of the journey, it is far from being the main course.

This leads to confusion as to the real goal. People practice in the hope of reaching "enlightenment" and "self realisation" as quickly as possible, in order to move away from the material world, leaving the planet and its inhabitants to their sorry fate. They confuse the act of "liberating oneself from the bonds of attraction to the world of matter" with "disconnecting oneself from the world of matter". This confusion is carefully nurtured by the ego, since it works to its advantage.[9] We cannot dissociate our self from the fate of Mother Earth or of humanity. It is quite right, indeed essential, that we get rid of the attraction exerted by matter on our consciousness, but this does not mean that we must run away from matter. This is where the confusion lies.[10]

Let us not forget that the ultimate goal of the journey is not to try to fly away as quickly as possible from this world on the wings of transcendence or to feed our ego with spectacular experiences, but to gain mastery over the three aspects of our lower nature (the physical, emotional and mental aspects), in order to create, in concrete terms, a world of beauty and love on this planet. Only through this kind of mastery will we attain genuine transcendence, and the ecstasy, the power and the freedom of our soul.

> To liberate oneself from matter is to master it, not run away from it.

Psychic Powers

Another form of confusion is to interpret lower psychic powers (clairvoyance, clairaudience, channelling) as signs of spiritual advancement and manifestations of the Self. In fact, this is far from being the case. While it is true that when our consciousness expands, we gain a more refined perception of subtle forms of energy. What we call psychic powers are, for the most part, nothing more than signs of a connection with the astral plane. They are not a sign of spiritual advancement.

In order to access the higher reality of spiritual worlds, we must be able to establish a connection with the higher mental world. This is a totally different dynamic from what happens in the case of typical psychic phenomena or incidents of channelling. It involves what might be called higher psychic powers: telepathy, genuine intuition, higher understanding, direct knowledge. In the future, these higher faculties will no longer be considered as "psychic powers" but as part of the normal attributes of any human being. The lower psychic powers, which are more and more common these days, will disappear since, by maintaining one's consciousness focused on the astral plane, they do not really contribute to one's evolution unless they are used by a higher consciousness through which the emotional plane has been totally mastered. This means that one's higher mind will need to have reached an advanced stage of development so as to be able to sort things out through direct knowledge stemming from the Self. But at that level of awareness, one is usually equipped with other more adequate and more reliable tools.11

There is no direct link between psychic powers and one's level of spiritual evolution. We should not mistake powers for consciousness. There is a vast difference between ego mastery and the possession of psychic powers: the soul's mastery of the ego is what characterises white magicians, while powers can lead to anything.

> The surest sign of the expression of the soul, of genuine spiritual realization, is measured by the qualities of love, wisdom, intelligence, detachment and genuine service that one is able to contribute to the world, whatever one's field of activity may be.

The Real Goal

Our main concern here is not to come up with a description of the type of "journey" we might experience in the world of transcendence, but rather to determine how the presence of the soul can manifest itself in practical terms every moment of our life. We want to know how we can bring all the richness of higher consciousness into the world, how we can build a world of peace and love, both inwardly and outwardly, and thus put an end not only to our own suffering and alienation, but to the suffering of all human beings. We want to know how we can regain a state of true freedom.

In fact, it is through concrete achievements in terms of contribution and the creation of beauty, goodness and truth, that we will attain an imperturbable state of happiness and serenity, every moment of our life, even if we have never had any great experience of mystical illumination. This quest for the manifestation of soul qualities in the world through love, intelligent creation and service will generate joy, freedom and a permanent state of serenity that cannot be diminished or limited in any way. This will form a solid foundation for genuine spiritual realisation.

It is said that, on our way to this realisation,

*"...Man goes forward blindly. He hopes, but he does not know; he expects that it may be so, but no tangible assurance is given... with care he watches his acts, guards his words, and controls his thoughts... he proceeds with his work but intensifies his meditation; he searches his motives; **he seeks to equip his mental body; he sets before himself the ideal of service** and seeks ever to serve; and then when he is so engrossed in the work on hand that he has forgotten himself, suddenly one day he sees the One Who has for so long seen him."[12]*

The path to genuine realisation is arduous, for it requires that we develop mastery in all aspects of our physical, emotional and mental life. Our day-to-day existence is where we are confronted most intensely with our self. The confusion remains, in fact, largely because it is far easier to dream of taking off and moving upward than to look at all the suffering we and the rest of the world are undergoing, and to get down to the task of healing simply out of love. The experience of the soul, of God within us and all around us, can be had only through this simple and humble love, which is totally detached and expressed in this world through intelligent service.

Though he led a relatively comfortable life, Roma, a young man in his twenties, did not feel good living in this ordinary world where it seemed to him that everyone was just looking out for themselves, where he saw so much violence, nonsense and injustice. He wanted something else. He had heard of a great spiritual Master living high up on a mountain. He dreamed of living close to the Master and listening to his teachings day after day, for the Master seemed to know the secret of happiness and wisdom. But though he had often been approached, the Master had always refused any company whatsoever. Roma decided to try his luck nevertheless, and submitted a request. Much to his surprise, the Master accepted to have him live in a tiny house next to his own. This was a great privilege. Roma was very happy and his heart was filled with gratitude. The Master gave him several practices to perform on a daily basis. Roma diligently followed the instructions. He was delighted and full of hope, for he felt sure that this privileged contact with the Master, in the silence and beauty of Nature, would certainly lead to a great spiritual realisation. After several years, Roma has indeed managed to control his thoughts, and he had had several wonderful inner experiences.

Yet as time went by, Roma felt more and more that something was missing. He talked about it with the Master, saying, "Master, you have taught me to find silence within me, you have taught me to listen to the sound of the wind, the song of the rain, the sighs of the earth, and to know the wisdom of the animals in the forest, to speak to the stars and come into contact with the Divine Mother. Yet something is missing in my heart. What should I do?" The Master remained silent for a moment, looked at Roma straight in the eyes, and said: "Roma, you will have to go down from the mountain, back into the world. I give you this little leather gourd. You must bring it back to me filled with water". Roma thought he had heard wrong, but no, he was indeed to leave the mountain to go and find the water, which seemed to him a ridiculous assignment. He hated the prospect of going back into the ordinary world, even for just a moment. He tried to argue a little, but the Master stood firm, saying he was to leave the next morning and that he could return as soon as the gourd was filled. Roma was perplexed, yet confident that this would not take too long, so he put his little house in order and the very next day, made the trip down from the mountain.

He got to the village toward midday, and found himself in the middle of the market-place, where there were all kinds of people, all very busy buying or selling goods. A repul-sively filthy beggar asked him for some money. Roma turned away in disgust, and went to buy some fruit for his lunch. The lady at the fruit stand was very angry and vociferat-ing at a child who had upset her fruit display. The boy tried to hide in the folds of Roma's robes, but the latter pushed him away, not wanting to get into any trouble with the lady or to be involved in any way in all this turmoil. He felt completely estranged from these people, and above all this, remaining cold and aloof from everyone. He was just anxious to get back to the top of the mountain. He knew there was a lovely fountain in the mid-dle of the village, and this is where he wanted to fill his gourd with water so that he could bring it back to the Master as instructed. In his haste, he bumped into several people as he moved toward the fountain to fill the gourd. Satisfied, he quickly headed back toward the mountain. An old man, stopped by the roadside next to a broken cart, asked him for help, but Roma declined, saying that other villagers, who were less busy than him, would soon pass by and would be able to lend a hand. He was too anxious to get back to the peace and quiet of the mountain to be willing to stop along the way.

Back in the presence of his Master, he happily knelt before him and deposited the gourd at his feet. The latter took the gourd, turned it upside down, and nothing came out of it. "Roma, this gourd is empty, said the Master. Go back to the world and fill this gourd." Roma frowned. He was sure that he had filled it and properly sealed it. He took the gourd and, without taking the time to rest in his haste to get this stupid task over with, went back to the village to fill the gourd up again. He made sure the gourd was not punctured and that it was properly sealed. But once he got back to the Master, the gourd was empty, once again. Roma was totally confused. The Master then said, "Roma, it takes a very spe-cial kind of water to fill this gourd, not just any water. Go back to the world and find the right kind of water." Roma obeyed, and went to the river. The water at the fountain was sure to be polluted by all those people around with their rather low vibrations. The water from the river was beautiful, clear and free: this had to be the water he was looking for. The gourd was filled, but once again, back in the presence of the Master, it was empty. He tried again and again, having to go further and further afield to find other springs. There was no need to go back to the Master. A little while after being filled, it would always end up empty. This went on for months. Roma felt more and more anxious, depressed and discouraged. He was even beginning to doubt the teachings and the mer-its of his Master. One day, he thought that his Master was making fun of him, and that he was not a real Master after all, and he decided not to go back to him, since in any case, the latter would send him away without a word of explanation, leaving him with no hope of ever getting back to the top of the mountain as long as the gourd was not filled.

Roma went back to live in the village, just like everybody else, but he was really un-happy. Then one day, as life was getting more and more intolerable, he decided to find the right spring, even if he had to spend the rest of his life trying to find it. So he started a great journey, trying out the water in all the rivers, brooks and lakes, all the springs and fountains he came upon. He often met people, with whom he spent more and more time talking. He even shared his secret with some of them. But they could not help him, and the gourd remained empty.

He had to start working again, to earn a living, for he had spent all the money the Master had given him before he left. He learned the woodworker's trade, met a young woman, and they decided to start a family. He was kept more and more busy with his work and his obligations at home. He had little time to look for other springs, but he always kept the little gourd attached to his belt, in memory of his Master. He learned to love his work and, when his children were born, he quietly learned to play with them and to love them. His heart was once again filled with joy as he went into the forest to find wood. His youngest son now went with him, and he taught him woodworking, as well as the secrets of the forest, which his Master had revealed to him.

One day, as he was walking by the edge of the river on his way home, he spotted his wife sitting at the foot of a tree, holding their last-born child in her arms. She was singing softly as she gently rocked him back and forth. Her eldest son was playing right next to her. The tree was in bloom, forming a protective dome above their heads. Watching this scene, so simple yet so beautiful, he felt moved deep down in his heart. For the first time in his life, a tear ran down his cheek. It ran down his face and fell onto the little gourd. Instantly, the gourd filled up and became quite heavy. Roma touched it, opened it just to be sure, and waited a few moments. The gourd was not emptying as before. He waited a while longer, and the gourd remained full. His heart surged with joy. He would be able to go back to see the Master, and live once again at the top of the mountain. Then suddenly he realised that he no longer felt the need, nor even the inclination, to go back to the mountain. At that moment, in a great burst of light, his Master appeared, looked at him with great love, and said, "What you are feeling is right, Roma, there is no longer any need for you to return to the mountain. You have just opened your heart to beauty, simplicity and love. You have realised everything I could possibly teach you. All you need to do now is to find judicious ways of expressing it in your day-to-day existence, in each of your thoughts, words and actions. Know that I will always be there by your side, closer to you than I have ever been. The light will thus continue to grow within you, lighting up not only your own path, but also the path of everyone you will be able to love."

---

[1] Translated from Krishnamurti, *La première et dernière liberté*, éd. Stock. page 296.

[2] In fact, as soon as we are truly liberated from our ego, the very notion of time disappears: the past no longer exists (has no further impact on our awareness at any given moment), and

neither does the future (no more expectations, hopes or fears). All there is left is the eternal present, experienced from moment to moment, in a state of peace, fulfilment and creativity. This is a beautiful prospect, which will nevertheless remain an abstraction within the mind as long as it has not been integrated and fully experienced. In the meantime, in order to play this game that our consciousness has chosen, it is necessary for us to respect the rule of time, until the moment when the goal of the great journey has been reached. Our consciousness is then liberated from duality and time, and totally free. We can then move on to other games, with different rules.

3 Words recorded by Colette Chabot in her book entitled *À moitié sage (Only Half Wise)*, page 189.

4 A paradox is what leads us from the lower mind to the higher mind when we manage to fully integrate its meaning. It places the mind in a state of "unexpected perplexity", which may open a window on a more expanded perception of reality. When Zen masters use Koans, those apparently paradoxical short stories or riddles, they are using this dynamic of the paradox to drive their disciples "out of their heads" and into their higher minds. A classic example: "What is the sound of one hand clapping?" Our rational mind is caught short and freezes, and the Self laughs because it knows the answer.

5 In order to express this reality directly, without the need to name it, humankind has used art, among other things, in its purest expression.

6 Krishnamurti, *Le livre de la méditation et de la vie,* Stock, page 308.

7 The quest for divine ecstasy can easily be reclaimed by the ego in its hunger for personal well-being. Here again we are faced with a paradox: any contact with the soul produces ecstasy, yet if we seek this ecstasy for the sake of ecstasy, we have lost our way, and all we are doing is reinforcing the walls that separate us from this wonderful state of bliss.

8 The book entitled *The Storming Search for the Self,* by Stanislav Grof, is a good source of information on this topic.

9 Having examined the structures of the ego, we can indeed see how these theories can be attractive—we will find excellent justification for withdrawal, for refusing to feel and to truly experience life, for developing spiritual pride and the conviction that this world is no good, etc., depending on the character structures. Thus, one way or another, the ego will pass the buck in order to go on satisfying its alienating desires and avoid doing the real work that is needed. Where does love and self-sacrifice fit in?

10 The pseudo-spiritual attitude of turning away from matter seems right because it appears to be the opposite of the materialistic attitude that places too much emphasis on material achievements (well paid job, nice house, travels, etc.). And we think that because we are no longer interested in material things, we must be very spiritually oriented. But **"opposites are just two sides of the same coin"**. Both parties despise each other, with materialists treating spiritual people as a bunch of disconnected dreamers not without reason sometimes, and spiritual people looking upon materialists as selfish, consciously deprived morons and sometimes that is also not far off the mark. In the end neither of these approaches lead to liberation and fulfilment. We must find the middle ground, that is a living, conscious spirituality that leads to right action on the worldly plane, action that reflects mastery and inner freedom. And this "middle ground" is not a halfway point between two poles, but rather another level that involves a blending of the two approaches and total commitment to both of them.

11 On this subject, please refer to Alice Bailey's, *A Treatise on White Magic.*

12 Alice Bailey, *A Treatise on White Magic,* page 170.

chapter 9

Functioning at the Level of the Self

OR

LIVING UNBOUND

When our consciousness breaks free of the ego's hold, our soul takes possession more and more of its instrument, (i.e., the personality). All of humanity is presently in an accelerated phase of evolution, and the process involved in this transfer of consciousness is about to become more and more evident. Of course this evolution occurs at varying rates, depending on each individual. But whether this process takes place as a result of a multitude of experiences over a succession of lifetimes—each of them carrying its particular learning and knowledge content—or as a result of conscious inner work (both paths become simultaneous once a person awakens to a higher level of awareness), all of us, sooner or later, will find our way back to the path of the soul. At that point, our life changes, as does the kind of impact our life has on our environment.

In Chapter 2, we described the kinds of behaviours we exhibit when we are caught up in ego-level consciousness. We can now go on to describe some of the concrete consequences, in terms of our day-to-day existence, of a state of consciousness related to the higher mind, which is when we have reconnected with our true spiritual nature.

Practical Consequences of Being in Contact with the Self

or the daily practice of God

WISDOM

Contact with the soul turns us into an intelligent being

A fundamental characteristic of this state of awareness, from which will flow many other characteristics, is the development of higher intelligence. This point was explored in Chapter 6.

The supple and open intelligence of the higher mind, powered by the Self, includes all of the qualities of the mind and allows an individual to express two of the major qualities of the soul: love and wisdom.

> *Wisdom concerns the development of a connection with Life that dwells in all form. It helps to shift one's attention from appearance to deeper meaning. It focuses on the essence of things, rather than on things as such; it allows one to discriminate between what is true and what is false, what is real and what is unreal. Wisdom is knowledge that has been transcended. Wisdom is the science of the Spirit, just as knowledge is the science of Matter. Wisdom is synthetic, for it unites and merges.*[1]

The manifestation of the Self through this higher intelligence will have major consequences on the quality of our existence. The first of these, a rather considerable one at that, is that it guarantees our access to freedom.

FREEDOM

Contact with the Self makes us a free being

Freedom because we are no longer subject to the pressure of desires and false needs.

We have seen how past experiences are recorded in our unconscious, making us slaves of our desires, of our preferences, and of our choices which, in actual fact, are not really ours but those dictated by our particular mechanisms. (The driver does not steer the vehicle as he would like; instead the itinerary is chosen by the vehicle according to its pre-programmed automatic pilot.)

Once these memories are no longer active, the tensions—the "false needs"—disappear. We no longer expect our life to fulfil the illusions of our desires. In addition, the soul's higher consciousness confers such a natural sense of inner well-being that the problem of dependency can no longer exist, at any level. Thus we regain the freedom to live our life to the fullest, without demands, without dependency, without fear, without expectations, be it at the physical, mental, emotional, material, spiritual or any other level. We are free to celebrate life independent of circumstances.

Freedom because we are no longer subject to manipulation by anyone or anything outside of our self

When we are in contact with the Self through the higher mind, we no longer function as a machine, we are no longer predictable. Our happiness and satisfaction no longer depend on any outside factor, so we are no longer subject to manipulation. Our reactions, based on the wisdom of our soul, are right and appropriate with respect to the truth of the present moment, and they can no longer be determined by any form of manipulation.

On the level of relationships, in particular, not only is our behaviour no longer controlled by our desires, but also others can no longer manipulate us through emotional blackmail. We thus maintain complete freedom.

To be free of outside influences does not mean that we remain impervious to potential input from people, things and events all around us. On the contrary, we become receptive to all the information coming to us from our environment, and we are able to process this information in a flexible, open and objective manner rather than the automatic, emotional and predetermined manner we were accustomed to. We are thus free to use new information intelligently and appropriately.

Through the higher mind the voice of our soul guides us with all its wisdom, and we know, each and every moment, what is the correct and right thing to do, for our self and for others. We have a solid, inner sense of our authenticity, of our own truth. No one can make us do anything that is not in total harmony with our innermost self.

We should note that this "voice" of the soul, which we described as intuition in the foregoing chapter, does not require extraordinary circumstances in order to be heard. Our soul is very interested in "talking" to us every moment of our life so as to be able to express its will in the phenomenal world. It is up to us to learn to tune into it constantly, not just during moments of meditation or mystical bliss.

Freedom thanks to the autonomy and discernment that spring from an accurate perception of things

This kind of discernment based on intuition makes it impossible for anyone to destabilise our right perception of things. This is quite different from the rigid attitude of the lower mind, which can also refuse to be destabilised, but on the basis of an inflexible fixed viewpoint that is limited and out of synch with reality. In this instance, sooner or later, some external circumstance or a strong enough person will eventually turn up to undo this false stability.

No one can manipulate someone who lives in contact with his or her soul.

Maud is invited by one of her friends to the opening of an exhibition of paintings by several well-known artists. She is an artist herself, and is very interested in this exhibition. So she makes her way to the event, which promises to be rather pleasant. In the course of the evening, her friend introduces her to Randy, one of the exhibiting artists whose work she finds particularly interesting. Maud and Randy strike up a conversation where Randy talks a lot, being his usual exuberant self, while Maud says little. At one point however, Maud manages to talk a little about her own research. At which point Randy proposes to have her visit his studio after the show. He has some material, especially some silk flowers, for which he has no further use, and he might let her have them as a gift. This could be very interesting for her.

Maud then faces the possibility of receiving this offer and making a choice (to accept or refuse) either through the lower mind or through the Self, via the higher mind.

If Maud interprets this situation through her lower mind, she will not be able to determine what it is in reality; she does not know what Randy's real intentions are. She will, however, be subject to unconscious automatic responses, following the dynamics described earlier. In this case, various types of automatic responses may kick in. For example, let us look at three very familiar possibilities:

- If the activated response is one of fear of being had, Maud sees Randy as a manipulator, becomes suspicious, and turns down his offer without thinking. It may be that Randy did indeed intend to manipulate her with promises (in which case her refusal is an appropriate response), or maybe he was sincere, open and genuine in his invitation (in which case she has just passed up a great opportunity that life had just brought her). She is making a blind choice.

- Another possible automatic response: let us imagine that some of Randy's facial features resemble those of Maud's father. Now Maud had a cold, austere father, who never gave her anything, and she was deeply hurt by this. Something may click in Maud's unconscious, "Finally, my dad loves me and he's offering me a gift, something I've wanted for so long." So Maud accepts the offer without thinking, being quite unaware of what just happened within her. Perhaps Randy was indeed sincere, open and truthful in his invitation (in which case her acceptance is appropriate to a certain extent, though it remains charged with a number of expectations), or perhaps Randy sought to manipulate her with promises (her acceptance is leading her into a trap). Here too, she is making a blind choice.

- Another possible automatic response: if Maud is caught in an unconscious feeling of deprivation (oral structure), she may jump at the opportunity to acquire something for free, and accept the invitation without thinking. Once again, she is making a blind choice.

In all three cases, her life was directed by the mechanism of her lower mind, which made the decision for her. Thus, when our consciousness is caught in the lower mind, we make choices that are disconnected from reality, and most often, inappropriate, causing disappointments and pain. We then blame life for being so tough, or other people for not being on the level.

If Maud is in contact with her Self through her higher mind, she can tune into what is actually happening. She is not caught up in past reactivations; she has an accurate and objective perception of the situation. If Randy wants to manipulate her, she knows it. So she will act accordingly, and probably turn down the invitation, which would not lead to anything good for her in any case. If he is sincere, she will also know it. She can then accept the invitation without fear, receive the material that Randy wants to give her, and perhaps begin a beautiful friendship with this person. Either way she comes out a winner.

How does Maud know? This is the big question we often ask our self. In fact, this ever-accurate perception is available to us once the lower mind has calmed down and the higher mind is able to tune into the wisdom of the soul through genuine intuition. This is how human beings function. Discernment is not something that comes out of nowhere. It comes from that state of higher intelligence that comes with being in contact with the Self through the higher mind.

> Discernment is what ensures the quality of our lives, especially our freedom.

LIVING IN THE HERE AND NOW

Every spiritual teaching points to the fact that we must be here now if we want to be happy, free of the future (free of expectations and fear), and free of the past (free of emotional charges that generate expectations and fears). This is indeed true, and this is the way we would like to be, but how do we get there? In fact, this occurs spontaneously once our contact with the soul is well established.

The soul does not function on the basis of the past. Thanks to its direct knowledge of reality at every instant, it allows us to experience the present moment with full knowledge and mastery, totally free of the past and future, totally unbound by time, in the fullness of the infinite now. This soul connection generates a state of presence in life such that there is no need to hope that tomorrow will be better or to regret what happened yesterday. Each instant is precious and perfect as it is, and we experience it in a state of serenity and simplicity. What was once a nice theory now becomes a genuine experience.

> The ability to live in the here and now is a natural manifestation of the soul.

OTHER STATES OF BEING
AND BEHAVIOURS STEMMING FROM THE SELF

The behaviours described earlier, and that are so typical of the personality, are transformed once the Self takes over via the higher mind. Some new characteristics also naturally emerge.

*These tendencies [instinctive to the lower mind] based on fear have acted as a
tremendous stimulation of man's entire nature, and have carried him forward to
his present point of wide comprehension and usefulness... Out of these instincts
carried forward into infinity, and out of the process of their transmutation into
their higher correspondences, the full flower of soul expression will emerge.[2]*

Let us now take a look at some of these different aspects:

A sense of security

Fear, anxiety and stress are replaced with a relaxed sense of security, for the soul
is constantly aware of its power and of its indestructible nature. Rich or poor, surrounded with people or alone in the desert, no matter what the situation may be,
we feel inwardly serene.

The fact remains that life can place us in situations that are truly dangerous. But
the way we handle such situations will be quite different from the way the personality would respond. If, for example, we find our self in a dangerous neighbourhood in New York City at 2:00 a.m., fear is not the most effective way to protect our self. Indeed fear can generate automatic, primary defence reactions,
which may ultimately control the damage but can also paralyse our higher intelligence. At the level of the Self, we get a direct intuitive sense of what we should
do or not do, where we should go or not go, which will totally protect us. This
direct inner knowledge allows us to live in a very relaxed state and with a natural
trust in life.

Psychological fears and insecurities also disappear. The fear of others, the fear
of losing, of displeasing, of losing control, the fear of being taken in (one of the
major ego mechanisms), these fears and all the other types of fear disappear in
the clear light of the soul, because no external circumstance can cut us off from
our source of power, knowledge and energy.

Creative vitality

As we tap into an ever-available source of energy, creative vitality soon replaces
fatigue, passiveness and sleepiness. Instead of being half dead, we become fully
alive. The Self allows us to be constantly in action in a way that is both natural and
effective, as it generates all the energy required to complete any given task. Fatigue
rarely appears, and it disappears very quickly with just a few hours of sleep. Indeed
fatigue mostly stems from our resistance to life; our emotional mechanism burns
away the major portion of our energy. At the level of the Self, the amount of energy
available for acting and creating becomes almost limitless. We can be constantly
in action, in a state of joy and dynamic energy, and we are ever replenished from
within. As we mentioned in Chapter 2, this state of dynamic energy is not a function of age. Loss of energy and degeneration as the years go by are rather due to
the fact that we use our time to reinforce our unconscious defence patterns and
rigidify our unconscious mental/emotional structures: thus our ego is reinforced,
our connection to the Self weakens, and our energy vanishes.

Yet this is not unavoidable. If we use our time to do some conscious work on our self and liberate our self from the grip of old memories instead of reinforcing them, then the energy of the soul becomes more and more available to us. Time will then allow us to gain more knowledge, wisdom, talents, and to develop a more sensitive openness to the world, greater strength and stability, as well as the capacity to make more extensive contributions, etc. As time goes by, instead of degenerating, we flourish and life becomes more and more interesting.[3] As an old saying goes:

Old age is like winter for the ignorant, and harvest time for the wise.

Some of us are able to **turn our life into this crescendo towards higher and higher levels of consciousness,** creative energy and influence. Great artists are a good example: most often they produce their best work towards the end of their life. Like them, we can turn our life into a fascinating adventure leading to ever-increasing freedom, creativity and joy of living.

A sense of fulfilment

Inner emptiness is replaced with a sense of fulfilment; the need for stuffing simply disappears. The energy of the soul is so life-giving that we no longer need to look for external means of filling our life. The frantic quest for pleasure in all its forms, whether direct or indirect, simple or sophisticated, is replaced with a

> In all circumstances, the soul is ever satisfied.

state of unalterable stillness, serenity and fulfilment. It is through this sense of fulfilment springing from the soul, regardless of external circumstances or of other people, that we can regain our true freedom.

> *He who is able to content himself will always be content.*
> —*Lao-Tzu*

At the level of the personality, we do not believe that we can be motivated if there is not some area of dissatisfaction to be dealt with somehow. Yet the sense of fulfilment we get from the soul does not mean that we will blissfully stay at home gazing at the sky (or watching television!). On the contrary, we feel so full that we spontaneously want to act and to celebrate life, for the joy of discovering, creating, sharing, and contributing, propelled simply and naturally by the energy of life, without any expectation. This dynamic is the complete opposite of what happens at the ego level.

Creative discontent

The state of fulfilment just described can be experienced when the soul is totally in control of the personality. However, on our way to this realisation, when the will of the soul and that of the ego are simultaneously present (as is the case for most of us), the richness of the soul can paradoxically generate a kind of dissatisfaction of the personality. Indeed, as long as we remain prisoners of ego mechanisms, we will continue to suffer. This state of discontent should not be anaesthetised: it can be the dynamic that leads to genuine inner inquiry. The fullness of the soul has nothing to do with the blissful satisfaction of an individual ensconced in comfort and routine, glossing over his fears and settling for a mediocre life. The soul pushes us to want more, to live more truthfully and more justly. This soul-generated discontent is a very positive thing. We must simply be vigilant as to how we deal with this sense of dissatisfaction. We will go into this at greater depth further along, when we look at the characteristics and paradoxes of the path leading from the ego to the soul, from shadow into light.

> *Does discontent not stand as an indispensable part of life, essential to any form of questioning, of inquiry, of examination, of discovery regarding what is real and true, of what forms the basis of existence?... One must keep this flame alive, from beginning to end, so that there can be genuine inquiry, genuine in-depth questioning as to the nature of this discontent.*[4]

Young people who are still in contact with the energy of life, particularly during adolescence, still have this positive discontent, this rebellion against the routine and stiffness of the adult world. If it is properly dealt with, this rebellion can be very positive, leading to an original form of fulfilment, and to the dismantling of old structures in favour of an emerging approach to life that is more encompassing and unfettered.

Openness to the unknown, to growth and to change

While the ego clings to what is known, which gives it an illusion of security and identity, the Self is more interested in exploring and discovering what we do not already know. This is not a quest for novelty stemming from a need for stuffing, for external short-lived pleasure and excitement. It is the will to discover the unknown, a desire to know and to understand more, a motivation that moves the personality to expand its perception and understanding of things.

In particular, the need to always be right is dissolved by the energy of the soul. While at the ego level we cling to what is known by maintaining we are right and trying to impose our point of view, at the level of the Self we are more interested in other people's viewpoints and we try to expand our own. When we are energised by the Self, we are permanent students of life. Our minds open up, we listen attentively, being ever ready to expand the way we perceive things after taking some time to think and observe. This attitude is evidence of a major change in consciousness, which obviously generates high quality relationships.

Does a cluttered mind, buried in facts and knowledge, have any chance of being receptive to any new, sudden, spontaneous flash of understanding? When your mind is cluttered by known facts, is there any room to receive anything coming from the realm of the unknown?

This openness to learning also involves **openness to changing,** even in the little things in life. When we live in the awareness of the Self, we can be flexible and adapt instantly to situations. This ability to adapt may look like weakness in the eyes of ignorant people, yet it actually leads to a great capacity for powerful and effective action. We are talking about just the right and proper amount of flexibility, stemming from a capacity to adapt intelligently and appropriately to circumstances.

Dynamic energy

Laziness and the desire for comfort are replaced with a desire to constantly extend one's limitations and to take risks.

Our ego yearns for easy living, yet once our Self is active, we ceaselessly look for new challenges. We lose interest in whatever we have mastered. This quest for challenges and new experiences is not fuelled by some false need springing from old memories (withdrawal, performance, big thrills). It is an inherent part of the will of the soul to dare go out in search of the unknown, to play freely and attain ever more refined levels of mastery in the world.

Young children, who tend to be closer to their Self than most adults, set an example of this search for new experiences and this lack of interest in comfort and ease of living. When a game is too easy, they lose interest. If there are not enough challenges in their life, they will create some so that their life become exciting. This is quite the opposite of adults who, more often than not, will tend to resist any difficulty and wait for something external to happen in order to make life interesting.

Comfort is the cemetery of consciousness.
—Sri Adi Dadi

I was on holiday with my daughter, who was six years old at the time, and we were staying in a hotel that had a swimming pool. My daughter had been playing in the water for a while when she came to get me. "Come on, Mom, I want to show you something." Back at the pool, she got in the water and said, "Look, Mom, I can do a somersault in the water." She did a somersault, and then came happily out of the water; I congratulated her, and went back to whatever I was doing. A moment later, she came back to get me once again to bring me to the pool. Once there, she said, "Look closely…now I can do two somersaults under water in one shot." She did the two somersaults, and then came out of the water, proud as a peacock. That big smile on her face and the joy she exuded made her simply radiant.

This incident is quite a metaphor. As human beings, we are truly happy only when we are creating and extending our self voluntarily, freely, for the sheer joy of it. This joy and this energy are natural responses to the life force emanating from the Self.

Problems?

The ego would rather have a problem-free life, a life of ease where everything comes effortlessly. Who among us has not dreamed of a life where we could have everything we want, as if this were the pinnacle of happiness? We are all caught up in the same illusion. We may all want a life without problems, but "Life", which is intended to help us become free and fully in command of all our potential, will make sure to give us "problems", or opportunities for self extension so that we can learn to master our personality and integrate the qualities of our soul. We may refer to these opportunities for growth as "problems", and resist them, deny them, or hope to get rid of them some day. But then, as we mentioned with regard to any form of resistance, they persist and we do not make any progress; or we can perceive them as opportunities for learning and assimilating the qualities of the Self. In which case we no longer have problems, only opportunities for growth. We know that when we cease to resist, our energy and creativity become totally available, and solutions emerge much more readily.

Does this mean that there will be nothing left for us to do, once we have ceased to resist and have resolved our old problems, once we have managed to let go and find ways to defuse memories that have beset us perhaps for a very long time? No! A life without problems, without challenges, would be nothing but deadly boredom. Once we have mastered one difficulty in our life, pressed by the energy of our soul, we will consciously and deliberately choose new problems, new challenges, in order to make an even greater contribution to the great game of life. This is a far cry from a selfish quest for comfort and from stupefying routine. Will we finally some day have a comfortable and easy life? Certainly not in the limited ego sense. In fact we will have much more: our life will be fascinating.

In any case, if we do not consciously and deliberately choose to give our self opportunities to grow, such as activities requiring that we surpass our limitations, life will make sure we get such opportunities, and these usually come in far more unpleasant forms: illness, accidents, losses, etc. We will have to face these challenges one way or another.

Accepting and creating challenges for our self keeps us in touch with the will of the Self, which is geared towards constantly experiencing and experimenting. By staying in tune with this will, we are constantly regenerated, and we naturally live in a creative, dynamic and energised state. This is the best rejuvenating cure. In order to stay fit, both physically and inwardly, what we need is not rest,

> To stay in shape, what we need is not rest, but self-expansion and self-sacrifice.

but self-expansion, though once again self-expansion that is freely chosen and soul-generated, rather than forced by alienating ego expectations. The soul knows how to rest, and loves to be in that state. It knows when it is time for rest. Inaction then becomes an integrated part of action, rather than an end in itself.

A sense of identity

A natural, simple, free and profound sense of identity, that is totally independent of the opinion of others, supersedes the quest for approval and the need to perform. This sense of identity brings a deep sense of inner peace, and eliminates all the stress related to the value we place on other people's opinion. We stop judging our self, since our system of comparison and evaluation is foreign to the soul.

Furthermore, this identity is naturally original. At the ego level, we are anything but original. We all have just about the same defence mechanisms, the same programmings stemming from our human past. On the other hand, the Self has its own original character that does not need to prove its worth, as it is part of the very essence of our being.

We could even go a step further, as identity still carries a sense of separation. Yet at the soul level, there is no longer any sense of "your identity" and "my identity". The experience is different. More than a sense of identity, we could say that, for the Self, there is a profound sense of existence, whereby we no longer need to feel different or separate from others in order to feel that we exist. We no longer need to put so much stock in our own personality. This profound and natural sense of existence brings great peace and great freedom.

While we are on this subject, there are many people, especially in the New Age movement, who are involved in this process of seeking their own identity. This is a sincere quest, but the ego is very skilled at redirecting this quest towards reinforcing its own mechanisms and finding justifications for navel gazing. "I want to know who I am." The ultimate answer is simple: at the ego level, we are nothing...nothing but a mechanism that will disappear some time in the future to merge with universal energy. At the soul level, we are everything, we are God. The only way to answer the question of knowing who we are is to try to tune into our soul. At that point, there is no longer any need to ask the question, for we have a direct sense of existence that is free from any reference to others.

Simplicity, spontaneity and humility

These qualities spring from that natural soul-generated sense of self. When we engage in inner work, we can still confuse true soul-generated spontaneity with automatic ego reactions. A distinction was made when we presented the mechanism of intuition (which generates true spontaneity leading to right, simple, free and appropriate reactions to the reality of the moment), in comparison with the emotional mechanisms of the ego (which only generate emotionally charged impulsiveness). This confusion is fostered by some New Age teachings that recommend that we "follow our feelings". That is fine, as long as we know the source of these feelings. It may be the voice of the Self, and it can also be an automatic emotional reaction springing from the unconscious.

Learning to see the difference is a major part of the work to be done along the path.

Well do the teachers of the race instruct the budding initiate to practise discrimination and train him in the arduous task of distinguishing between:

- *Instinct and intuition*
- *Higher and lower mind*
- *Desire and spiritual impulse*
- *Selfish aspiration and divine incentive*[5]

Along with simplicity comes **humility,** which is one of the greatest qualities of the Self. Not humility as it was often interpreted in our old moral teachings, where we were told to practice humility in the sense of self-denial. Like genuine spontaneity, humility as it springs from the Self is simple, light, joyful and free. It is a natural, uncontrived way of being, marked by great beauty and dignity, the way a flower is happy as it is, without arrogance nor any need to prove anything in order to define itself.

Self-confidence

Paradoxically, this genuine humility generates a natural state of self-confidence, a state of inner calm that is not the result of external approval, or of any comparison with others, or one's social status. It comes from simple acceptance of our limitations and qualities, from the will to learn and to grow, not for the sake of meeting external standards, but because the energy of love compels us to do so. We learn to know our self, to know our instrument. The lack of self-confidence stems from fear, and fear disappears the moment the soul enters the picture. Thus the very concept of self-confidence disappears.

A sense of unity

Separateness yields to altruism, a sense of unity, sensitivity and great openness to others, along with total independence. The illusion of separateness was useful for a time, as we mentioned earlier. However, the reality of the Self is quite different. The Self does not draw its definition from separateness, but from its essence, which is the same as in any other human being.

A direct experience of the power of the soul

First of all, our irresponsibility, our "victimitis" and sense of powerlessness make way for genuine **creative power** and responsibility. Being in touch with our soul allows us to feel close to the source of our own destiny. This gives profound meaning to our life (to all our lives), no matter what trials may have befallen us. With a heavily loaded past filled with suffering, our collective unconscious is burdened with a strong sense of powerlessness. Coming into contact with the creative power of the soul has a profoundly healing effect with regard to the past.

It also brings the experience of simple, reliable, unshakeable **power** that is beneficial to all, and which makes the quest for personal external power or resistance to other people's power appear totally pointless. The problem of power is one of the major issues facing humankind these days. At the ego level, power is used for personal, selfish, separative, and therefore destructive ends. Human history is an illustration of our constant struggle for power in various forms. This struggle fades the moment we get in touch with our soul, because at that moment, we have found the true source of genuine power. At that point, we are no longer interested in possession or domination, because what we have inside is so fulfilling that we need nothing else. In addition, the quest for ego power is based on fear; once this fear has vanished, the need to dominate others also disappears. This experience of power brings freedom and allows others to be free as well.

What do we do with this power? We use it with love and respect to create whatever is beautiful and good, to serve and to contribute. We use our power to give power to others, so that they also can become more creative.

> The most beautiful gift we can bestow on others is to help them reclaim their own power.

Autonomy

This freedom from automatic behaviours also generates autonomy. When we are no longer subject to manipulation, we know how to function on our own, and we become truly autonomous.

The kind of autonomy we are describing here does not necessarily mean that we function alone.[6]

We are truly autonomous when we can function smoothly, either alone or with others, and make a contribution within a group of people (such as our work environment, our family, our community, an organisation of some sort, and ultimately all of humankind). Autonomy means that we no longer need approval, as our Self naturally gives us an inner sense of what is right and what is not. It means that we have nothing to prove; that we can accept support and comments from others and use them creatively; that we can spontaneously and naturally make our viewpoint known while being always ready to listen to other people's viewpoint and eventually, if we sense that it is right, to change or expand our own without feeling like a loser; it means that we can stay in touch with our self with a flexible, right attitude, while being in contact with others in an open, non-judgemental way; and that we are able and free to receive from others, as well as to give. Autonomy means that we are no longer afraid. That kind of autonomy comes from being in touch with our soul.

Joy, humour, lightness and non-dramatisation

When the soul is present, a natural state of inner joy emerges in our daily living in the form of lightness, humour, and non-dramatisation.

He who has ceased to laugh has ceased to live.
—Anonymous

The ego is always very serious. As it is totally engrossed in its search for identity, being able to laugh at itself is out of the question; whatever it is concerned with is heavily charged. The computer's automatic responses lead to overdramatising. In this state of seriousness and dramatisation, the ego has only brief moments of joy, whenever its programming is fulfilled. And then again, this joy is of a limited quality since it is largely dependent on others and on circumstances. In addition, at this level, fun is generally a complicated thing (unconscious expectations must always be met), it often comes at a high cost (in terms of money, energy, disappointments and pain), and it is always built from scratch.

When the soul becomes dominant, our inner state is totally different. The higher and finer vibrational frequency of the soul generates a permanent state of natural joy that is not dependent on circumstance…it is simply the joy of living. The joy of the soul is ever present, and costs nothing (except to let go of the ego!).

Gratitude

This vibration of joy that we carry deep in our hearts naturally generates a permanent state of gratitude. This in no way prevents us from being aware of human suffering

> Dissatisfaction is a typical ego characteristic. Gratitude is a typical quality of the soul.

and being sensitive to it. In fact the opposite is true, as our sensitivity only increases, along with our desire and ability to offer help and healing wherever possible.

Creativity

We have seen that, when our soul is active, we are unafraid of the unknown and, at the same time, we are moved to take action. In addition, through the mechanism of intuition, which is now active, we have access to all the wealth of knowledge of the universal mind. We can then move off the beaten path, free our self from routine and habitual thought patterns, and access a level of creativity that is out of the ordinary. Great scientists, artists, and creators of all sorts have drawn their inspiration and new "ideas" from the higher consciousness levels of their soul, which made it possible for them to bring new knowledge and more and more original beauty into the world.

This higher creativity is not the exclusive characteristic of great artists or scientists. Anyone can develop and use such creativity in his or her daily life and work, down to the simplest aspects, turning them into opportunities for creation and permanent sources of joy. Creativity is not generated by circumstances: we, on the other hand, can use our creativity to affect circumstances, whatever they may be, through the creative power of our Self.

The power to act

As was stated earlier, when the Self takes over its vehicle, it has no intention of letting it remain inactive. It will use this vehicle very actively to produce concrete manifestations of its will on the worldly plane. Whenever the energy of the soul is present, we experience a very strong motivation to act, yet in an impersonal, detached way. In addition, through the soul's accurate perception of reality, its intelligence and its wisdom, we can act in ways that are perfectly appropriate and therefore highly effective.

Work, a joyful act of creation

In particular, this level of being allows one to "work" in a state of joy. There are two ways of dealing with work, as with anything else.

From the viewpoint of the personality, work is seen as a chore or, at best, a necessity that we have to contend with in order to survive and buy security and pleasure. We could do without, and the interesting moments of our life are usually outside of working hours: evenings, weekends or "holidays", when we do nothing and, most often, are content to seek pleasure and stuffing. At this level, we resist work. We try to do as little as possible, just the number of hours for which we are paid, not a minute more.

This attitude blocks the creative process and everything goes wrong. We are quickly tired, we can never achieve what we want, people are unsupportive, circumstances are unfavourable, etc., and we blame people, or life, for being so difficult.

On the other hand, when the energy of the Self prevails, we have a completely different approach to work. From the soul's perspective, any action, any work, is an opportunity to create, to serve, to play and to manifest itself in some form or other. This is why the soul loves work, because it loves to create, which is its main goal. As soon as our consciousness changes and we live in the presence of the soul, work naturally becomes a very exciting and interesting thing.[7]

When the energy of the soul is present, along with everything this means in terms of truly letting go of ego expectations, a creative energy emerges that allows us to generate "working" conditions that really suit us. Under such conditions, we find that our talents and creativity can truly blossom and be put to good use. We can then find original answers to problems, which become interesting opportunities to play more and to create more. We stop resisting difficult situations, and in fact welcome them, as they stimulate our creativity. We thus find our self constantly energised, whether we experience easy or hard times. For interesting work is not always easy work. Our state of mind as we work makes all the difference.

Our jobs, thankless though they may have been, become a way to manifest our soul's beauty, creativity and infinite love of life, no matter what our external circumstances may be.

Service, contribution

The soul's main interest is creating and playing in the world, and the dynamic underscoring all of its actions is that of love expressed through **service**. When the soul prevails, there is a natural emergence of the will to serve, to contribute, and to offer something to the world. This is, in fact, its fundamental goal.

Service is a soul instinct. It is the outstanding characteristic of the soul, just as desire is the outstanding characteristic of the lower nature. It is group desire, just as in the lower nature it is personality desire. It is the urge to group good. It cannot, therefore, be taught or imposed upon a person... **It is simply the first real effect, evidenced upon the physical plane, of the fact that the soul is beginning to express itself in outer manifestation.**[8]

As soon as the soul manifests itself, there is indeed a major natural shift in one's focus of interest. The ego desire for satisfaction of any kind makes way for a natural desire to serve. This desire to serve is the clearest sign of the presence of the energy of the soul.

> A person's level of spiritual evolution can be seen not in that person's words or powers, but in the quality of service that person contributes to the world.

When one is ego bound, serving is absolute torture, as giving makes the ego feel depleted. Of course the ego can reclaim service for its own ends. For example, this could be a way to gain recognition or play the martyr, to boost one's image or impose one's point of view. But if we play the game of service at the ego level, sooner or later we are bound to be disappointed or to burn out. Service is not exhausting in itself: the same cannot be said in the case of misguided or mixed motivation, which often underscores service.

At the soul level, we have a completely different dynamic: we serve without any expectation, for the sole joy of serving. Whether this service is recognised or not is unimportant. The mere act of serving brings its own joy and its own reward.

Alberto was getting on in years, in terms of his physical age. Yet, at over seventy years of age, he continued all of his activities as a psychotherapist during weekdays. On the weekend, he would take part as a volunteer in various service organisations. He was married, and he took care of his personal life. He was joyful and available to a remarkable degree, always ready to lend a hand or just to play; he was a pleasure to be around. He firmly believed in life and in the wealth buried within each human being. For nearly twenty years, people around him had been telling him to slow down and take a rest. He just laughed and went right on living his life of service to the fullest. Then one day, while he was shovelling snow around his car, his heart stopped beating. Thus ended his life, in a simple, direct manner, without having to carry any burden of illness. His passion for serving had kept him young and useful until the very last minute. When his soul decided it was time to move on to other things, he put an end to this lifetime and passed on to the other side, most likely to continue serving in another form.

To live in a state of service at this level is both energising and inspiring. We feel a deep sense of inner satisfaction, no matter what the external outcome of our efforts may be, as long as we feel we did our best. As we go about all of our activities in this state of mind, we live in a state of love and joy, a state of grace. To paraphrase Khalil Gibran: *Service is love made visible.*

Concentration, attention, emotional self-control and mental centredness

When the mental/emotional mechanism of the ego is active, there is no way to master our thought processes and we end up subject to disorganised and inefficient mental activity. When this mechanism is brought under control, we can access the higher mind's capacity for concentration. This brings about qualities of centredness and attention that make it possible to face any situation in our life in a state of calm, objectivity, efficiency and truth.

Krishnamurti, who spent a lifetime of work tracking down the dynamics of the lower mind, places great emphasis on this state of attentiveness where we remain without fear, without tension or resistance, available and open, and where the now silent lower mind makes way for an accurate perception of what really is.

> If you are fully aware and totally attentive when you look at something, you will realise that a radical transformation takes place, and that this total attention is, in fact, what we refer to as good.[9]

This kind of attentiveness is quite different from that of the ego, which burns energy and eventually tires a person out. The soul's attention is relaxed, supple and serene, and thus infinitely more efficient. This particular state of attentiveness is well known in various spiritual traditions. Robert Linssen speaks of it as *"a state much like "Wu-Nien" as practised by Chinese Ch'an masters: a state of attention without thought, where the Doors of the Heart open and reveal "Cosmic Ananda", the state of supreme love and bliss."*[10]

Strength and passion

One outcome of the soul's many qualities is that, whenever it's presence is manifested, one is filled with great strength, with unwavering toughness, while at the same time one is inspired with great "passions". Of course these are not the emotional, unhinging and destructive passions of the ego. In this case all the power of the emotional body is channelled by the "will to good" for the purpose of doing good and beautiful things, of daring to go off the beaten path and do extraordinary things. It is the passion for learning, for knowledge, for understanding; it is the passion for discovery and self-expansion; it is the passion for creating, contributing, helping; a passion for life in all its beautiful and creative aspects.

> At the soul level, life is far from comfortable. It is exciting, full of unforeseen events, creative activities and opportunities for self-expansion.

All of these passions are experienced in a state of great inner silence, as long as they are not mixed with ego desires. They are completely free of expectations and are rewarding in themselves. They generate an almost infinite flow of energy, the energy of Love. This is the passion of a musician for writing music, of a dancer tirelessly practising her art for years; the passion of a medical doctor for his work driving him to travel through the countryside at night to help a patient; the passion of a teacher who never watches the clock in her efforts to help her students; it is a passion springing from the depths of the heart and from the love of Life. It is a form of passion that leads a human being to go beyond mere comfort, and thus become truly alive. For living in comfort is to live with one foot in the grave. This strength and this passion are often referred to as "the sacred fire", a very apt expression: it is the fire of the soul burning in our hearts, giving meaning to our life.[11]

> The most beautiful thing that can happen to a human being is to discover this sacred fire, the fire in one's soul, and to act in such a way that one's whole life becomes an expression of this inner fire.

Abundance, mastering our creative power

When the soul's creative power is active, we have the potential to generate a state of abundance, as the soul's deepest desire is to have abundance and beauty for all who inhabit this planet. But we need to understand what is meant by abundance in this case.

In ordinary terms, when we speak of abundance, we are most often referring to the accumulation of money or material possessions. This is not a sign of abundance and, in fact, beyond our desires for material things, the concept of abundance is the source of a great deal of confusion.

There is a trend, in many personal development seminars, to work on abundance and one's "creative power", saying that we deserve to be prosperous. This is true to some extent, yet this approach can also serve as camouflage for a great illusion. We may seek abundance under the illusion that satisfying our worldly desires will make us feel better. So we practice certain techniques focusing on "creation", visualisation, meditation, and other areas, which are fine in and of themselves; but we fail to see that what we are doing is feeding the desire mill and remaining prisoners of our personality. Working to create "abundance", as the personality sees it, is to live in a state of illusion, and illusions lead, sooner or later, to disappointment and suffering. Whether or not we get what we want, we will end up spinning in the "circle of dissatisfaction".

There is indeed a form of creative power at the mental level. Mercifully, at the ego level, our creative power is relatively limited. We know that whatever we attract is the product of our thoughts, at the conscious and especially at the unconscious level. Knowing what our collective unconscious is burdened with these days, it is a good thing that our creative power is limited! If, by some magic trick, everyone could instantly actualise his or her desires, we can imagine the chaos that would ensue.

It is very important to specify that the soul's creative power is not focused on filling the needs of our personality, but on meeting its own level of necessities. For a violinist, abundance is not about owning three Cadillacs and a couple of homes, but about having the best possible instrument to play on, and having supportive people and adequate practical conditions fostering the practice and expression of his art. This is a far cry from our ordinary definition of abundance: this is no longer about the accumulation of anything. On

> Genuine abundance, at the soul level, is the capacity to create what we need in order to manifest our soul's will on a worldly plane.

the contrary, this is a state of free and permanent creative energy, which at any given moment (yet never in advance) allows us to create whatever is necessary to support the soul's manifestation—basically to be able to serve and contribute to the best of our ability. When we tune into this kind of abundance, we manage to create the resources we need at every level (material resources, people, energy, inspiration, etc.) in a way that seems magical. **This abundance is not in any way based on desire. It is based on the soul's intention to create and to serve,** in silence, in peace, and without resistance.

Caught as we are in the dynamics of involution and attraction to the material world, our ego seeks physical or psychological stuffing/abundance; our soul seeks abundance in order to be able to serve better. These opposite types of motivation will determine the type of "abundance" we seek, the intent underscoring our actions, and the quality of our life.[12]

Possession

At the level of the Self, we do not "possess" anything, nor do we have any desire to possess. The very notion of possession is foreign to this level of consciousness. If we happen to "own" some material thing, we do not see our self as masters of that thing but as custodians, protectors, guardians, or managers. For we know that, in this universe, everything belongs to our souls, which are all

> To possess means to be in charge of proper maintenance of whatever we "possess", and to ensure that its usefulness for the greater good of all is maximized.

One; nothing belongs to any one personality except the responsibility to make sure that it works well and fulfils its intended purpose.

The best way to create abundance and gain mastery on the material plane is to work on liberating our self from ego mechanisms, and dedicate our self to fulfilling the will of our soul. Like any other manifestation of the Self, this attitude obviously requires a great deal of letting go, especially with regard to fear, insecurity, and possession. We often seek to create abundance because we hope that we will then feel more secure. Yet in order to create the "magical" abundance that is possible at the level of the Self, we must be able to live in a state of detachment, intuition, constant vigilance, and serene "insecurity", remaining intelligently confident in the soul's creative power, knowing that it will never manifest itself in advance.[13] This places the personality in a state of intolerable insecurity unless we have learned to master the desire machine. This level of mastery always brings its own rewards, and the abundance created from moment to moment by the creative power of the soul is one such reward.

We were told, *"Seek you the Kingdom of God, and these things shall be yours as well."* In our own words, look for the path that leads to your own soul, and the rest will come. The great sages know that there is no other alternative.

So abundance can mean very different things depending on whether it is seen from the viewpoint of the soul or that of the personality. It is, first of all, about simplicity. The soul always respects the "law of thrift", which in fact is the law pointing to the right use of energy. To quote Ghandi's famous words, *"To live simply so that others can simply live."*

It also leads to a certain quality of life, love, sharing and contribution. Thus we become empowered to create "magically", with highly effective action.

Health

The highly positive states engendered through this contact with the soul, as we have just described, naturally tend to generate a good state of health. The interest we take in life and in others, along with loving service and self-sacrifice, joyful sharing, detachment and high spirits, all foster energy circulation through the three bodies, and thus good health.

Yet each human being carries memories accumulated over millennia, especially at the physical level, and a great deal of debugging remains to be done. This is the reason why, as we proceed along the path to transformation, we may have to face illness at some point or other. But when this happens, the presence of the Self generates such inner strength and detachment that the physical handicap will be more easily overcome, and used in a positive manner in order to speed up the process of transforming the personality, without really undermining the individual's service and contribution to the world.

> [People who have reached an advanced stage along the path] *often have an uncanny ability to continue their work no matter what happens to them physically. The physical brain can so well reflect the life of the soul that the person is not at all affected by external circumstances. He learns to live with his weaknesses and with adverse conditions, and his work continues at its usual high level.*[14]

Ultimately, when the Self is totally in charge of the personality and there is no longer any energy blockage, human beings will have total mastery of their physical bodies, and will therefore enjoy perfect health.

Quality Relationships

Human beings have a natural, legitimate desire to relate to others. Yet this is an area where the most challenging difficulties arise. In fact, if we were able to create right human relations everywhere, the kingdom of God would be an imminent reality on this Earth.

The source of all the difficulties arising between human beings lies in the stock of unresolved memories that each of us carries within, as well as in the lack of development of our higher mind. Indeed, we have seen that these memories are the source of all desires, expectations, and demands, of all the dominant/dominated power games being played out on a daily basis in ordinary human relationships. This is why these relationships are often so difficult or unsatisfactory.

The moment we move closer to the soul level, relationship difficulties disappear, especially in couple relationships, where expectations and unconscious mental/emotional mechanisms are particularly felt. For when we are filled with the presence of the soul, we feel deeply loved and nurtured, whether we happen to be alone or with somebody.

A feeling of brotherhood, of kinship with fellow human beings

The dynamics of our relationships undergo a radical change the moment the presence of the soul is felt. In particular, we become less and less interested in satisfying the affective needs of our personality. We relate to others for the sake of helping, serving, supporting, inspiring...in a word, giving instead of taking. A sense of kinship with fellow human beings emerges, which brings us to the subject of love.

Unconditional love, compassion

Love is obviously the fundamental quality that emerges when a connection with the soul is established. But what are we talking about when we speak of love? We were told that God is love, that the soul is love, and that everything in the universe is sustained by the energy of love. Countless volumes have been written on the subject of love; poems, music, and works of art of all kinds have celebrated love. Yet there is very little we can say regarding this cosmic dynamic of love. In its universal form, it is the great law of attraction, covering vastly different realities, depending on the environment where it is applied.

Love, when it is experienced at the level of the Self, is quite different from "emotional love". The latter mainly springs from mechanisms such as desire, affective emptiness, or the need to possess or dominate, projecting old memories that have yet to be defused onto others. It is an emotional, conditional reaction which in fact has nothing to do with love: "I love you" IF you satisfy the requirements of my computer. Otherwise "I hate you" or, at the very least, "I am not interested in you". This pseudo-love is, in fact, a struggle for energy, an opportunity for taking, or if we are giving, our ego is keeping tabs and it is with some expectation of some form of return. It is an emotional bind that locks us into a state of stress and unhappiness, keeping us prisoners of our own mechanisms. All our love stories, passionate melodramas and other stories we have been telling for centuries illustrate how hard it is to experience genuine love, beyond the mechanism of our personality.

Do not mistake desire for love. Desire frantically seeks one form
of gratification after another. Love is satisfied in itself.
—Anonymous

Love, at the level of the soul, is quite a different thing. The soul is in a permanent state of fulfilment, and it is easy and natural for it to offer unconditional love
in the form of self-sacrifice, openness, acceptance, compassion, and service. This
kind of love is based on great inner freedom, and a high level of maturity. It is the
expression of the very essence of the soul and it includes every other quality.

> *Love is neither a feeling nor an emotion... Love is the higher force that guides*
> *the worlds and leads to integration, unity and inclusiveness, all of which impel*
> *Divinity itself toward action. Love is a daunting thing to cultivate, as egoism is*
> *such an inherent part of human nature.*[15]

> *The motivation behind true love is a passionate desire that the beloved person*
> *(or object) fully actualise his/her inherent perfection, regardless of the conse-*
> *quences for the one who loves; it is a state of service.*[16]

> *The truth is, unless we have gone through a lengthy process leading to profound*
> *transformation, it is not possible for us to love in the true sense of the word. This*
> *truth must be perceived and acknowledged, and one can then set a goal for one-*
> *self of reaching the state of fulfilment of our humanness, that is a genuine capac-*
> *ity to love.*[17]

It is perhaps easier to understand now why it is so difficult to love. As long as
we are out of touch with this freedom and bliss of the soul, as long as our computer is loaded with old memories, it is impossible for us to really love. We often
think that love hurts. The root of our suffering is not love, but our inability to
truly love.

Love depression is the inability to cope with a situation
from the viewpoint of the soul.
—Anonymous

The true force of love impels us to give, to forget our self, to become detached
from our old ego, and this is painful to our personality. There is no need to beat
our self up with guilt for that; all we need is healing, and this will come through
the practice of soul values, the practice of love.

Genuine love is not experienced just in the context of relationships, far from it.
In fact, this is where it is often the most distorted. This source of love and respect
nurtures our relationship with everything around us, especially with the Earth,
which translates into respect for nature (the ecological movement is a manifestation of a new loving consciousness that is spreading across the planet), and love
for animals. This is not sentimentalism; it is the expression of a deep love and
respect for all of creation.

To live with this love energy springing from the soul is to live in freedom, in a
state of grace.

Good Will

While the word love may lead to confusion, there is a more discreet quality that is nonetheless a powerful and direct expression of genuine love: Good Will. While this may not seem very spectacular, it is one of the major manifestations of the presence of the Self. Good Will involves the fundamental qualities of the soul: a flexible and open mind, detachment, self-sacrifice, humility and genuine love; it directly implies that one has ceased to identify with one's ego. If there were but one quality to work on as we proceed along the spiritual path, this would be it.

The manifestation of the Self—Heaven on Earth?

Yes and no. It all depends on what we mean by Heaven. All of these outcomes of the manifestation of the Self may seem very positive, yet they are of little significance when compared with the actual experience. Indeed, when we eventually succeed in bringing our ego totally under control, and our soul is completely in charge of our personality, we will be able to live in a state of consciousness that is difficult to describe, as it is far beyond everything we have just examined or could possibly imagine.

For the time being, our ego is still not completely flexible, and we are caught in a mixture of two wills: that of the ego and that of the soul. We are in a learning process, and the hazards of the path must be well understood if we want to be able to move towards this state of higher consciousness and absolute freedom.

In fact, as we have emphasised at the beginning of this chapter, we cannot move towards the expression of the soul by gradually improving our ego. We evolve through successive and increasingly difficult stages of letting go. This means that when we strive to unleash the energy of the soul so that it becomes active within us, while our ego is still present, our life will not necessarily become easier or more pleasant. On the contrary, while we remain in this in-between phase, life in the light of the soul can actually be anything but comfortable, since this light shines on all the unresolved aspects of our ego and reactivates them.

> Life on the path that leads to a complete expression of the soul is essentially a life of self-extension.

It is important to be aware of this dynamic, for as we proceed along the path of transformation, we can indeed get the feeling for a while that the more the soul's energy is felt, the more difficult and challenging life becomes. The path to ego liberation and to the manifestation of the Self is no picnic. It is a saga involving inner triumphs, self-expansion, failure and despair followed by major liberation, patience, giving and letting go, perseverance and courage.

While life under such conditions is far from comfortable, it is nevertheless exciting; it is not easy, but it is inspiring. It is about forgetting our self in order to discover our true identity, it is a constant act of giving that naturally enriches us from within; it brings no satisfaction to our personality, but brings great joy and freedom within our being.

The soul wants to fully manifest itself through the personality. Comfort is the least of its concern, for its satisfaction lays elsewhere. It is satisfied whenever a service has been rendered, or a wound has been healed, or help has been given, whenever love has triumphed over fear, whenever an area of darkness has been turned into light within us and on this planet. The fact that the personality still maintains its last bastions of resistance, and finds this game demanding, is of little concern to the soul. The soul loves its instrument, but it also expects it to perform to its full capacity.

This is where a great deal of confusion is still to be found. Some New Age or personal development teachings sometimes convey the illusion that when we "tune in" spiritually, we will live in a state of increasing happiness, abundance and health, we will realise all of our dreams, and all will be well. That is simply not the case. As we proceed along the spiritual path, as we gain higher levels of mastery, we certainly have more and more chances to tune into the joy and fulfilment of the soul as well as all the positive aspects we have just described. But *at the same time,* as long as we remain unable to totally identify with the soul, as long as the slightest part of our will remains ego bound, we can expect the latter to be confronted and life will not necessarily be easy. On the contrary, there will be great challenges, difficult tests, yet we will have all the strength and inner resources needed to cope with such challenges, and, for those interested in genuine personal growth, the game is worth it.

All of the qualities of the soul's manifestation that we have just described are not designed to bring satisfaction to our ego. They can only be experienced through the energy of the soul, which requires a totally different state of consciousness. This most important consideration is often forgotten. In order to gain access to all of these wonderful outcomes, we have to have reached the point where we have let go of our fears and insecurities, of all the ego's mental/emotional expectations, of all our desires for comfort, easy living, possession, stuffing or whatever. The soul's motivation is not to satisfy the mental/emotional garbage in our computer; it is in fact totally opposed to this. It is naturally oriented towards service and self-sacrifice, which the ego abhors. For this reason, no matter how wonderful these positive aspects stemming from one's connection to the soul may be, it must be clearly understood that they come at a very high price for the ego. And there will be pain, for as long as it takes for the ego to let go. To embark on a spiritual quest with the hope (be it conscious or unconscious) of satisfying some desire or false ego need is an illusion that still leads many people astray on so-called paths of spiritual or personal growth, which actually turn out to be dead ends.

In order to find peace, we have to cease to desire peace; in order to find security, we must cease to desire security; in order to find love, we must cease to desire love; in order to find freedom, we must cease to desire…and replace personality desires with the radiant will of the soul.

And when the ego is completely under control, then the bliss, magic and absolute freedom of our innermost being will be ours.

> *It is possible to reach a point where naught that occurs can ruffle the inner calm; where the peace that passeth understanding is known and experienced, because the consciousness is centred in the Ego, who is peace itself, being the circle of the buddhic life; … where bliss itself is reached that is based not on circumstances in the three worlds, but on that inner realisation of existence apart from the not-self, an existence that persists when time and space, and all that is contained therein, are not; that is known when all the illusions of the lower planes are experienced, passed through, transmuted and transcended; that endures when the little world of human endeavour has dissipated and gone, being seen as naught; and that is based on the knowledge that I AM THAT.*[18]

Even though we cannot have any real idea of the infinite beauty, power and freedom afforded to us when we experience the presence of the soul, and though we know that the path can be demanding, we can nevertheless realise the extent to which a change in consciousness might bring us what we are all looking for: peace, joy, power, love, bliss and, finally, the gift of LIVING UNBOUND, free to experience the full essence of who we are.

The questions that arise then are: How do we go about strengthening and fully realising this connection with the soul? Can we take conscious action in order to speed up the process? For thousands of years, human beings have been looking for the means to answer such questions. Every spiritual discipline, every approach to personal growth has been, and still remains, a more or less successful attempt to answer this call. The answers found thus far are numerous and varied, but the path is not an easy one to follow and it is riddled with pitfalls. In the following chapters, we shall offer a global perspective on the transformation process, which might help to develop a better understanding of the actual dynamic involved in this process. This deeper understanding may help the seeker along the path towards his or her own light and freedom, regardless of what method is applied, just as a good road map or effective directions can facilitate travelling, regardless of what means of transportation we end up using. I shall also present a few approaches that I have explored in depth through my own experience, and which have proved useful along my path.

Comparison Charts on
How the Ego and the Soul Function

I ~ HOW THEY FUNCTION

EGO	SOUL
The will of the ego	**The will of the soul**
maintain defence systems stemming from the past	is to bring peace and love on Earth
motivations for action: desire and pleasure	the motivation for action: service
functions on the basis of automatic responses (via the lower mind)	functions on the basis of intuition and right knowledge (via the higher mind)
seeks self-affirmation, wants to take	wants to give and serve
survives	is fully alive
is a prisoner of all that is material or emotional	is free to play and to create
lives in a state of illusion	lives in reality
thinks of itself	thinks of others
inaccurate perception of reality	right perception of reality
materialism	idealism
manipulates and is manipulated	respect, integrity, discernment
self-centredness, selfishness	selflessness
price, false humility	genuine humility
ill will	good will
seeks and is dependent on material	is free of any form of possessions or affective possessions
wants to work as little as possible	wants to work (to create) as much as possible
stuffing	fulfilment
fear, separativeness	unconditional love, unity

II ~ CONSEQUENCES

EGO	SOUL
The will of the ego	**The will of the soul**
stress, tension, anxiety	relaxed state, inner peace
fatigue, lack of energy or hyperactivity	calm and balanced energy, always plentifully available
powerlessness or abuse of power	power, ability to empower others
violence	respect, compassion
scatteredness, weakness	centredness, strength
illness	health
solitude or alienating relationships	genuine, free, fulfilling relationships
insecurity	security
sense of deprivation, dependency	fulfilment, autonomy
seriousness, dramatisation	playfulness, light heartedness
narrow mindedness	intelligence
closed mindedness	open mindedness
routine	creativity
judgement	compassion, understanding
inner inquiry is either non-existent, or separate from daily life	inner inquiry that is integrated and manifested in daily life
instability	mastery
momentary satisfaction	permanent satisfaction
fleeting moments of happiness	deep and permanent joy
enslavement due to automatic responses	freedom
separation, selfishness	genuine love

1 Excerpt from the Glossary of the World Goodwill Association.

2 Alice Bailey, *A Treatise on White Magic,* pages 627–628.

3 In other cultures and other traditions more balanced than our own, "elders" were respected and honoured for their wisdom and understanding of life. In these traditions, human beings were less disconnected from themselves, often through constant contact with nature or through spiritual practices that allow people to remain in a more wholesome state of awareness than that which prevails in our materialistic society.

4 Translated from Krishnamurti, *Le Livre de la méditation et de la vie,* page 278.

5 Alice Bailey, *A Treatise on White Magic,* page 585.

6 Our ego is very interested in operating alone because it wants to do things its own way and no other, according to its programming. It wants to prove its own rightness, its competence, and perhaps also that it is better than others. Functioning on one's own can be useful for some people whose egos are still partially formed, so that they can define themselves at the ego level. But this has little to do with genuine autonomy.

7 Of course we could say that, given the prevailing difficult economic conditions, we have no choice but to put up with uninteresting jobs in order to "earn a living". This attitude, which is deeply embedded in our collective consciousness, actually stems from the way the ego functions. This is the way to "lose one's life by earning it". In addition, it feeds a vicious circle, as difficult economic conditions are merely the product of our collective level of consciousness. When the majority of people eventually attain a higher state of awareness, this will automatically result in far more positive economic conditions, and everyone will experience a sense of creating and contributing in every one of their activities. Our economy is not the product of "chance", but of people.

8 Alice Bailey, *Esoteric Psychology,* Vol. 2, page 125.

9 Translated from Krishnamurti, *Le Livre de la méditation et de la vie.*

10 Translated from Robert Linssen, *La méditation véritable,* éd. Le courrier du Livre.

11 Many of the stories that touch us deeply are stories involving this sacred fire. The film entitled *Dead Poets' Society,* now a classic in its genre, is a fine example.

12 Let us note that it is possible that the soul's will is to have the personality experience certain material limitations so as to allow it to gain higher levels of mastery, to develop humility, courage, will power and creativity, to practice letting go, to learn to identify what is essential, especially where past lives have been marked by abuse and lack of consciousness, or powerlessness.

13 Alan Watts, a well-known trailblazer in the field of renewed awareness in the United States, wrote a book entitled *The Wisdom of Insecurity,* a title that says it all.

14 Alice Bailey, *Discipleship in the New Age,* page 82.

15 Alice Bailey, *Discipleship in the New Age,* Vol. 1, page 31.

16 Stewart Emery, *Actualisation.*

17 Translated from: Arnaud Desjardins, *À la recherche du Soi,* éd. de la Table Ronde.

18 Alice Bailey, *Initiation, Human and Solar,* page 77–78.

PART THREE

The Transformation Process

✦

On Our Way to Freedom

The age-old identification with the form aspect is not easy to overcome; the task expected of the disciple is a long and arduous one.
But in the end it holds the promise of success, providing there is
clear thinking, sincere motivation and scientifically organised work.[1]

Introduction

TO PART THREE

The potential for evolution exists, and it can be developed among distinct individuals, with the appropriate knowledge and methods... The forces that restrain the evolution of the masses also restrain the evolution of each human being. It is up to each of us to overcome these forces... Later you will understand that all of these hurdles are in fact very useful; if they did not exist, we would have to create them deliberately. For it is only through overcoming obstacles that one can develop the qualities one needs within oneself.[2]

Now that we have become aware of the various mechanisms of consciousness, the next step is to know how to better control them. This form of inquiry is shared by increasing numbers of people today, especially since, as we noted earlier on, humankind is at a crucial point in its history, a time when our collective consciousness is ready to take a leap forward to take us from the human era to the spiritual era.

This explains why we are now seeing such a vast array of methods for inner work (through books, courses, workshops, conferences, internships, training sessions, spiritual practices and all sorts of techniques), from the most serious to the most hare-brained, the most authentic to the most deceiving, the most profound to the most superficial. This is a most auspicious sign of a collective blossoming of consciousness. Even though all is not perfect, and though our ego is still busy trying to reclaim much of these efforts, all these activities are nevertheless a sign of an intense desire for change. And rather than focus on the shortcomings of many of these approaches, we would rather see them as a valiant, though sometimes misguided, effort on the part of humankind to attain another level of awareness.

With all these different approaches, a seeker may feel somewhat bewildered, not knowing what criteria to use as a basis for making a choice. There are now a number of effective teachings dealing with this or that aspect of consciousness, yet a more global understanding of the process is often lacking.

This understanding is all the more necessary since there are numerous pitfalls along the path to inner liberation. This is a difficult path. One overly simplistic New Age view is the belief that if we engage in a process of inner work, everything will get better and better. That is simply not the case. So it is important to get a clearer understanding of what the work of inner transformation involves and, more specifically, of the stages we can expect to go through along the way. Each of us, of course, will follow his or her own path, but there are some general principles that one should be aware of as they are very useful in helping us to avoid wasting energy on fruitless quests or disappointing experiences, and thus more easily find the way that works for us.

Thus a clearer understanding of the dynamics underscoring the process of changing our consciousness will make the following possible:

- we can more consciously choose our own methods of inner work;

- we can deal more serenely with the difficulties encountered along the path and all the typical human reactions (discouragement, doubt, fear, etc.) that will not fail to arise when we want to engage in a genuine process of transformation.

For centuries, we as human beings had not reached a high enough stage of development to seek our own path, and we were given practices to follow for which we often did not see the reason. In this perspective, this is why we needed a particular Master or certain "moral" values that acted as necessary safeguards, but that were also rather limiting. These days, for many of us, the mind is sufficiently developed to enable us to work more directly with the "inner Master", with the force of our own soul. This is why the work of transformation must inevitably go through the development of intelligence, which enables us to understand and to totally take charge of our own process of transformation. This makes it all the more demanding, and we must be that much more vigilant if we want to avoid getting lost in paths that lead nowhere.

In the following chapters, we will go over certain fundamental principles in an effort to clarify the dynamics of the transformation process—in practical and concrete terms—and thus facilitate the use of any given method or teaching.

chapter 10

Context and Clarity of Intention

Quality of the Context

When it comes to inner work, no matter what approach we end up using, the context in which this approach is used, rather that the technique itself, **is essentially what will determine how effective and how real this work will be.** With our materialistic conditioning, we tend to place too much emphasis on techniques. Yet when we truly work on changing our consciousness, we end up noticing that the most important factor is not the technique as such, but the context: that is the state of mind, the capacity for intelligent perception, the inner motivation, the intention, the mental clarity, and the vision with which we engage in this work. As human beings, we have a vehicle, but we are more than the vehicle. This is why any technique, no matter how interesting or sophisticated, will never be enough to accomplish genuine inner work. The quality of the context may seem like a detail; yet it will determine whether or not we get effective results from our efforts. Instead of running around looking for "the" technique, or "the" master, as the quickest path to spiritual enlightenment, it is more effective to work first of all on developing a broad, intelligent context.

How does one define a context? The context is the totality of the thoughts (both conscious and unconscious) that colour our actions. It can also be defined as a point of view, a way of seeing things, a philosophy, a model, or a system of beliefs. It is the basis on which the method is built. Most often, we take the context as a matter of course, without realising that it is just one model. For example, science has until now been working in a materialistic context: its belief system holds that nothing is real unless it is material and can be experienced through the five senses or through physical instruments. Spiritual teachings and practices are also based on a philosophy, on a specific approach to reality. Most often, these basic models are not questioned when in fact they should be, for they determine how clearly we perceive reality.

The broader and clearer the context, the richer our potential experience will be,[3] no matter what technique we use.

Since the context is made up of conscious and unconscious thought systems, if we want to be able to use an effective context that supports our inner work, we will need to examine it from two angles: first, at the conscious level, we can try to broaden our conscious perception (e.g., through new knowledge, and more generally speaking, through cultivating an open mind); and second, as far as our unconscious thoughts are concerned, we should try to defuse the automatic systems of perception that are rooted in our unconscious. We shall go into this second aspect in greater depth further along in this book, as the work to be done at this level is quite different.

As far as the **context at the conscious level** is concerned, we can mention some elements that will just about guarantee that we have a context already broad enough to allow us to experience rapid and effective growth, no matter what method is used:

- **Gain clear knowledge and understanding of human mechanisms** as much as possible, and always be prepared to broaden this knowledge. The more we get to know our inner mechanisms, the more we will know what to do about them. There is nothing new in this. A long time ago, the Delphic Oracle said, "Man, know thyself". The suggestion is very broad in its scope, but it is fundamental. We cannot achieve ultimate liberation if we do not become aware of certain mechanisms that are part of our human nature. While it is possible to have a mystical experience, or to get results from effective therapy, sooner or later we will have to take full and conscious responsibility for our own vehicle in order to get to the point of genuine mastery.

- **Integrate the responsibility-attraction-creation principle.** This principle is becoming more and more familiar in the present movement towards a new level of awareness, yet it is sometimes poorly understood. In my previous book, I sometimes took pains to clarify this principle since, once it is properly integrated, it forms a very solid basis for any consciousness development work. This principle sets up a context that enables us to reclaim our power, makes it easier for us to let go in concrete terms, and allows us to use each moment of our life as an opportunity for consciousness development. It makes it possible for us to have a far more relaxed and serene attitude towards life.

- **Treat the soul as a fact of life,** either as evident, if that is how we perceive it, or as a working hypothesis. This hypothesis generates more concrete results than the materialistic approach in terms of healing and well-being.

- **Be aware of basic ego dynamics** (fear, power seeking, victimitis, selfishness, wanting to be right, etc., as well as all the dynamics I presented in Volume 1 in the form of character structures), and develop a clear intention to become free of these dynamics.

- **Be free of the dominant/dominated dynamic,** or at least develop a clear intention to become free of this dynamic, and be ready to do the inner work required to achieve this (quite a program!). This clears the way towards being able to work freely in a state of respect for oneself and for others.

- **Consciously choose simplicity, integrity,** impersonality and detachment as much as possible (yet another program that will also require stringent inner work).

- **Practice the witness stance,** as I will describe it further on.

- **Be prepared to expand our thought context,** broaden our viewpoint when we come across new data or knowledge and be open to constantly expanding knowledge. Be free of the dynamics of always wanting to be right.

- **Be ready to put in all the effort required** and to persevere in order to access the light of the soul, knowing that the going is likely to get tough at times; stop focusing on ease and comfort; and develop enough inner enthusiasm for this quest to be ready to let go of all the things our ego clings to the most (security, pleasure, power). Many people stumble on this issue. They were led to believe that the transformation process would quickly and easily lead to a heavenly existence. Heaven is indeed within our reach, but the price to pay is quite high in ego terms. We need to know that the transformation process is not a comfortable one, and to have a deep enough understanding of the benefits of this process to be determined to pay little attention to discomfort at the personality level.

These inner attitudes will keep our consciousness awake and ready to open up to broader dimensions.

Beyond this effort to open up our general context, certain basic conditions are essential to ensure that the work will be authentic and effective. Among the most important, let us focus on the purity and strength of our intention.

Purity of Intention

> *The time has come when the first and major principle governing true esotericism must be grasped as conditioning all hierarchical workers: Right Motive.*[4]

Purity of intention and clear motivation are not often stressed in various teachings, perhaps because they may be less appealing than some spectacular technique. Indeed they require, from the outset, that we ask the real questions. If we are sincere, they quickly shed light on our ego mechanisms. Yet these are among the main factors that condition genuine inner work, and in any process of inner inquiry, one should regularly ask the question, "Why am I following this teaching, or performing this practice?" And we should not be content with beautiful, vague answers to this question.

The answer is far from obvious because in fact, most of the time, our intention is twofold: there is the ego's intention, which is to feed its mechanisms, and there is the soul's intention, which calls for genuine transformation. For this reason, it is good to take a look at what our personality might get out of this quest, through the eyes of a compassionate, non-judgemental witness. We then create the potential for having a clearer perception of things, and our true intention—that of our soul—can more fully manifest itself. The degree to which our intention is pure, and the motivation of our personality is clear, will attract our soul's attention, which then sends a wave of healing and transforming energy into our personality.

This has often been mentioned by our masters, as they reminded us to clarify our motives, to find the "right motive".

> A "pure" motive is rare; when it does occur, it always leads to success. Our motive can be selfish and personal, or selfless and spiritual; where spiritual aspirants are concerned, it is a more or less mixed motive. Power thus depends on purity of intention and one-pointed focus.[5]

In fact, no matter what level we may be at, or what field of endeavour we may be involved in, it is **our intention, rather than our outward actions, that ultimately determines the outcome.** This is true as much for the material actions we take in our ordinary world as for the steps we take along the spiritual path. We may meditate ten hours a day, yet if our intention is ultimately to gain certain powers and feed our pride, to prove that life is hard, or to withdraw from the world, all we will be doing is reinforcing our unconscious patterns. Enlightenment will not come just because we meditated. It is essential that we develop genuine self-knowledge if we do not want to lose our self in the illusion of "good intentions", which in fact stem directly from the unconscious part of our ego. The same goes for all disciplines, all techniques for inner transformation, and all methods of personal development or spiritual practices. If, from the outset, we do not take pains to figure out the workings of our ego, we run the risk of reinforcing the wall of illusion and becoming more and more entrapped in the mechanisms of our lower nature.

> The development of right motive is a progressive effort, and constantly one shifts the focus of one's incentive when one discovers himself, as the Light shines ever more steadily upon one's way, and constantly a newer and higher motive emerges.[6]

Figuring out the workings of our ego is a very demanding task, yet sooner or later we have to face the real facts if we truly want to access the freedom and power of the soul. Clarifying our motive as much as possible will lend strength to any approach. This clarification will be a conscious effort. Becoming aware of our unconscious defence patterns is very useful for acknowledging the motivations that spring from our ego mechanisms.

In support of our conscious intention, it will be necessary at some point to work on the unconscious level, as this is where our most active motivations are to be found. What we think on a conscious level is often a far cry from what lies in our unconscious, which conditions our life as long as it is not sufficiently cleared up. When I described the various character structures in Volume 1, we saw how each structure can reclaim spiritual seeking for its own ends, and how the roots of these structures go deep into the unconscious. The more we work on clearing up our unconscious, the easier it will become to have a truly clear intention.

Strength of Intention

Our intention must not only be clear, it must also be strong.

> Yet, though man may understand his potential, even in the clearest terms, this would not be enough for him to advance even one step towards its realisation. In order to be able to realise this potential, he must have an all-consuming desire for liberation, he must be prepared to sacrifice everything, to risk all, in order to attain liberation.[7]

We could go back to the analogy of learning to play a musical instrument: we may have access to the best methods, to excellent teachers, and be passionately involved in music; however, if our intention is weak, if we are not interested in learning and putting a lot of effort into practising, we will never reach the stage of mastering our instrument.

If we want to engage in a process of inner inquiry, we need to be impelled by a free, yet burning desire. The soul does not force anything at the personality level; the latter must decide, out of a conscious and free choice, to open up to the impulse coming from the soul. No one is obliged to engage in a process of transformation. We may continue to live at the ego level for as long as we like. There is nothing wrong with this…it just happens to be unsatisfactory. The choice is ours, and ours alone.

This is where will power comes in. You need will power, determination and courage to move forward along the spiritual path, for as we mentioned before, when the soul manifests itself, the ego will concentrate all its energy into putting up defences and the inner battle can be intense. Only with unshakeable will, bolstered by what some call faith, can we overcome the difficulties encountered along the path.

The concept of will power is often poorly understood. What we are talking about here is the will that springs from the soul, with all the flexibility, openness and awareness that implies—not the will stemming from an ego structure, which makes the whole personality subject to automatic behaviours that are often inappropriate for the circumstances. This confusion is so easy to fall into that this component of spiritual advancement is often left unmentioned. Our will is often associated with power with negative connotations, as if it were practically the opposite of love. All of these confusions stem from the fact that will and power have very different aspects depending on whether they come from the ego or from the Self.[8] It is essential to cultivate the quality of genuine will. In an excellent book entitled *The Act of Will*, Roberto Assagioli presents a very accurate analysis of this dynamic of human nature. He makes a distinction between several aspects, such as strong will, good will, transpersonal will, universal will, and joyful will. Combined with practical exercises, this book is an excellent working tool.[9] Here is one example:

The gymnastics of will: "useless" exercises… to reinforce the will; it is prefer-able to exercise this psychological function apart from all the others. This can be done by performing deliberate acts that have no other purpose than to train the will. The application of such apparently "useless" exercises has been hotly de-fended by William James in the following terms:

Keep alive in you the capacity to make efforts with small daily purposeless exer-cises, that is by being systematically heroic each day in little non-necessary things; every day, do something for the sole and simple reason that it is difficult and that you would rather not do it, so that when a cruel moment of danger strikes, you will not be dismayed or poorly prepared. (…) He who has developed a regular, daily habit of focusing his attention, channelling his energy, will be well reward-ed for his efforts. Should disaster strike, he will remain steady as a rock, even though he may face ruin at every turn, while his partners in misfortune will be swept away like leaves in the wind.

In fact a person's dedication to transformation and the strength of his or her will are directly related to that person's level of evolution. If he or she is inward-ly ready to make that step, to let go of old structures and to live more at the level of the soul, his or her dedication to the process of liberation will be very strong. A less-evolved person will not be genuinely interested in this type of work. It will be more appropriate for this person to carry on with the ego-building process, to fully experience his or her limitations, along with limited joys and inevitable sor-rows. That person's intent to go through the process of transformation cannot be strong, because the time is not yet right for that to happen.

Using one's intent towards transformation as a motivating force may seem sim-ple, yet it is not easy, as the ego has no intention to change or to question itself. When a person awakens to his or her true self, he or she may then experience inner conflicts that are not always conscious. The will of the Self is to speed up the process of transformation through a radical change in the mechanism of con-sciousness; the will of the ego is to maintain the status quo.

Once the individual is aware of the work to be done and is ready to engage in this work in the context of the soul, that is the point where methods become highly effective. No matter what method is used, we could say that a weak intent produces weak results, while a strong intent produces powerful results. And for equal measures of intent, a so-so method may produce good results, while a very good method will give excellent results. On the other hand, without a clear and strong intent, even a very good method will not produce any lasting outcomes.

What we have here is the theme of freedom in another form. Indeed, if what determines the successful outcome of a process of inner work is not so much the method at hand but the will and clear motivation of the individual engaging in this process, this means that each human being is free and totally in charge of cre-ating his or her own outcomes. No one, and nothing external, can possibly effect our transformation for us. This means that **human beings are totally free with**

regard to choosing self-transformation, that this choice is strictly dependent on each of us. There is no need to depend on a method, a brilliant therapist or an enlightened spiritual teacher to take us in charge. Genuine inner work, particularly with regard to the unconscious, can only take place if an individual has made a free and conscious choice, and is deliberately taking charge of his or her life.

But don't we need a teacher?

This is a frequently asked question. The answer is simple if we do not tack an emotional charge onto it. In any discipline, it is very useful to have one or more teachers to guide us. It would be a huge waste of time to try to reinvent mathematics for the sake of independence. We can benefit from the accumulation of centuries of acquired human knowledge. The greatest artists have their masters.

In the same way, as we proceed on our way to self mastery, it is good to seek knowledge, teachings, information and inspiration from real teachers, those who share their knowledge but refuse to play the game of illusion and dependency. It is also totally normal to offer respect and gratitude for what they give us. But indeed the pitfall to be avoided at this level is to fall into some form of affective projection, and to use the "Master" to discharge emotional excess baggage that we are unable to manage by our self.

To give and to receive teachings is part of the law of sharing. We receive these teachings or this inspiration with gratitude, yet knowing that it is up to each of us to use them according to our own intention and resources, rather than with the hope that someone is going to do the work for us.

When we place our self in an appropriate context, and our conscious intent is clear and strong, the power of the soul kicks in, and we can look to it for support. The method is less important than purity and strength of intent, and the intelligence with which we go about doing the

> When the personality clearly declares its intent to transform within a conscious context, the soul gets the green light to take action.

work. These aspects will not constitute the actual work of liberation, but they are the **essential keys** needed to open the door to genuine inner transformation.

---

[1] Translated from Alice Bailey, *Glamour: A World Problem,* Lucis Trust.

[2] Ouspensky, *In Search of the Miraculous, Fragments of an Unknown Teaching.*

[3] See *The Power of Free Will, Chapter 2.*

[4] Alice Bailey, *Externalisation of the Hierarchy,* p. 666.

[5] Idem.

[6] Id., *A Treatise on White Magic,* page 203.

7 Ouspensky, op. cit.

8 When our intention to do the real work is very strong, it will not be long before we get results. However, if we are mainly motivated by the rigid structure, we will have to be vigilant as to how we use our will. Indeed, this activates a very specific energetic process, which could be explained by saying that this force of intention opens the door to the energy of the soul, which will then use any available method to generate a real and profound transformation.

9 Roberto Assagioli, *The Act of Will,* Viking Press.

chapter 11

Working on the Three Aspects of Consciousness

Along the spiritual path, there is a great deal of confusion with regard to the methods one should use. Some people swear by meditation, by the teachings of some Master, by oriental techniques, by modern western techniques, by techniques centred on the body, on emotions, by strictly mental techniques, or by ascetic, strictly spiritual practices. In fact, we often proceed blindly through this maze without any clear idea of what we are doing, or we are sure that we are right, which is even worse. We will not discuss methods here, but rather the fundamental principles on which any method should be based in order to be effective.

In light of everything we have seen in the preceding chapters, we can see that, in order to engage in a complete process of inner work, it will be necessary to work on the three aspects of consciousness, not necessarily in the order in which they are presented. Further on, we will examine the interaction between these three aspects, as well as the flexibility required to approach them:

- **The unconscious aspect** involves a process of defusing memories from the past, which will pave the way to emotional and mental mastery (taming the horse). The principle on which this is based was partly explored in Chapter 9, where we saw that the more the unconscious is free of these old memories, the easier it gets to access the higher mind.

- **The conscious aspect** involves gaining conscious mastery, which essentially means controlling our thoughts and developing our higher mental capacities (transformation, heightened awareness of the coachman).

- **The supraconscious aspect** involves bringing soul awareness into the consciousness of the personality (conscious connection with the inner Master).[1]

No matter what spiritual practices or personal growth disciplines we engage in, we invariably encounter one or several of these aspects, which are more or less well managed as the case may be. Often, only one aspect (or two at the most) of the transformation process is considered, and this is why the results we get are not always durable or satisfactory in terms of a genuine transformation that is concretely manifested on the worldly plane. In many cases, personal growth seminars work only at the conscious level, and merely skim the unconscious and supraconscious levels (assuming they are at all concerned with these levels). Therapeutic practices are aimed at liberating the unconscious, but without calling upon the energy of the soul. Spiritual practices are more focused on working "in the light", and thus place more emphasis on the supraconscious, and eventually the conscious aspect, yet they omit the fact that there are also shadowy areas. In addition, many of these approaches omit the aspect of service and concrete manifestation in worldly terms. All of these approaches, many of them excellent, would gain from broadening their perspective on the issue, and would become all the more effective and fulfilling if used in combination with the other.

As far as I am concerned, I have perfected certain methods over a number of years of research, and have realized **the importance of a complete, comprehensive and coherent approach working on all three levels: the conscious, the unconscious and the supraconscious.** In fact, the process involves all three levels in a lively dynamic, working by successive approximations, as the work on one level always supports the work at the other levels.

Indeed, these three aspects interact with one another. For example, debugging the unconscious may create an opening for a sudden inflow of spiritual energy; conscious mastery may pave the way to unravelling certain aspects of the unconscious, and make it easier to function on the basis of higher consciousness; calling upon spiritual energy may facilitate a healing of past wounds, etc. The process is very personal, as there is no predetermined path. The only thing that must be kept in focus is the **necessity to work on the three levels in a flexible, vigilant manner, and according to the specific dynamics of each individual.**

In order to facilitate our inquiry and shed some light on the essence of this process as well as its complexity, we will observe how the work is to be approached more specifically for each of these three aspects. As these are interdependent, we need to recognize and complete several different steps, each involving one or more of these aspects, so as to ensure that the process is both effective and safe. These different steps are very often overlooked, and this is why the path often seems so difficult, and so full of dead ends. When we become aware of the dynamics underscoring the entire process, it makes an enormous difference in terms of facilitating the healing process and allowing us to gain mastery, and thus our freedom.

The steps along the way

To begin with, it is helpful to lay down the strongest possible foundation for the work at the conscious level. Then we can move on to working on the unconscious, which will allow us to expand the conscious aspect, which in turn will lead to more in-depth work on the unconscious, etc. At the same time, the energy of the soul will be called upon, to varying degrees of intensity, which will involve the supraconscious level. And this is how we can proceed with the work, through successive approximations, in a cyclical rather than linear fashion. I will therefore need to have appropriate methods available to us at each step. We have ours, and we will mention some of their features further on. If we continually follow up on this progression, and have access to a set of coherent tools, then we can move ahead in a genuine, safe manner towards higher and higher levels of mastery and freedom.

The First Step: The Foundation

Working at the Conscious Level: First Encounter with the Soul
The First Initiation

Before we can work effectively and safely on the unconscious, and then work in greater depth at other levels, it is important to begin by building a solid foundation. This is done by working first of all at the conscious level. This is the first step, the most important since it will have a bearing on the quality of our subsequent development work.

When we want to build a house, we make sure to build a good foundation before raising the walls; this is considered obvious in the physical world. The same goes for the world of consciousness, although we may think we can go about it any way we want to because it is less tangible. So we start working on our self, perhaps full of enthusiasm for the latest technique, yet without knowing exactly what we are doing. The results will end up the same as in the physical world: at best momentarily spectacular but short-lived and ultimately disappointing, or at worst downright destabilizing.

We have noted, in fact, that our practical observations match the more classic teachings of esoteric science. According to the Tibetan teacher, the first stages of spiritual development are the following:

- *character development;*
- *right motivation; and*
- *service.*

Then come six other levels (the fourth being meditation), which correspond to more specific work, but which can only be safe and effective if the first stages have been sufficiently integrated. These first three stages are the first basic step.

> *This work of imposing the higher vibration on the lower is character building, the first prerequisite upon the Path. [At this moment] the earnest student can begin to sum up his energy assets; he can tabulate the forces which he feels control his life, and thus arrive at a reasonable and truthful understanding of the forces which require to be subordinated and those which require to be strengthened. Then in the light of the true knowledge, let him go forward upon the path of his destiny.[2]*

Many seekers are unaware of this first step, and consequently end up getting lost in more or less sophisticated, often oriental techniques, that are all the more attractive because they are exotic, and going round and round in ever-deepening circles of illusion. To practice these techniques without having reached a high enough level of self-awareness is just a shot in the dark, and it ends up feeding our ego one way or another. Often, what is nurtured in such cases is either more or less obvious spiritual pride, or withdrawal. It takes a lot of humility, patience, and perseverance to focus our work simply on character development, as the Tibetan teacher calls it, which in our language translates into the development of soul-based control of the personality. This is perhaps the most difficult stage, as our ego refuses to play along with this, wanting instead to achieve spectacular and easy results so as to avoid having to truly let go of old habits and patterns; in the end, our ego is opposed to self-questioning, and yet this is an essential first step.

Based on my practical experience, I have observed that in order to build a solid foundation, to ensure that the first step is sufficiently integrated, it is good to work on the following three aspects simultaneously:

- begin by working on **developing awareness and self-knowledge** in terms of personality mechanisms and the presence of the soul. The more deeply this conscious knowledge is developed, the easier it will be to get through the next steps;

- **open a doorway to the energy of the Self;** and

- **put all of this into practice.**

If you have already moved ahead in your exploration of various techniques without having integrated these three aspects to a sufficient degree, it is better to backtrack and take care of the foundations before the house caves in, or you may end up stalled in your other work for a long time.

Let us now take a closer look at these three aspects.

Self Knowledge

There are several ways to approach this work. All the teachings we find in books, magazines, conferences, personal development seminars, spiritual teachings, as well as self-observation, stimulate inquiry and begin to pave the way to a more refined level of awareness. This knowledge may be more or less developed, as the case may be, but the fact remains that this is the way each of us begins to develop self-awareness and to ask questions on the meaning of life, instead of cruising on automatic pilot. At this level, developing an increasingly clear understanding of the human mechanism is an essential part of the work. There are now some excellent books and seminars, some reflecting age-old wisdom, some written by contemporary authors, and these are valuable sources of information to help us get to know our self better.

On the other hand, if we stick to a strictly intellectual understanding, we will remain unable to radiate and to manifest the qualities of the soul in concrete ways in everyday life. We may acquire a great deal of philosophical knowledge, but we will go on living as we always have. If we want to really integrate these teachings, we need to bring another dynamic into play.

First Contact with the Soul

For this reason, when I present this kind of knowledge in my seminars, I always combine this transfer of information with the potential for having a direct, free experience of the soul. This can be done in various ways, and I have mine: practical exercises, meditations, and symbolic processes that make the personality receptive to soul-generated energies.

Even at this first stage, as the soul's energy is activated, several latent qualities can already become available and actualised in our daily existence. At this level, many people recover a deep sense of inner peace; a capacity to un-dramatize situations; a sense of liberation from judgement (other people's and their own); a greater capacity for self-acceptance; better health; more energy; a capacity for love, humour and joy; and a much deeper sense of self—all of which bring a whole new level of meaning to their day-to-day life. All of these outcomes have nothing to do with magic: this is what happens when the energy of the Self becomes more active within a person. This is what transforms the quality of our life, rather than any reorganization of our external living conditions. In many personal development seminars, spiritual teachings and consciousness-raising sessions, this is a stage that many people experience with more or less clarity or distortion, as the case may be.

This stage corresponds to what is called the "first initiation", or "birth", in traditional esoteric teachings. The term "initiation" does not refer to anything mysterious. It simply means recognition that **a certain level of awareness has been reached.** This level is reached when a person becomes aware that he or she has this undeveloped potential, and chooses to engage in conscious inner work in order to develop that potential. It is usually characterized by **open heartedness and a desire to contribute,** which is simply the early manifestation and expression of the soul's energy. The Tibetan teacher describes this stage as follows:

> *The first initiation simply stands for commencement. A certain structure of right living, of thinking and of conduct has been attained. [It] marks the beginning of a totally new life and mode of living; it marks the commencement of a new manner of thinking, and of conscious perception. The life of the personality in the three worlds has for aeons nurtured the germ of this new life, and fostered the tiny spark of light within the relative darkness of the lower nature. ... The lives of initiates of the first initiation are beginning to be controlled by the Christ-consciousness, which is the consciousness of responsibility and service.*[3]

Many people are presently at this stage. Indeed there is a growing interest in everything referred to as "New Age", or spirituality, everywhere in the world. This is merely an expression of the fact that a vast number of people have reached the level of awareness of the first initiation, even if they have no idea that this is happening.

Consciousness in Action

The acquisition of a certain amount of knowledge is only useful if there is a conscious, simultaneous effort to put theory into practice. This is where real difficulties arise. This is why we need at least some soul energy input even at this stage, otherwise we run the risk of becoming discouraged with the magnitude of the task, or of remaining ensconced in our intellect in order to protect our self.

First of all, if we want to put our knowledge into practice in a conscious manner, we need to constantly cultivate a specific attitude: the witness stance.

The Witness Stance

Once we have gained enough knowledge of human mechanisms, if we want to gain some level of mastery over these mechanisms, we have to be able to observe our self, to adopt what is called the witness stance. This practice is recommended right from the start, in some form or another, in all spiritual traditions. This implies that we are open enough, sincere enough with our self, and courageous enough to recognize our own mechanisms and dare to face the truth about our self. On the other hand, it is very important to be able to make such observations without judgement, and with a great deal of love for our personality. This observation is not intended as a form of self-evaluation, but as a way to get to know our self better, beyond any "moral" judgement. This is not an easy attitude to maintain. We are so used to trying to be "good" (in order to be loved) that we are very afraid of looking at our self squarely in the face.

This witness stance has often been adulterated in some teachings, where we are taught a certain way that we should be, otherwise we are not being good. How can we dare to tell our self the truth in such a context?

Adopting this witness stance requires a great deal of respect and compassion for our self. If, through self observation, we discover that we are caught in a specific automatic pattern, it is important not to pass judgement on our self, but instead to rejoice at having uncovered one of our mechanisms and get on with the work of defusing these mechanisms. Recognizing our mechanisms is an indication that we are already on the path towards liberating our self from them: we are already halfway there. So we observe our self with love, understanding and humour. Everything we have seen regarding the mechanisms of the ego, as well as the history of consciousness, can help us maintain this non-judgemental witness stance. Indeed, we understand that, although we may not have reached perfection yet, it is not because we are mean or stupid; it is simply that we are involved in an normal process of evolution, with a great deal of suffering that still needs to be healed.

Daily Soul Practice

As we observe our mechanisms in action by taking the witness stance, we can already start to gain some level of control over them, to a certain extent, by putting into practice certain basic values that feel right to us: not moral values stemming from our cultural conditioning, but **values that we have freely chosen to reaffirm as being in synch with our own inner truth.**

Once we have become aware of some of our flawed behaviours, we can begin to try to consciously change these. There is no way around the fact that the roots of any negative or limiting behaviour go deep into the unconscious. We cannot expect therefore to be able to instantly shed some basic automatic responses simply because we have recognized them. In order to truly rid our self of these responses, we will need to work also on the unconscious and supraconscious levels. However, certain personality aspects can be worked on right away through conscious choices. We thus lay the groundwork for an eventual transformation at the two other levels, when the time is right. This level of good will also allows the soul to begin to manifest itself. We shall go over some of the aspects that we can approach directly, to a certain extent, through an act of conscious will. These are simple aspects, which anyone can recognize. Yet in a world that is now lacking certain basic value systems, it is good to go over some of these values. As we mentioned earlier, it may seem trivial to list these values, yet **if you put them into practice, you can begin to gain control over your lower mechanisms in your day-to-day life.** In order to facilitate this process, you can refer to the facts presented in Chapters 8 and 9 concerning the comparative functioning of the higher and lower mind.

Defuse the strategies of the lower mind, specifically:

Stop insisting on being right and imposing your point of view. As soon as you realize that you are playing this game, you just stop, plain and simple. This does not mean you do not have the right to have your own viewpoint and to express it, but you learn to do this while being ready to hear and to respect other people's viewpoints as well. Insisting on being right and imposing one's viewpoint is a very strong lower consciousness mechanism, which can manifest itself in very subtle ways. Through an act of conscious will, you can eventually gain control over this mechanism, and this is a great step in the right direction.

A practical suggestion: Observe every occasion when you find yourself thinking you are right and others are wrong. As you witness this dynamic, take a deep breath, call upon the energies of compassion and soul openness, and use the process of context modification as described in Chapter 9; if need be, you can clearly and simply communicate with the other person, without placing the other at fault, in a state of mind characterized by openness and mutual support.

A good course on communication can help in this respect.[4]

Develop flexibility in the face of change. Be attentive to your reactions when your world is rocked by unexpected upheavals. You can then consciously choose to be flexible and open, instead of getting caught up in the ego mechanism of resisting and closing up. This is real daily training, which can be very helpful in making lower mental mechanisms more flexible.

Tolerance: This naturally springs from a deeper understanding of oneself and others. Careful study, intelligent inquiry, and observation are all helpful in developing tolerance, as it is the expression of an open heart and an open mind. To this end, it is good to be with people who are very different from us (our ego does not like differences). *Travelling*, for instance (real travelling, not the materialistic and selfish tourist expeditions we usually associate with travelling), the kind of travelling that allows us to really come into contact with other cultures and other ways of looking at life, is very helpful to broaden our consciousness in this sense.[5]

The absence of destructive criticism: The tendency to criticize is deeply embedded in our collective consciousness, to the point where we often do not realize that we are criticizing someone: we think that we are right and that our perception is the only accurate way of seeing things! If we care to be vigilant with regard to the words we use, we might be astonished to realize how much negativity they carry.

As a conscious act, we can decide to stop all criticism.[6] All we need to do is to constantly maintain a witness stance so as to remain attentive to our words, and simply *shut up whenever some useless criticism is about to come out.* This may seem simple, but it is already quite an exercise in mastery over the mechanisms of our lower mind and of our emotional body. It is a conscious act that allows us to make sure the energy within us and around us is kept clear, thus fostering the expression of our soul.

By the same token, we will need to learn detachment in the face of criticism from others. Over-sensitivity to other people's criticism points to a lack of emotional mastery. Now this problem most often stems from powerful memories that have accumulated in our mental computer, and this is more difficult to resolve through an act of conscious will. This needs to be worked on at the unconscious level, using methods we will examine further on in this book. Gaining this kind of serene independence is a sign of psychological maturity.

Innocuousness and right speech: The absence of criticism is part of an even broader quality, that of innocuousness.

> But let him who so thinks practice that positive harmlessness which works out
> in right thought (because based on intelligent love), right speech (because gov-
> erned by self-control), and right action (because founded on an understanding
> the Law), and he will find that the attempt will call forth all the resources
> being and take much time to achieve.[7]

This is a far cry from any kind of spectacular technique, and ye
innocuousness leads to the development of such a pure heart t
instantly finds its way into our life.

Integrity, authenticity and sincerity: These are well-known q
we really practice in our daily life, will also create an inner sp
the manifestation of soul energy.

Good will: We have already mentioned good will as being one of the distinctive qualities of the soul. As we really try to understand what this quality involves and we make it part of our daily practice, we make it possible for our life to become enlightened.

A practical suggestion: We may, for example (just to try it out), choose a day when we will make a point of practicing good will, and observe how our personality reacts and in what circumstances this quality eludes us.

This quality will be particularly difficult to manifest if we happen to be caught in masochist or rigid structure. These two structures, with their strong component of dissatisfaction and arrogance, usually generate a permanent attitude of ill will. As a deliberate act of conscious choice, we can begin to defuse this mechanism and develop the habit of practicing good will.

> *Good will is the first attempt by man to express God's love. Its outcome on Earth will be peace. It is so simple and so practical that one fails to appreciate its force or its scientific and dynamic effect.*[8]

Humility: Goes together with impersonality. Our ego is always trying to make itself important, to play a role. In particular, as we progress along the Path, and we begin to build knowledge in certain areas and to develop certain powers, our ego may very quickly grab hold of this to play the role of a teacher, a saviour, or a resource person who helps others. This is in fact one of the temptations of power, and it is more and more prevalent as we progress along the path. From the outset, cultivating humility and true self-extension in the form of impersonality is a very beneficial practice in order to really access the pure energies of the soul. In fact, the purity of these energies is what eventually manifests as a genuine power to help others, essentially by allowing them to reclaim their own power.

Knowing how to choose what is essential: If we want to experience a genuine process of transformation, we need to pay more conscious attention to what we ᵊnd our energy on, in terms of time, money, and concrete actions in our day-
ʰife.

thoughtful, intelligent look at how we live our life, we can clearly
ᵗial and what is less so. This simple exercise makes it possible
ᶠ our true values. For though we may often subscribe to
b be surprised to note that our actions, *where we choose
crete terms,* do not necessarily reflect these values as a
not, we get wrapped up in routines, materialistic con-
ypnosis or emotional mechanisms, so that only a very
dedicated to what is essential.

th of us to define what is essential. Depending on our
e, it will be essential to experience life at the personal-
materialistic activities in keeping with ordinary collec-
ers, the main focus will be on studies, meditation,
us forms of inner inquiry, and the quality of the con-

tribution they bring to their professional activities. We do not all live by the same criteria. We simply need to become aware of the motivation that underscores our actions, in order to see whether we act in a manner that is consistent with our vision of the world. And, as we move ahead along the path, clearly what we see as being essential will change, as will our priorities. As we do this simple inner work, we are often surprised to note the many things we do unconsciously, often on the basis of our parents' behaviour or certain societal conditionings. Today our collective conditioning is very strong, as it is constantly being reinforced through the means of powerful media. It is of primary importance that we remove our self from this influence if we want to make clear and free choices as to what is true for us on the basis of our own values.

May I suggest that you ask yourself this question: What is really essential, what is really important to you, what do you treat as a priority? Everything you see as being important will become part of your conditioning. I can suggest one criterion, one among many, to distinguish what is essential from what is not: anything that can be eroded over time is not essential.

A practical suggestion: *Make an initial list of all the things you consider essential or important in your life, along with the fundamental values related to each of these things. Then make a second list describing all the things you spend your energy on, in your daily life, in terms of time, money, and creativity. Then compare the two lists. This comparison can help you come to some very interesting realizations, which may eventually lead to some changes in the way you live your life. From the outset, you can free yourself from certain automatic conditionings or from certain emotional mechanisms that limit your life and make it unsatisfactory; you can make more conscious choices and be more at peace with life.*

Mastering time management: Many people complain they have no time, and experience stress and frustration as a result. This did not seem to be a problem for previous generations. What is going on here? In fact, humankind is presently being tested in the area of emotional mastery, controlling desires. It is natural to

> We do not lack for time, we just have too many useless desires.

want to create and to contribute more, but when we experience frustrat[ion] because "we have no time", it is because the number of our desires is greater [than] our capacity to meet these desires; indeed it is because the ever-growing b[urden] of our desires has reached critical proportions. In a social context where [we are] continuously activated by the consumer machine and its push towards [instant] gratification, we are under constant pressure to have or to do more [and more] things. This collective conditioning actively feeds our emotional bod[y and] its desires. In order to liberate our self from this conditioning [there is an] unavoidable necessity of consciously choosing to focus on what i[s essential if we] want to have the time to live and to experience deep satisfaction [every] day, **what we need is not more time, but less desires at the** [source.] Michelangelo and Einstein did not have any more time av[ailable] any other mortal. They were subject to the same human constraints. What did they do with their time? They chose to focus on the essential.

In fact, what is essential is whatever serves the purposes of our soul, our creative and service-oriented activities. We need to ask our self the following question: How much time do I spend satisfying my personal desires, and how much time do I spend creating, contributing and serving?

More specifically, in the case of the masochist structure, time is seen as a source of complaints and as a cause for a sense of powerlessness. To get free of this dynamic, we can decide to take our fate into our own hands and consciously choose what we want to spend our time on. Our soul has given us a certain capital of hours to spend on this planet...what are we going to do with it?

A practical suggestion: As a way out of this impasse regarding time, rather than saying, "I didn't have time to do this thing," we can say, "I didn't take the time to do this thing." This constantly confronts us with our own choices. It then becomes easier to see how we organize our life. Is it focused on the essential?

We can also make a list of all the things we would like to do but that "we have no time for", and **choose to let go of certain desires.** *We choose those we can realistically meet, and take action. As for the others, we make our peace with them, and let go of them, which then allows us to live in peace.*

Simplicity: We can consciously choose to live as simply as possible, which will specifically result in bringing us back to what is essential.

Joy, contentment, gratitude: Joy is a fundamental quality of the soul. We can begin to develop this quality by cultivating a sense of contentment: simply choosing to *"see one's cup as being half full rather than half empty."* This is one way to perceive things that we can consciously choose to adopt.

Cultivate happiness, knowing that depression... and undue sensitiveness to the criticism of others leads to a condition wherein a disciple is almost useless. ...piness is based on confidence in the God within, a just appreciation of time, ...getfulness of self... Suffering comes as the lower self rebels. Control that ...inate desire, and all is joy.[9]

...heavily charged, joy will obviously elude us, as will many ...though we may make conscious efforts to manifest ...ed to work on our emotional healing, and on liberat- ...emories, in order to recover a kind of serene and pro- ...ot dependent on circumstances. Yet at this initial stage, ...or to this energy by consciously choosing our attitude.

...precious ally to help us along the path.[10] The more dis- ...e will bring us reasons to be dissatisfied. The more we ...life will bring us reasons to be thankful. This is just ...of energy happen to work.

A practical suggestion: Every morning, be thankful for every positive aspect of your life, being as specific as possible; also, think of all the people on this planet who do not have one tenth of what you have, and send them thoughts of love and light; put a sign up on the bathroom mirror saying, for example, "Today, I choose to be happy, and I am thankful for all that I have and for all that I am."

Detachment: This is more difficult to put into practice by an act of conscious choice, yet we can still succeed to a certain extent. Context changing, a dynamic described in Chapter 7, is very helpful as a first step towards experiencing detachment, in situations that are not too heavily charged emotionally.

Humour: If we pay attention to the way we think and talk, we catch our self fairly quickly whenever we fall into excessive seriousness and dramatisation. Practicing humour is a way to put things back in their proper place. It allows us to take the melodrama out of situations. People who are caught in masochist and oral structures especially need to cultivate this quality. We can all find "tricks" we can use to make our self laugh when things become overly dramatic.

The ability to use times of crisis in a positive way: Knowing how to make creative use of problems and crises instead of resisting them is a determining factor in our progress along the path. The following quote from Christiane Singer on this issue is right on the mark:

> *Along the way, I became convinced that catastrophes happen in order to preserve us from the worst. As for the worst, how could I express what is the worst? The worst is actually going through life without shipwrecks, always just skimming the surface of everything, dancing in a hall of shadows, staying mired in the marshlands of hearsay, of appearances, never being thrown into another dimension. Crises, in the kind of society we live in, are actually the best we could come up with (unless we happen to have a perfect teacher on hand), to gain access to another dimension. In our society, we put all our ambition and all our concentration on turning our attention away from what is important... This is an enormous conspiracy, the most gigantic conspiracy of a civilization against our soul, against our spirit. In such a society, where we are bound up in every way, where there are no road signs to guide us to a deeper realm, all we have is crises to break down the walls standing all around us.* [11]

We can take great strides towards the light of our soul just by accepting our daily trials, from the chronic to the most intense, as a teaching and an opportunity for growth that life brings our way.

A practical suggestion: In order to meet problems in a constructive, dynamic way, we can choose to remove the word "problem" from our vocabulary, since it is very negatively charged, and replace it with the word "opportunity".

This change in vocabulary is not unwarranted. It represents a fundamental change in attitude whereby we move away from ego resistance and towards the creative power of the Self. Indeed, when we stop resisting our problems, and instead we welcome and face them as being opportunities life brings our way so that we can develop certain qualities, we gain access to a number of inner resources to solve these problems. Doing this is actually an essential step towards freeing our self from the constraints of ego mechanisms, which block our access to the power of our soul by reinforcing our attachment to the path of least resistance and effort.

Welcoming difficulties with serenity and using them as opportunities for personal growth is not necessarily always an easy thing to do, especially when these difficulties come with a heavy burden of strong emotional charges. The principle of responsibility-attraction-creation, as presented in my previous book, can be used as an effective consciousness-building tool to facilitate this process of acceptance and thus enable us to begin to recover our power.

Giving up inertia: We have seen how our ego hates difficulties, always seeking a "problem free" existence with maximum returns for the least amount of effort. It is a well-known fact among spiritual traditions that one of the forces impeding our progress along the path of transformation is the force of inertia, also referred to as "tamas". We will certainly be called upon to struggle with this dynamic, and this will indeed require the exercise of will power. Easy solutions have never led anywhere. If we hope to move ahead along the path doing whatever we want, whenever we want to, all we are doing is living as falling leaves blowing whichever way our emotional winds take us. Mastering the force of inertia is tackling one of the most limiting of all ego forces.

Remember, the context of our daily existence is where we are tested and trained to gain mastery over our personality through the teachings of life, not just through our moments of meditation or whatever specific exercises we may practice.

A practical suggestion: In fact any activity requiring regular practice (playing the recorder, jogging, trapeze arts, archery) can do the trick; stick to the practice, no matter what, especially when you don't feel like it; practice any form of discipline in order to train yourself to overcome the force of inertia, and perhaps extend yourself in service to others.

Exercising will power: We went over this point, in part, in the course of Chapter 10. It is indeed easy to see how we need to exercise will power in order to use the above mentioned practices successfully, and we need to temper that will with flexibility, intelligence and love, as we have previously seen. Without will power, no amount of progress is possible.

Besides these soul qualities that we can put into practice on a daily basis, there is one aspect of human activity especially that we can use as a **powerful instrument of transformation...practicing selfless service.**

The Spirit of Service

It is curious to note that this theme is not often included in personal development programs, except perhaps partially in certain spiritual practices, and mainly in the form of service to a master or to a specific community, rather than as the development of the spirit of service no matter where one happens to be. And yet service is a fundamental aspect of the kind of inner work that will have to take place along with every other phase of development. Any service activity reinforces the presence of the soul as it liberates us from ego limitations. No matter what spiritual teaching or course we choose to follow, offering service from the perspective of the soul will speed us on our way to a high level of spiritual realisation. The healing and transforming power of service is very strong, and yet we hear so little about it: that is because the ego does not like to serve and finds it difficult to reclaim this activity to its own advantage.[12]

> Service is the crucible where the work of forging the personality can be performed with the greatest degree of effectiveness, in order to receive the light of the soul.

Service, in and of itself, definitely stems from an extraordinary inner event, and when we see this outcome, it is a sign that a number of secondary creative wellsprings have also been generated. First of all, it points to a change in one's lower consciousness, a tendency to turn away from things related to our personal selves and to move towards broader group problems, a genuine, outwardly expressed change in orientation, and a new-found potential for changing one's living conditions (through creative activity) that is evidence of something dynamically new. The first perceivable effect of the power of the soul arising, which is a major factor leading to the manifestation of service, is to integrate the personality and to unite each of the three lower aspects of a human being into one whole being destined to serve.[13]

Obviously what we are talking about here is service that is freely chosen, rather than service as sacrifice. If we serve as free beings taking full responsibility for our choice, the energy of our soul is strongly activated and it speeds up the process of inner transformation. Soul energy is a reality, and when we begin to experience it by activating it through service, we sense the full extent of the good that it does, not just inwardly, but in all our activities. This is when auspicious "coincidences" happen, or appropriate support turns up at the right time, and possibilities for fulfilment begin to multiply.

> Service offered in a free and disinterested manner is sometimes more valuable than months of therapy or self-centred "spiritual practice".

I was asleep, and I dreamt that life is joy.
I awakened, and saw that life is service.
I served, and saw that service is joy.
—*R. Tagore*

Let us note that serving does not necessarily mean acting like Mother Theresa. It is a **state of being** that one can experience in any kind of work or activity. Whether we are teachers, bakers, engineers, artists, business people, housewives, no matter what our activities may be, we can perform our tasks while remaining caught up in ego mechanisms, or we can do them to manifest the creative and beneficial power of our soul in a spirit of service. The choice is ours, and the consequences follow suit. In fact, as in all other areas, **what counts is not the external form of action we take, but the motivation that underscores our action.** So it is not necessary to engage in so-called "spiritual" activity in order to serve. Indeed, these so-called spiritual activities are often reclaimed by the ego, and do not lead to any genuine form of service. Engaging in a simple, unassuming, not necessarily recognized form of activity, where we are genuinely serving, is a far more reliable demonstration of the presence of soul energy.

> Any activity can be considered "spiritual" if it enables us to love and to serve our fellow human beings.

True service, without personal agendas or expectations, at work, at home, in a community project, or through some global contribution, makes it possible for the ego to disengage itself in a fundamental way from all of its mechanisms. It is **a major means of self-transformation.**

With each step along the path, each healing process, each new level of awareness that is integrated into our daily existence, a change in consciousness takes place, raising our vibrational frequency. When we have had the privilege of raising our vibrational frequency, all we are required to do is to serve even more and to extend our self in a spirit of simplicity and love. Our responsibility for our own and the world's evolution increases. This is no time to rest on our laurels: the more we manifest our potential, the more demanding our work becomes. **A high level of vibrational frequency is anything but a passport to a more comfortable life, but it can make this life more useful.**

And what else?

I could comment on a number of other qualities worth cultivating in order to foster the emergence of the Self. In so doing, I would be covering all the qualities described in all spiritual teachings. This would appear to lack originality. In a materialistic, licentious, and easy-going society, where the most beautiful values are often ridiculed, all this may seem like moralistic nagging. Yet the fact that these same things have been repeated over and over for centuries should alert us to their undying truth.

If we find our self reacting to that, it is because these values have often been presented in the form of good and evil, which led to a great deal of repression and guilt. As we get to know the mechanisms of human nature, in its lower and higher aspects, and understand the grand journey towards consciousness that humankind is engaged in, we find that this perspective confers far more genuine and vibrant meaning to these values. We can then see a far deeper meaning to life, where such values are naturally integrated.

We all know the qualities of the soul, and if we are aware enough to get past the cynicism that plagues our contemporary world, we want to manifest these in our life: love, wisdom, centeredness, peace, joy, energy, freedom, etc. As a first step, we can then strive to put them into practice through an act of conscious will, even though this may be far from easy. For this reason it is important, right from the start, to give our self an opportunity to experience an initial contact with the soul, as we mentioned earlier. Purely theoretical teachings are generally not enough to cause a definitive change in the way we handle our self in daily situations. On the other hand, clear guidance combined with some form of contact with the soul will enable us to start manifesting the qualities of the Self to a certain extent. From that moment on, we can get a sense of our progress along the path to self-discovery and self-mastery. Yet this will not make our life any easier, for a number of difficulties are likely to arise at that stage. It is essential to know that our inner work can and should be combined with another aspect, if we want to avoid getting stuck along the way.

Problems Encountered in the First Step

The next step: the need to clear up the unconscious

Indeed we soon come to realize that, despite these fine principles, there seems to be a mountain separating our stated ideal and the way we handle our self on a daily basis. We know, for example, that practicing unconditional love will make us free and blissful. Yet we often find our self unable to experience that in our personal relationships; we catch our self being jealous, dependant or domineering. We know that we are supposed to stay calm and centred under any circumstance, and yet it still happens that our horse goes out of control and we lose our temper. We understand that it is good to serve, yet we have no desire to do so. We know how important it is to keep an open mind, yet we still get caught in the mechanism of the need to be right. We know many things, and at this stage we do our best to conduct our self as much as possible so as to promote harmony, yet we note that a part of us is putting up a strong resistance, despite our best intentions. Old memories resurface, and our unconscious defence patterns deprive us of our freedom. All aspects of our life are affected: difficult relationships, low levels of energy, negative emotions, poor health, or limited creativity. Peace, joy and the capacity for positive outreach keep eluding us despite the fact that we know so much and are putting in so much effort.

Many people stop at this stage, and continually stumble on resistance stemming from their personality. This is where it is important to understand the process, to know that these problems are to be expected along the path, and that **we must initiate the next step**, which is to clear up the unconscious.

Yet all this conscious preparation is far from lost. Combined with the initial soul contact we have been given to experience, it will constitute a solid basis on which to start working on the unconscious. If this stage is not integrated to a sufficient extent, we run the risk of facing further difficulties. This is often what happens when individuals seeking increased inner well-being initially turn their attention to working on the unconscious, generally through the great variety of "healing" or "purification" techniques offered on the New Age market. If this is approached as a process focused purely on the personality level, it will have a limited impact and there is nothing wrong with that. On the other hand, if we apply these techniques in the context of a more in-depth process, we may encounter some serious difficulties.

Indeed, as we begin to work on the unconscious, old wounds and painful experiences are reactivated, and if we really want to work at a deeper level, it is of primary importance that we integrate both of the above mentioned aspects:

- **consciousness development work,** whereby we can come to understand the mechanisms we want to free our self from; and

- **a fairly solid connection with the soul,** as described earlier, from which we can draw maximum inner strength and constancy to face the momentary storms that may emerge from the unconscious.

While we pointed out the ineffectiveness, or even the danger, of getting involved in seemingly advanced "spiritual" techniques without the benefit of solid groundwork, we must also emphasize the importance of engaging in the various aspects of conscious work, and of reinforcing the energy of the Self, *before we start working on the unconscious.* Many people of good will, in their effort to liberate themselves from old stuff from the past, will launch into direct healing practices focused on the past without this preparation at the conscious and supraconscious levels, and end up either facing serious problems or being stuck in some way without understanding why. What they lack is this inner strength and clarity that would enable them to deal with the powerful undercurrents of the unconscious. Generally speaking, when that happens, their defence systems are reinforced for the sake of self-protection, and the work becomes more and more difficult. The problem does not necessarily have to do with the method, but with a lack of preparation.

There is no question that it is necessary to clean up the basement as well as the rest of the house; otherwise the upper levels may be infested with odours, insects and decay. The foundations may sustain water damage due to rusty plumbing. Though we may change the wallpaper every year, it will keep getting unglued due to the humidity rising from the basement. In other words, no matter how much good will we want to exercise on a conscious level, it is not easy to constantly maintain a soul-inspired conduct in our day-to-day life. We will need to clear away our old memories from the past in order to live a more liberated, soul-illuminated life. This is what we need to do at the second stage. But we have to be ready!

Indeed, in order to clean up the basement of the house, before we empty its contents and bring it all up to the first floor, we must make sure that we clear away some space on that floor, and that we have adequate cleaning apparatus and appropriate tools for any needed repair work. Otherwise, the whole house will be cluttered with old dusty rubbish, rats may turn up along the way, and we may end up finding our house quite uncomfortable, even more uncomfortable than before. It is therefore necessary to make sure that the rest of the house is ready to absorb the momentary impact of this clean-up operation. This is the purpose of the first stage of the work as we have just described.

These two points, in fact, are often ignored in many practices that focus on healing the past, and this is why these practices are at best lengthy and inefficient. We need only to think of the decades it takes under conventional psychoanalysis to clear up certain aspects of the unconscious, a process that can take only a few hours, or days or at most a few months, using more modern methods in an appropriate context of awareness. Or, if other more modern and more powerful methods involving direct work on the unconscious are used without adequate preparation, they can be destabilizing and leave a person feeling even more at loose ends than before. The more powerful the method used, the more important it is to take these preliminary precautions.

On the other hand, once our conscious work and our connection with the Self have been established to a sufficient degree, we can engage both safely and efficiently in this second stage, involving a more direct clearing of the unconscious.

---

[1] We have mentioned that any process of inner work may be considered as a way to bring the unconscious in contact with the conscious mind, and the supraconscious with the conscious mind. This indeed amounts to liberating our consciousness from the grips of the unconscious, and to creating the potential for a concrete and conscious manifestation of the transcendental qualities of the soul on the ordinary, worldly plane, which then becomes an extraordinary world. We thus go far beyond the sole aspect of personal growth aimed at coping better with the world as it is, as we strive to attain complete fulfilment so that our true being can express itself totally.

[2] Alice Bailey, *A Treatise on White Magic,* page 203.

[3] Alice Bailey, *Ponder on This,* pages 206–208.

[4] Among others, Jacques Salomé's books and conferences provide very valuable insights along these lines.

[5] By the way, please note that any one of our daily activities can be used for the purpose of spiritual training, if we are willing. A trip abroad, for instance, can be an occasion for opening

one's consciousness in a big way, or it can be a form of withdrawal and stuffing. It all depends on the state of mind we are in at each moment of our life, and on the nature of our intention.

6 This does not refer to constructive criticism, which is always expressed quietly and directly to the person concerned, without emotional turmoil, in a spirit of contribution and good will. Destructive criticism is never aimed at the right people. All it does is to feed negativity and our ego-need to justify our self and to be right.

7 Alice Bailey, *A Treatise on White Magic,* Lucis Trust, page 317.

8 Id., *The Problems of Humanity,* Lucis Trust.

9 Alice Bailey, *Initiation Human and Solar,* page 76.

10 The oral and masochist aspects of the personality, which we described in Volume 1, will block access to this energy, which is nevertheless highly beneficial.

11 Translated from Christiane Singer, *Du bon usage des crises,* éd. Albin Michel.

12 It can still do it, as we have seen earlier, for there are obvious advantages (mostly in the oral and psychopath character structures). But if the service is of a totally disinterested kind, the ego prefers to abstain.

13 Alice Bailey, *Esoteric Psychology, Vol. II.*

chapter 12

Mastery of the Emotional Body

WORKING ON THE UNCONSCIOUS, HEALING THE PAST MOVING TOWARDS THE SECOND INITIATION

Features of the Second Step

No matter what good results we may have had in the course of the first step, once the transformation process has been set in motion, we can be sure that our ego will raise its head, and in particular, that all the emotional charges buried in our past will resurface. Taken by surprise, our old mechanisms will want to reclaim lost ground. This explains why, after a marvellous period of awakening based on a broader understanding of our self and a deeper than usual soul connection, we will often be confronted with violent emotional storms, periods of doubt, emotional fears and torn up feelings that make us question the validity of our work. **It is very important to know that this dynamic is part of a normal process, and to understand why this is happening.** Otherwise, we begin to worry and we may give up on the whole idea, thinking that our progress to date has led nowhere, or may even have made things worse.

• **Moving toward the second initiation**

According to esoteric tradition, once the first initiation is passed, once the first step has been integrated to a sufficient degree, the seeker's task consists of purifying and mastering his or her emotional nature. This level of mastery will lead to an inner state described as being the second initiation stage, also referred to symbolically as a "baptism". This is known to be the most difficult stage along the path for most average human beings.

> The initiatory process between the first and second initiations, is for many the worst time of distress, difficulty, realisation of problems, and the constant effort to "clear himself", to which the disciple is at any time subjected. ... The storm aroused by his emotional nature, the dark clouds and mists in which he constantly walks, and which he has created throughout the entire cycle of incarnated living, have all to be cleared away in order that the initiate can say that—for him—the astral plane no longer exists, and that all that remains of that ancient

and potent aspect of his being, is aspiration, a sensitive response to all forms of divine life, and a form (the physical body) through which the lowest aspects of divine love, goodwill, can flow without impediment.[1]

It is of the utmost importance to know what to expect at this stage of the journey. This is where we will be tempted to the deepest recess of our being. This is where the greatest doubts and the greatest fears will emerge and we will be left to our self to constantly affirm and reaffirm our choice to move ahead towards the light. Knowing the meaning of these trials and their place in the transformation process makes it a lot easier to persevere in spite of these difficulties. Also, the fact of having made that initial contact with the presence of the soul, during the first stage, gives us the strength to go through all the inner trials that will turn up one after the other during this stage of gaining emotional mastery.

Many people today have reached the first initiation, and are now struggling along this difficult part of the journey. As we can see, at this stage we are far from the promises of easy fulfilment offered by many personal development philosophies. Not that these are useless; they are part of the first stage. It is simply important to know that our evolution does not end at that stage, and that sooner or later, the life force will propel us onward so that we move towards a richer and more complete manifestation of our soul.

In order to gain a better understanding of what goes on over this stretch of the path, let us go over certain aspects of the transformation process, which will show up especially during this stage.

• The cyclical nature of the process: expansion and contraction

These difficulties along the path will show up in a very specific manner. Indeed, personal development does not occur in a linear fashion, and we find our self dealing alternatively with moments when all is well and moments that seem more like an ordeal.

In accordance with the laws of nature, the transformation process follows the law of ebb and flow, of **expansion and contraction.** A period of expansion, where everything seems to be coming up roses, will invariably be followed by a period of contraction, where everything appears to lose meaning. It is important not to resist these periods, for they are part of the process itself and are essential steps leading to the integration of soul energies into the personality.

One of the reasons for this cyclical aspect is that, from the moment a seeker has declared his or her intention to achieve transformation, the soul begins to send waves of energy to the personality, and *this happens in a cyclical manner.* When we receive the light of the soul, this at first creates a sense of opening up and a beautiful experience of life: this is the expansion phase. But after a while the ego is reactivated and resists: this is the contraction phase. During this time of contraction, the ego replays all its mechanisms to the fullest: hence the pain, uncertainty, doubts, fears, and confusion. Yet, at the same time, it is also a time when the personality integrates this newly received dose of soul energy. So this time is important, and it is not without purpose, even though it can be arduous. Once this integration has taken place, the soul will send another wave of energy to the personality, which leads to another period of expansion that will be greater than the previous one. This explains why our "inner demons" resurface just when we are seeking inner peace; or why, after a period of clarity and certainty, we find our self in the shadow of doubt. The soul gives the ego time to react with its mechanisms and then be more prepared to let in a little more of its light with each new cycle. Thus the personality is able to integrate more and more of the light of the soul.

Those difficult periods of contraction should therefore be welcomed as essential periods when we let in and integrate all that was received during the expansion phase. This is often the point where people become discouraged and quit the process, thinking they have failed and that their efforts have been fruitless, that transformation is an unattainable or utopian goal. It is good to be forewarned, and to know how to recognise such periods so as to be able to go through them in relative peace and tranquillity, without trying to force anything, knowing that a period of greater expansion will come in due time. This requires higher and higher levels of mastery, and sustained effort. We are a far cry from the easy promises of certain simplistic theories that feed the expectation that the more we work on our self, the easier and more comfortable our life will become. We will certainly not find comfort on the path to transformation; we will, however, find far more valuable treasures.

The soul's meditation is rhythmic and cyclic in its nature as is all else in the cosmos. The soul breathes and its form lives thereby... There is an ebb and flow in all nature, and in the tides of the ocean we have a wonderful picturing of an eternal law. As the aspirant adjusts himself to the tides of the soul life he begins to realise that there is ever a flowing in, a vitalising and a stimulating which is followed by a flowing out as sure and as inevitable as the immutable laws of force... However, these cyclic impulses in the life of the disciple are of a greater frequency and speed and forcefulness than in the life of the average man. They alternate with a distressing rapidity. The hill and valley experience of the mystic is but one way of expressing this ebb and flow. Sometimes the disciple is walking in the sunlight and other times in the dark; sometimes he knows the joy of full communion and again all seems dull and sterile; his service is on occasion a fruitful and satisfying experience and he seems to be able to really aid; at other times he feels that he has naught to offer and his service is arid and apparently without results. All is clear to him some days and he seems to stand on the mountaintop looking out over a sunlit landscape, where all is clear to his vision. He knows and feels himself to be a Son of God. Later, however, the clouds seem to descend and he is sure of nothing, and seems to know nothing... and wonders how long this uneven experience and the violent alternation of these opposites is to go on.

Once however that he grasps the fact he is watching the fact of the cyclic impulses and the effect of the soul's meditation upon his form nature, the meaning becomes clearer and he realises that it is that form aspect which is fail-ing in its response, and re-acting to energy with unevenness. He then learns that once he can live in the soul consciousness and attain that "high altitude" (if I might so express it) at will, the fluctuations of the form life will not touch him. He then perceives the narrow-edged razor path, which leads from the plane of physical life to the soul realm, and finds that when he can tread it with steadi-ness it leads him out of the ever-changing world of the senses into the clear light of day and into the world of reality.[2]

Saint John of the Cross talks about the "dark night of the soul". While we want to avoid over-dramatising, we must simply be aware that if we are truly interest-ed in receiving the energy of the soul and spreading it around in our world, this will require constant will power and persistent effort. On the other hand, if we hang on, our efforts will be rewarded, and we will recover the power and freedom that are our birthright.

This impression we get sometimes of not moving ahead along the path is also due to the fact that the transformation process occurs not just in a cyclical man-ner, but also in the form of a spiral. We work on certain aspects of our personal-ity to the extent possible given where we are in terms of awareness at any given moment, and then we move on to other things, to another level on the spiral. And so, later on, we will find our self apparently in the same general area as the ini-tial point we were working on, but we are dealing with it at a higher level. We are not necessarily aware of this reality, and it seems to us that problems we thought were dealt with are resurfacing once again. At that point, it is good to know that we are not exactly at the same place, and that we are in a position to work far more deeply on whatever turns up.

- **Solitude**

Another aspect we are likely to be confronted with at this particular point of the journey is solitude. Indeed, when the Self begins to be manifested, our values change, our way of looking at life changes. We may then find our self out of synch with the "ordinary" world, which, by the way, is not the "real" world; it is the world of illusion, of separation and of fear; it is the world created through lower consciousness. The real world, the world beyond the lower mind's illusions, is the world of the soul, from which we can see reality as it is. Nevertheless, when we begin to see through the mists of illusion, we may experience a temporary sense of separation from our familiar environment, if the latter does not harmonise with that same vibration. This experience of separation is not a negative thing. It is in fact **a test of our emotional mastery,** in terms of authenticity, inner truth-fulness, and detachment. It leads to the realisation of ever higher levels of love, contribution, and service. This time of apparent solitude is also a time when peo-ple, with whom we have a connection at the soul level, rather than at the personality level, begin to cross our path. We then reconnect with the right people to travel with on our way to a more complete manifestation of the essence of who we are.

• Acceptance of non-recognition

For those more advanced along the journey, those whose lives have turned to service as the primary form of activity, forsaking the rush to meet the needs of the personality (in both material and affective terms), another test will inevitably turn up.[3]

This desire to contribute stemming from the will of the soul is not always easy to manage from the point of view of the personality. Indeed, the latter is always on the lookout for a little more approval and love, and is likely to expect some form of recognition for whatever service is rendered. This recognition will not necessarily come, in fact the opposite may happen. One of the major tests for the authenticity of one's service is to be able to offer this service without concern for the recognition that may or may not be forthcoming.

Very often, in fact, our inner light is a disturbing factor, and we can expect to encounter criticism, lack of understanding, defamation and ingratitude. This is the test whereby a seeker can measure how far he or she has come in terms of emotional mastery, freedom, and the capacity for unconditional love. This is a tough test to pass, for at this stage, we are called upon to give without getting anything in return from the outside. The soul is the only place where we can find the strength and love required for true service. It is our only recourse. But it is also a safeguard for the authenticity of our inner work and the quality of our contribution. Being aware of the fact that this constitutes a major test along the path allows us to avoid falling prey to discouragement, and to continue to move ahead, no matter what adverse reactions we may get from our environment.

> *And do not be afraid of serving an ungrateful master. Offer him even more service.*
> *And in his place, let me be the one indebted to you, for then you will know that each minute,*
> *each additional service you render will always come back to you.*
> —*Og Mandino*

❖ ❖ ❖

As we become aware of the difficulties of the journey, let us not get discouraged. On the contrary, this awareness should allow us to get through the difficulties with greater strength and perseverance. *At that first piano lesson, a student may be discouraged with the size of the task, and all there is to be learnt and the efforts this will require. Yet if he is confident, if his motivation is strong and if, with proper support, he practices regularly no matter what mood he is in, then one day he will gain mastery in an area that, years before, seemed unattainable.*

The same goes for the path that leads to mastery of the personality. If we hang on and stay the course along this part of the journey, which may seem quite bumpy at times, we realise in the long run that we are gaining more and more mastery over our lower nature, that we can go even deeper in our inner work, and especially that we have the power to offer ever more authentic and beneficial forms of service to those around us. This has been my observation over the years as I have helped people go through this deep cleansing process.

As difficult as this period may seem to us, we must never lose sight of the fact that we have what it takes to get through it, by working directly on clearing away old memories. For, as we have seen in the course of this book, it is these memories that account for our lack of emotional mastery, to a large extent, and this stage of the journey is mostly about emotional liberation. This aspect of the work was often lacking in many spiritual disciplines, where one put a great deal of good will into practising soul values, yet without any direct method to clear away old memories. The emotional charges laying in the unconscious would then jump out at the bewildered disciple who didn't quite know what to do about these inner "demons". This is why the work dragged on and seemed so difficult, why it generated a great deal of guilt, and was ultimately achieved by only a few highly motivated or more spiritually advanced individuals. This purification process would span lifetimes, and required the presence of an individual Master who had the knowledge and could provide step-by-step guidance to the disciple. For a long time, it was appropriate that things would evolve in this manner. These days, however, as the average level of consciousness and mental development of human beings has reached a higher level, it is possible to clear up the unconscious more quickly, using effective approaches along with appropriate knowledge, as long as *we remain in contact with the inner Master, and continue to integrate all of the aspects of the first stage.*[4]

Being aware of the necessity to work on the shadow at the same time as we seek to find the light, and having a more specific understanding of the mechanisms of the unconscious, we can find effective methods to liberate the emotional charges buried in the unconscious, and thus facilitate our access to the light of the Self.

Clearing Up the Individual Unconscious

Personal Healing

◆ **Working at the Energy Level—General Principles**

Since the time of Sigmund Freud, whose efforts were aimed at gaining access to the unconscious through verbal channels, we have come to realise that the deeper levels of the unconscious responded poorly, albeit not at all, to conscious or semi-conscious verbal approaches. For this reason, seekers turned to "energetic" approaches, for psychological blocks have an energetic counterpart. By working at the energetic level, we can clear away psychological blocks that would otherwise remain inaccessible.

Energy and consciousness are indeed closely linked. When we transform our consciousness, our vibrational frequency rises and the quality of our energy changes. When we change and improve the quality of our energy, our consciousness changes. This, however, does not imply that the two are interchangeable.

A Golden Rule

One essential reality that should not be forgotten in the course of any work at the energetic level is that **energy follows thought.** The moment we change our energetic state, we need to be aware that the latter will tend to be shaped according to the thoughts that come with it. This may seem like an obvious remark, yet it is of vital importance in order to ensure the safety and effectiveness of any energetic process. We shall go over this again a little further on in this book.

There are a multitude of approaches now available for this type of work, some more effective than others, working at a more or less deep level.

As far as I am concerned, I have chosen to work with the breath at the initial stage. In the course of more than twenty years of practice, I have observed that a certain breathing technique, used with caution in an appropriate context and in conjunction with certain other conditions for advanced work, makes it possible to clear away old memories safely and effectively.

Working with the breath is a technique that has been around for thousands of years to foster the development of consciousness. This work has many facets, and it is not my purpose to go into this in detail. I will simply mention some of its principles, as an example, as well as the effects I have observed with regard to working on the unconscious.

I use two types of techniques: simple breathing for basic work, and breathing in combination with other types of energy, for more advanced work.

◆ The Power of the Breath

My experience with breath work started more than thirty years ago with yoga. I had already observed the impact of breath control on one's state of awareness. Then, like many other people, I became involved in the Rebirthing movement that started in the seventies and spread like a tidal wave in the world of personal growth. Many inquisitive people of good will began to breathe, without really knowing what they were getting into. I witnessed marvellous experiences, incredible journeys, and miracles, but also some rather unpleasant casualties that gave the technique a bad name. Some more or less inspired theories were associated with this practice, and in the end everyone was doing whatever felt right, each and everyone believing theirs was the only way. This mess was not necessarily a bad thing: it was a creative mess. Nature rarely creates in an orderly fashion. The creative process usually occurs in a state of disorder that allows an old order to be transformed into a new order. So without dwelling on the weaknesses of this movement, I shall focus on its positive aspects, which many people were able to use to great benefit. Other seekers, including Stanislav Grof, have their own way of using the breath as a technique to access the unconscious. So this is a basic technique that is familiar to many people.

As far as my approach to the unconscious is concerned, I begin with a specific, relatively simple way of breathing, "rebirth breathing". A professionally trained guide individually monitors the person breathing. It is important to have appropriate guidance at this first stage. This phenomenon is well-known among therapists who work with the unconscious, regardless of the method used: without guidance, the breathing experience may eventually be pleasant (though not always), but it is certainly of little effect in terms of any in-depth defusing of old memories. For our unconscious refuses to reveal itself to us; the ego insists on maintaining control. The presence of a competent, positive guide brings an energy level that supports the person's conscious intention. The role of the guide is to support the individual as he or she moves along the path that naturally takes shape through his or her individual process. The true guide is the Self of the person with whom we have initially made contact. The guide will have to be able to stay in tune with the inner process occurring in the person being guided, so as not to interfere with the process and simply input the required energy through his or her presence and through appropriate interventions.

I do not bring in any other factors at this initial stage. This is very important in order to allow the person to work on *his/her own energy with his/her own energy* in a way that is both safe and autonomous. This is the beauty and the power of this process. There is no outside intervention to direct the experience, either in the form of a person or some kind of technology. The experience must take place as naturally and organically as possible.

This works very well and is very effective, as all we are doing, in fact, is reactivating a natural process of self-healing. Nature knows what it's doing, and it has given us a natural capacity to clear away old hurts through our breath. When we know how to use this capacity, with appropriate monitoring, we get all the power and wisdom of nature working for us.

So this is a process whereby a person can work autonomously. The work is done through his/her own intention and his/her own energy. One might think that outside intervention could speed up and force the process along. My experience has shown that this serves no purpose. The results I get are more "ecological", in the sense of respecting the individual's integrity, and ultimately far more profound and durable. There can be no power play between the person undergoing the experience and the person acting as a guide. In addition, this ensures a high level of safety, as the person does only what he or she is capable of doing, in terms of energy level and awareness.

This technique is as old as the world. It may look simple, technically speaking. Yet mastering the process itself is far more demanding than it may appear at first glance. In oriental teachings, the more advanced breathing practices could only be done under the supervision of an enlightened master, and for good reason. It takes thorough knowledge of the dynamics involved, and of the safety measures to be taken in order to use this approach safely and appropriately. This, as far as we are concerned, is why we train professionals to provide adequate guidance at this stage. Otherwise, one might be playing with fire.

• The Application of the Golden Rule

Earlier on, I mentioned the golden rule: energy follows thought. We need to observe this rule particularly when doing breath work. Indeed, this work triggers some activity within the individual's energetic system. This energetic activity must not be left to chance. "Energy follows thought", so we must pay close attention to the thought context in which we carry out such experiences. For this reason, the **quality of the experience depends on the thought context** in which it takes place. If our thought is not clearly aligned with the manifestation of the soul, then we witness what amounts to chaotic emotional stirring, and the process amplifies emotional charges instead of defusing them. We have seen people who, after a number of breathing sessions, found themselves in an obvious state of emotional disorientation. Doing breath work without first defining a broad enough thought context can lead to many difficulties.[5]

This is why, before starting the actual breath work (and generally working on the unconscious, regardless of the method used), I suggest that people first experience the first stage, as I defined it in the preceding chapter. This allows us to clarify our thinking, to test the strength of our intention, and to ensure a sufficient level of self-knowledge and contact with our inner being so that the experience will be safe and effective.

When appropriate preparation has been followed, and breath work is approached in a manner that is conscious, well-mastered, and adapted to each individual, the results obtained are impressive. It is indeed a very direct means of liberating the unconscious.

As far as I am concerned, I have chosen to work with sane, well-balanced people who are involved in a growth process. This has allowed me to observe very clearly the process of clearing away old memories. In light of the results I get, it seems obvious to me that breath work could be used in other branches of psychology, or even psychiatry, with significant benefits. But air is free, while prescription drugs generate fortunes for pharmaceutical companies. In addition, this process is aimed at making people autonomous, which is not in everyone's best interest. I am nevertheless drawing attention among inquisitive and open-minded doctors and psychiatrists who want to develop new healing methods, and I invite them to explore this approach.

As my focus is not on therapy but on consciousness development among "normal" people who are already open, I will describe the type of results that can be obtained at this level, while others, who wish to innovate in their area of specialisation, may want to extend the method to more therapeutic applications.

The Results

The results are a direct outcome of clearing away unconscious blocks stemming from the past. They therefore show up concretely as a liberation from various automatic reactions that were limiting to an individual, whether they are physical or psychological, conscious or unconscious.

At the Physical Level

To begin with, I regularly observe recoveries from chronic illnesses after one or two weekends of this experience. A very great number of people thus find themselves free of such ailments as psoriasis, back pains, chronic migraine headaches spanning years, asthma, constipation, digestive problems, etc. I have recently seen several cases of fibromyalgia cleared up by more than eighty percent. When we consider how painful this illness can be, and how much of a handicap it can be for those affected, as well as how powerless conventional medicine seems to be with regard to this "illness", it is encouraging to know that other helpful methods exist. This is not theory, but concrete results. But, once again, these methods are inexpensive and do not translate into profits for the system in place.

These physical recoveries are a very sensitive issue. I would never claim that breath-rebirth is a cure for everything or that it is a substitute for medical care. Conventional medicine has its place, and it is essential for people's well-being. Yet other approaches also have their place, and if we could embrace them all in a broader perspective and cooperate openly and intelligently, we would be able to relieve a lot more suffering in this world, and at lower cost.

I understand why health professionals are reticent with regard to these relatively new techniques, which have often been used inappropriately. Yet the concrete and durable results obtained when the process is properly mastered would make it worthwhile to explore this area with more extensive scientific research.

Ever since her brother Jonathan was born, Paulette, being twelve years older, had taken care of him. Their mother, who was cold and often absent, had delegated her responsibilities to her daughter. When he was eight years old, Jonathan fell seriously ill. Paulette adored her little brother, and took care of him as best she could, but one morning she found him dead in his bed. This was a terrible shock to her. For a year following this sudden death, Paulette cried for hours every day. She ended up in a profound state of depression. She sought professional care, and in the course of her treatment decided that she would stop crying. Some time later, she developed serious chronic digestive problems. She was monitored by doctors who did their best, yet her condition failed to improve. Stomach surgery was considered. At this point she came to do some breath work for the sake of her own inner progress, without necessarily focusing on her physical condition. During the process, certain images filled her mental screen, including a scene where she spontaneously saw herself holding her little brother in her arms and telling him she loved him (something she hadn't been able to do before he died). She went home satisfied with her weekend, giving no more thought to these images. To her astonishment, the next day she noticed that she experienced none of her customary digestive symptoms. She thought this was a coincidence, yet as days went by, it became more and more obvious that she had recovered: no more stomach pains.

I have often witnessed this kind of result. Yet I never present my work as physical healing work, as indeed it is not. The physical recoveries are only consequences of the work done on one's consciousness. They do not occur systematically. I never make any promises of any kind to this effect, as I let the process take place naturally, and I use it as a specific tool for personal growth, not as a healing method. I make no attempt to determine in advance what the individual will naturally clear up through the experience, and whether or not this will have an influence on some physical problem. If physical recovery occurs, so much the better, but I do not make any attempt to bring it on.

The goal is not physical recovery; the goal is to defuse active memories that remain lodged in the unconscious. Yet I cannot help but note that when these memories are cleared up through this approach, a number of physical ailments disappear for good.

• **At the Psychological Level**

Beyond the physical limitations that may be dispelled, a number of psychological limitations disappear as soon as the energy block from the past has been deactivated by the breath-rebirth process. This is quite understandable given what I have seen regarding the process through which memories are recorded in the unconscious, and the behaviours triggered by these unconscious memories. These may be obvious limitations, such as the various fears generally referred to as phobias (fear of the dark, fear of crowds, claustrophobia, agoraphobia, fear of certain animals, fear of bridges, etc.), or fears of a more general nature (fear of men, of women, of authority, fear of self-expression, etc.). Some limitations are more difficult to detect, due to familiarity; these are the most insidious since we are not aware of them, and yet they strongly condition our life. These include all the limiting behaviours we described in Volume 1. These limitations generally go unnoticed, as we identify with them as part of our personality. We are not even keen on changing them, since we are generally unaware of the link between these structures and the problems that prevent us from leading a free and happy life. We do notice them, however, when the limitation disappears and we find our self liberated. Being aware of our structures, and seeing our behaviours in that new light, allows us to do the work of unblocking the unconscious more clearly and expeditiously. I have had many testimonials to that effect.

Following are three apparently quite simple examples, yet where a whole life context was changed:

Nancy tells me how things went when she returned home after in-depth breath work: "When I came home, I saw that my apartment had been broken into. The way I was before, I would have been in a state of shock. Three years ago, my handbag was stolen, and I had to take a week off from work in order to get over the shock; and I told the whole world about it. This time, I went around the house noting that many things that meant a lot to me had disappeared, and yet I was calm! I could not recognise myself, or rather, I was finally able to remain myself under difficult circumstances. And this was happening naturally, without having to force anything at all. I am so glad. I don't know what I cleared up this weekend, but the concrete results are there: I am experiencing emotional stability such as I have never known before. This has greatly changed the way I relate to others. I am finally daring to be myself, simply and naturally."

Among other things, this example illustrates the fact that it is not necessary to consciously reconnect with past stories where certain energy blocks were created. When we work at the energetic level, the story sometimes resurfaces in our conscious memory, sometimes not. Yet this is unimportant. What is important is that the memory is defused, and we see concrete evidence of this in our reactions to day-to-day situations, which, from being difficult and limited, spontaneously become far more balanced and free.

Norman's story is another, equally simple example:

Norman is a businessman. His character is founded on a rigid structure. Here is what he had to say, a few weeks after his own inner work with the breath-rebirth approach: "As I went back to the office Monday morning, I spontaneously went to see my secretaries to say hello and wish them a good day. They were quite surprised. They were even more surprised to learn that I planned to hitchhike to work once a week to break the routine, which I have been doing for the last few weeks. I don't know where this came from, but I find it a very good idea. I have rediscovered the pleasure of relating to people; my day of hitchhiking has allowed me to meet several new friends, and all the stress I was experiencing at the office just evaporated. I have reconnected with the child in me."

Norman was an educated man; he had read many psychology books and knew very well that he had lost his sense of joy and creativity. He had tried to relax, without much, or indeed any success at all, even with some very nice trips to tropical islands. The old memories held him hostage. Once these were cleared up, he was able to spontaneously find his true, playful, happy nature once again.

A third and final example:

Frances, whose personality is strongly based on a schizoid structure, tells us of her return home after the experience: First of all a strong chronic pain in the neck that no treatment could really cure disappeared that weekend without ever recurring. And she says: "I don't want to analyse, I just want to live. I used to find it such a chore to get up in the morning, and now I wake up singing and I watch my daughter sleeping and it's marvellous. I now have recovered a taste for living. I had never opened the door to the balcony, where I live, and ever since I've come back, I leave it open all day long: I am no longer afraid of some surprise attack."

These are the little details of our daily life that show how major fears and active memories have been defused. These energy blocks are cleared away spontaneously, with no need for explanations or verbal interventions. Yet this will have a direct impact on people's behaviours for the rest of their life, whether they are faced with major or minor events. There lies the beauty of this process, and the permanent quality of the results. When a memory is defused from the inside, our capacity to live as calm, happy, centred people in full command of all their assets naturally resurfaces. All this is not about miracles. Throughout this book, I have described how the unconscious gets loaded up with memories, as do the behaviours that stem from them. When we have a chance to clear up an energy block from the past, we cannot help but release the natural, ever-present flow of life, which only needed this opportunity to come through once again. We now have available means of undoing these memories and liberating our self from limiting reactions or behaviours.

However, I would not want to lead anyone to believe in miracle methods. Even though one can get impressive results in a few well-prepared and well-coached breathing sessions, the human psyche remains complex and heavily loaded, as we have seen throughout the course of this book. This explains why such results depend not only on a technique, but also more importantly on good preparation and on a combination of inner conditions that make this work more effective, on the surrounding context (Chapter 10). The reason I began by presenting the conscious context and the quality of one's intention is that these are the keys that open the door to potential healing.

Our ego would very much like to get rid of anything in its way, as long as it does not have to let go of anything. This is why so many people get caught up in hoping for miracle techniques that will solve all their problems once and for all, with minimal effort. Knowing the long evolutionary path followed by all human beings, we can see how unfounded this expectation can be. For this reason, it is an illusion to think we can inwardly free our self through some technique, without doing some in-depth consciousness development work as an integral part of our daily existence.

There are certainly some effective tools available to help us really clear up old memories, and I use several of these. Yet one also has to be ready to face the totality of the journey, with its joys and sorrows, **and to maintain a firm intention to work on loosening up the ego's hold on our daily existence.** Emotional mastery is not something one gains overnight, just as mastery of a musical instrument cannot be gained in a few hours through some miracle method. A good method certainly makes things easier, but one will have to put in the effort and the practice, even on days when we are out of sorts, and one will need to exercise will power and perseverance, in order to finally get to play to our heart's content. On the other hand, regular effort is always rewarded with progress and success. The same goes for spiritual practice.[7]

• But how does this work?

One might be curious to know how breath-rebirth can unblock memories locked in the unconscious. How is it that during a breathing session, one remembers long-forgotten childhood memories? How is it that one may experience one's own birth, or part of one's intrauterine experience, or highly charged stories that seem to come from past lives, so clearly that one has the feeling of "reliving" these experiences? And more importantly, how is it that breathing under certain conditions allows one to clear up these experiences, which form the basis of major blocks in the unconscious, and bring about very specific recoveries and liberations at both the physical level and the psychological level? This phenomenon is now fairly well-known, enough to generate interest in finding out what triggers such experiences.

It would take too long to explain the dynamic involved in the whole process. I have found interesting explanations based on my own observations as well as various sources (at the physical, energetic and esoteric levels, all of which are mutually reinforcing). These explanations also point to new avenues for more in-depth research in this area. Given the inherent power of the breath to transform our consciousness, it would make sense to invest in such research given its potential benefits for all humankind. I urge all inquisitive and open-minded scientists to get to work so as to provide a better understanding of this phenomenon, promote higher levels of mastery in the process, and make it possible to use it on an even broader scale for the benefit of all.

For me, these explanations are not the most convincing argument regarding the effectiveness of this method. From where I stand, the theory is not the most important thing. What I am interested in is how this approach can benefit all human beings. And it is the concrete outcomes, the testimonials from thousands of people, including the most sceptical, over years of experience, that have encouraged me to use and to perfect this approach to clearing up the unconscious. Scientists have been able to use electricity extensively to promote our well-being without fully understanding its mystery (as it is an etheric phenomenon); in the same way, even though we have yet to figure out the mystery surrounding the specific mechanism involved in clearing up the unconscious through breath work, I have experienced its benefits enough to understand its laws and to use it safely in order to generate beneficial concrete results.

This approach to clearing up active memories can be very helpful on the difficult path to learning emotional mastery. Knowing our inner mechanisms allows us to use this method far more consciously and effectively. We are not looking for miracle cures that would allow us to go on with our comfortable little routine; we are looking for liberation so that we can better manifest the qualities of our soul, so that we can love more fully and serve more effectively.

I use a more sophisticated approach to breath work in other contexts, combining it in particular with the transforming power of music. I can thus clear up some more deeply buried aspects of the unconscious. At this stage, we also begin to access the collective unconscious and we can then render simple and discreet, yet highly effective service to humankind. This advanced work requires a very broad level of consciousness expansion, and can allow an individual to experience states of transcendence. I take care that these states do not lead to some form of disconnection from reality, but rather to a desire to promote even more love and peace within us and all around us.

✦ ✦ ✦

This example of one of my approaches to clearing up the unconscious is mentioned only to confirm the fact that it is possible to free our self from the impact of our old memories and from the mechanisms of our mental/emotional make-up. There are now a great number of approaches working along these lines, using a wide variety of techniques. Their methods can be combined and be mutually reinforcing, under one condition: that we won't look for the miracle method that will do all the work for us and that we remain aware of what we are doing and of the clarity of our intention.

I found it interesting, for example, to consider using certain floral extracts to reinforce the work of clearing up the five unconscious defence patterns.[8] Following are some examples of flowers associated with structures:

- **Schizoid:** gentian, violet, cornflower, St-John's Wort, sunflower, ginger.
- **Oral:** bleeding heart, nasturtium, narcissus, daffodil, French marigold.
- **Masochist:** willow, mistletoe, camomile, zinnia, melissa, petunia, gardenia.
- **Psychopath:** *acute:* snapdragon, dandelion, water lily, pine, tigerlily; *mild:* buttercup, centaurea, goldenrod.
- **Rigid:** lilac, verbena, marigold, begonia, rose, echinacea.

These are only a few examples, yet for each psychological problem it seems that nature has given us one or several plants that can help us recover our inner harmony.

Taking a few drops of flower extract each day will not instantly free us from all the problems related to our ego mechanisms. It would be great if such were the case, but when we know the source of our structures, we know that the work to be done is a lot more demanding. On the other hand, if we use these flower extracts to support in-depth work on the unconscious, they can contribute to our well-being in a significant way.

I should also note that if these flower extracts can help us purify our energy field, conversely, the clearer our energy, the more effective they can be. Their use, like any other approach, must be part of a more comprehensive program of inner transformation that each person designs according to his/her own vision.

I could give a myriad other examples, as there are a great number and variety of methods available today to work on emotional purification and on clearing away the unconscious, from the most conventional psychoanalysis to healing with angels. These include approaches that are directly body-centred as well as others involving more mental work. It is up to each of us to find and experience what works for our specific needs. These approaches are often presented as being "healing techniques". Some are quite serious, and they open avenues to a more genuine comprehensive knowledge of the process of inner liberation. Others are questionable, as they are not founded on any real knowledge.[9]

Yet the existence of some rather flaky practices should not be a reason to remain closed to anything that is unfamiliar to us. New discoveries are being made at an ever-accelerating pace and we are witnessing a revolution in the art of healing, based not only on new approaches but also on ancient traditions that have been revived and reintroduced in the light of an even broader perspective. Faced with this profusion of methods—among which several are nothing but smoke and mirrors—it is extremely important to keep both feet firmly on the ground, and to use our common sense and discrimination so as not to get lost in dubious approaches.

If we can manage to remain highly vigilant with regard to the reclaiming mechanisms of our ego, we can naturally avoid many pitfalls. As we become more aware of the very dynamics of the transformation process and of the characteristics of the path, that will also be very helpful in order to find approaches that work for us, to harmonise several methods, and not to get lost on paths that lead nowhere.

We can thus use the principles presented earlier in this book to move ahead with greater assurance along this difficult part of the path, so as to make our practice safer, more effective and more satisfying, no matter what method we use.

We will also be greatly assisted in this process if, as we clear up our unconscious, we simultaneously work directly on developing the qualities of the higher mind. We will cover this subject in the next chapter.

_._._._._._._._._._._

[1] Alice Bailey, Ponder on This, page 210.

[2] Alice Bailey, A Treatise on White Magic, pages 62–63.

[3] This stage where our interest is redirected from the quest for personal satisfaction towards service activities is a sure sign of progress along the path. Yet there is no point in forcing matters. It is good to allow a little girl to play with dolls as long as she finds this interesting. Then, as she goes through the stages of growing up, she will naturally move on to other activities, because she has lost interest in dolls. In the same way, it is necessary for a human being to experience the desires of the personality, and then one naturally moves on to play other games in life; one then chooses service not as a duty, but because the rest has simply become uninteresting.

4 In school, while students gain new knowledge, one must make sure that previous concepts are well assimilated and revisited, if needed, and then integrated into whatever new concepts are being learned. All is reflected in all: we are all students in a school, the school of life and of transformation.

5 This is one of the reasons why breath work may have been perceived with some suspicion. It is not the actual breathing that needs to be redesigned, but rather the preparation in terms of the thought context. As we move forward in scientific knowledge, we will recognize the importance of thought in any work at the energetic level.

6 In fact they are not that new. For thousands of years, breathing techniques have been used in the context of certain teachings for working on states of consciousness. All we are doing is rediscovering what used to be taught only to a few initiates.

7 Let us remember that spiritual practice is essentially a matter of successive levels of letting go at the ego level. The parachute jumping analogy comes to mind (Chapter 7). When we talk of progress, it has nothing to do with the reality of the soul, which has always existed and will always exist. We are talking about mastery of the personality. One could say that, **on the spiritual path, all we do is prepare to let go.**

8 The properties of Bach Flowers are now well-known. A very good reference: *Flower Essence Repertory,* by Patricia Kaminski and Richard Katz, The Flower Essence Society. (http://www.flowersociety.org). In Quebec, Danièle Laberge's work with flowers and herbs is also good: L'Armoire aux herbes (http://www.armoireauxherbes.net).

9 Here again, there is a great deal of confusion regarding "energetic" techniques or approaches dealing with "subtle bodies". As these techniques are relatively new, they are often used indiscriminately and incompetently. The belief is that, because we are dealing with subtle bodies, we can approach the work any way we choose. It is easy to foster a number of illusions in this field, or to think of oneself as a great energy healer, when in fact we have no idea what we are doing. Just as one cannot become a surgeon overnight (one does not decide to operate on someone by "following one's intuition" or untested directives coming from subtle worlds), one does not become a healer at the energy level just like that. A great deal of illusions and pretensions still prevail in this field, as well as a lot of irresponsibility: we hope that some individual is going to rid us of our problems through some magical treatment.

For those who would like to develop real competencies in the field of energetic healing, we recommend, among others, the kind of training offered by Barbara Ann Brennan (www.barbarabrennan.com).

chapter 13

Developing the Higher Mind

REINFORCING OUR SOUL CONNECTION

Meditation

For thousands of years, as human beings unceasingly tried to reconnect with their soul, certain masters have been teaching the art of meditation. This can indeed be a direct way to come in contact with the light of the soul and to have it descend to the level of the personality.

Many people now meditate, and this certainly contributes to raising humanity's level of consciousness. This subject is of the utmost importance. We shall not go into this here, since that is not the purpose of this book, but we mention it in order to give it its rightful place within the perspective of our inquiry.

As is the case with other approaches, the results obtained through meditation will depend first of all on the purity of our intention and on the context in which this practice is used. Meditating, in and of itself, is meaningless. All depends, first of all, on the reason why we meditate, and *then* on the technique being used. To be effective, as we have seen (in Chapter 11), this practice should come in fourth place, so as to rest on the three basic foundations: first, character building (adequate mastery of the personality through self-knowledge); second, right motive; and third, service.

The contents of this book, to the extent that it has shed some light on our inner dynamics, should serve to build a good basis for meditation practice. If this basis is not strong enough, then, just like any other approach, meditation can end up being a way to feed the ego and to go on wandering in the valley of illusion.[1] On the other hand, once they have been properly integrated, these three elements become a firm foundation for the inner dwelling place we are trying to build, and all forms of meditation, whether active or receptive, take on their proper significance in this process.

Developing the Higher Mind

On the way to inner transformation, in addition to all that we have seen so far, there are a number of activities that can be used to work directly on developing the higher mind. The mental system we possess is one of the privileges of being human. Making this system work to the best of its abilities is an essential condition for building a bridge between the soul and the personality (in esoteric science, it is traditionally called "anthakarana"), clearing a path towards the light of the soul.

It is both easy and accurate to see our inner development as the development of our capacity to love. Yet in fact, love is always present, and the transformation required of humanity at this time is a **transformation of mental consciousness.** This transformation will lead to mastery of the two other bodies (the emotional and physical bodies), and to the possibility of handing over the direction of all three forms to the Self, through an act of conscious and constantly reaffirmed choice. It must be clearly understood that the development of mental mastery does not mean that we become coldly intellectual and live inside our minds. What it does mean is mastering our lower mental and emotional nature so that all the love, joy, compassion, beauty and freedom of the soul can naturally radiate within us and all around us. Looking after the horse is not the job of the Master riding in the coach, but that of the coachman, who must be able to control the latter intelligently, while maintaining its full power and remaining at the Master's service. So the mind is not to be rejected or blamed for our difficulties. It must be worked on, in the light of the soul, so that it becomes the seat of a fundamental transformation for which humankind has been preparing for thousands of years.

By making conscious choices, and engaging in specific activities, we can consciously nurture certain qualities of the higher mind. The qualities that should be practiced from the very beginning of the transformation process, as we pointed out earlier, should continue to be practiced all along the way. In principle, all spiritual disciplines and methods of inner development point towards this goal. We will not dwell on all these basic teachings, which are now readily accessible to all. We would simply like to clarify a few specific aspects that are often ignored or considered of secondary importance for various reasons, yet which may actually turn out to be fundamental and very helpful, no matter what method of inner work we choose to use.

It is interesting to look at this question from the perspective of the activity generated by the two hemispheres of the brain. Though it is not our purpose to engage in a thorough examination of this perspective, we will use this reality to specify two types of qualities that need to be developed, and to shed some light on some apparently contradictory aspects we may encounter as we proceed with our inner development.

In general, we tend to function with one hemisphere of the brain more than the other (right or left, depending on the baggage we carry from our past, either from parts of us that are already enlightened or from those that remain blocked), and it is difficult for us to arrive at an integration of both. Indeed it is a well-known fact that the two physical hemispheres of the brain generate different types of mental activity. The rational left-brain has often been opposed to the intuitive right brain. Yet the truth is not that simple.

In fact, both hemispheres of the brain are expressions of the mental system as a whole, and each has a "lower", automatic, unmastered level, as well as a "higher" level that is open to the energy of the soul.

> The lower mind uses the lower characteristics of the two hemispheres. The soul seeks to use the potential embedded in the higher characteristics of the two hemispheres through the higher mind.

By clearing away our memory-based conditionings, we can clear away behaviours stemming from the lower mind, **from the lower levels of both hemispheres.** Even though we did not make any obvious reference to this classification as we described the general dynamics of the personality and the automatic responses pertaining to the unconscious defence patterns, we were describing mechanisms that for some, are rooted at the level of the lower left brain, while for others, they stem from the level of the lower right brain. In the same way, by cultivating the higher qualities of the two hemispheres, we can open the door to mental mastery—to the higher mind—and thus to the energy of the Self. Neither of the two hemispheres should therefore be seen as particularly worthy of attention. Our task is to develop the higher aspects of both sides of the brain, while loosening the grip of the lower aspects of both the left and right brains.

If we tend to be more right brain oriented in the way we function, we will tend to mostly cultivate the higher qualities of the right brain, while neglecting the qualities of the left rain, and vice versa. Being aware of this will help us approach our inner work in a more thorough, and therefore more effective manner.

The Lower Characteristics of the Two Sides of the Brain

Among the lower characteristics of the two brains, it is easy to identify the specific conditionings of the unconscious.

In particular, the **lower left brain** is where we find mechanisms such as wanting to be right and holding onto one's point of view at all cost, resisting change, conformity, calculated selfishness, insensitivity, narrow rationality, avoidance of open-mindedness, fear of the unknown, cold manipulation, control at all cost through mental rigidity, arrogance and unfeeling pride, etc. These are characteristics mostly found in the rigid type of structure.

The **lower right brain** is essentially where we find lack of emotional control, emotional irrational behaviours, excessive sensitivity, laziness, pleasure seeking, irresponsibility, instability, lack of rigorous thinking, inability to stick to any discipline, emotional selfishness, avoidance of commitment, rebellion, submission, and a whole array of negative emotions. These characteristics are typical of the four other structures.

This leads to the realization that, though we may think of our culture as being rational and left-brain dominated, this is also a society of uncontrolled right brains. Though our society is ostensibly based on very rational principles, most people are caught in highly unconscious emotional mechanisms. The apparently left-brain characteristics of this society are expressions of the rigid structure (lower left brain) doing its best to control or repress emotional charges (uncontrolled lower right brain excesses).

If our goal is to use the higher mind to tap into the power of the soul, we will need to develop our higher qualities, whether they stem from the left-brain or the right brain. Often, people involved in inner work develop a fairly high level of sensitivity (right brain), but remain unknowingly limited by under-developed left-brain qualities. True spiritual development involves the totality of higher mental functioning, rather than just its sensitive and intuitive aspects.[2]

As we examine the higher qualities that are specific to each of the two brains, we can more clearly identify the various aspects of the higher mind that we can develop on a day-to-day basis. Some are more obvious, and are extolled in all spiritual teachings, while others are less well-known.

Developing our Higher Left Brain Qualities

It is especially important to draw attention to certain left-brain qualities that sometimes tend to be overlooked in the course of our inner work. This process obviously means developing an increasingly refined level of sensitivity as well as an open heart, as these are essential to further growth. Yet this sensitivity and openness, which have yet to be fully mastered, sometimes lead one to being excessively emotional. Certain higher left-brain qualities can prove to be valuable assets in terms of balancing the process. Our emotional ego will tend to resist working on these qualities, which are often mistakenly seen as irrelevant to spiritual development. Emotional people loathe an intelligent mind, just as a horse will momentarily hate the coachman trying to tame it. Yet these qualities act as safeguards ensuring the kind of authenticity, objectivity, balance, integrity and disciplined thinking that are so essential to progress along the path.

Among the higher left-brain qualities, the following are worth mentioning:

- A highly developed, rich and open intellect
- The ability to concentrate
- A capacity for intelligent thinking
- A capacity for clear and objective reasoning
- Disciplined thinking
- Will power
- Orderliness
- Clear thinking
- Discipline
- Centeredness
- Courage
- Silence and emotional mastery
- Action power

- Intelligent realism
- Clear vision

As we eventually pass through high peaks of love and light (very right brain) in our travels along the path of transformation, we may forget, or even look down on such qualities, which nevertheless are fundamental and essential for the development of mastery and intelligent creative power. All of these qualities are aspects of the higher mind that are indicative of mastery and independence in relation to the emotional mechanisms of the lower mind. They lead to intelligent, respectful mastery of the three worlds, and turn the coachman into an effective instrument of the will of the Self.

It is therefore highly beneficial to practice and develop anything that reinforces the development of these qualities on a day-to-day basis. For example, this can be done through **study** in an area of interest to us. In particular, we have found that the study of mathematics is very useful to develop objective reasoning, disciplined thinking and higher intuition. This can also be done through **reading, thinking, writing,** and through **activities that develop one's intellect and capacity for concentration.** Unfortunately these qualities are often ignored among spiritual seekers, though they are very useful indeed.

Apart from developing robot brains, our present society is not geared towards working on the best aspects of our intellects. Unfortunately many of our young people remain glued to their television sets, and are less and less interested in intellectual effort, even just to read a good book. This tends to lower people's level of mental mastery, and keep them mired in an uncontrolled emotional state, especially in North America.

In the preceding chapter, we mentioned the development of will power, which is also part of this training.

Many spiritual seekers, who are turned off by the ordinary, apparently rigid and unfeeling world, tend to look down on these qualities of the intellect as belonging at a lower level of consciousness, thus confusing rigidity and mastery, the automatic mind and the higher mind. Thus their power of transformation remains limited, and this also weakens their potential for establishing a solid channel for the energy of the Self in their own life and in the world at large. Such qualities are not easy to maintain, as our emotional self (lower right brain) puts up a formidable resistance. It is easier to ignore them, to think of our self as being above all this in our spiritual quest, as being guided by "divine" intuition (which is often nothing more than emotional reactivity), than to try to put these qualities into practice in our day-to-day existence.

Many approaches to spiritual and personal growth tend to be right brain oriented. There are some, however, that are geared more specifically to the development of some of the higher left brain qualities, especially will power, as is the case in Zen practice, for instance. These may appear to some as rather dreary approaches, yet as pathways to the soul they are just as effective as some of the more "touchy-feely" approaches. They also have their own pitfalls to watch out for, the main one being the temptation to remain ensconced in our unfeeling intellect, in a space that is disconnected from the heart. Yet this can be avoided if we remain vigilant and truthful to our self, and if we always make sure we integrate the qualities of both aspects. We then get a balanced and effective whole-being approach.

The capacity for intelligent observation and analysis, combined with a loving heart, is a most useful tool, especially in order to remain aware of our own mechanisms by practicing a *witness stance*. The conscious process of *changing the context*, which we described in Chapter 9 as a way to access the higher mind, is also based on such qualities of objectivity, analysis, and self-knowledge from a perspective that is both intelligent (left brain) and loving (right brain). It is easy to see how significant these left-brain qualities can be on the path to self-transformation, and how important it is to practice them in our daily life through activities that suit our individual needs.

Developing our Higher Right Brain Qualities

This perspective based on the two hemispheres of the brain allows us to emphasize how necessary it is to strive as much as possible for a balanced and complete synthesis of all our potentialities.

Referring to right brain qualities, we find, in fact, that many of these are qualities related to the manifestation of the Self through the higher mind, in particular:

- Intuition
- Creativity
- Living in the present
- Sensitivity
- Imagination
- The ability to innovate
- The capacity for loving communication
- Openness to the unknown
- Love, tenderness, warmth, compassion
- A channel for every positive emotion

There are now a number of different approaches specifically designed to develop right brain qualities, and these are found in a whole array of spiritual teachings and personal development seminars. It is up to each individual to choose the most appropriate one from a conscious and discerning perspective.

Besides these readily accessible approaches, we would also like to mention other activities which, though they may not necessarily be described as being spiritual, are nevertheless useful means of *practicing soul connection on a daily basis* (sometimes even more so than others, perhaps, as the mind has less of a tendency to reclaim them). Foremost among these is art as a daily practice.

Art

Art as a daily practice (not just during a special weekend), with no personal ulterior motive other than the pleasure of creating something and celebrating life, is a very supportive activity in terms of maintaining contact with soul energies.

In our society, art is most often reclaimed for commercial or materialistic purposes.[3] It seems to be reserved for a few great and exceptionally gifted artists, and some who do their very best to survive in a society ruled by performance and competition. Ordinary people are conditioned to maintain a passive consumer attitude. Yet any artistic activity can be a doorway to creating original works of art, generating beauty, joy, and a direct expression of the soul. It is not surprising that a society bent on materialistic exploitation tends to treat art as a very low priority in its school curriculum. This would give children far too much autonomy and freedom of expression. So they are assigned strictly intellectual tasks, which may have some value in themselves, but which eventually dry up the wells of soul energy if they are not matched with other activities of a different nature.

Whether the medium is music, painting, dance, theatre, poetry, or any other form of creativity, the practice of art and the creation of beauty give us direct access to soul energy. It is not necessary for us to be great artists in order to give our self the right to some artistic activity. If we can stop comparing our self to others or to the latest music on the airwaves, we can allow our self the pleasure of creating by and for our self, and maybe also for a few friends. Any process of inner work would gain from including the experience of artistic creation somewhere along the way.

More and more, over the past few years, art has become an integral part of various approaches to personal development. As far as I am concerned, besides the methods I use to work in depth on debugging the unconscious and to connect with the supraconscious, I have also developed some art-based transformational approaches. This is a very interesting path that allows the soul to express itself directly, short-circuiting the lower mind and transmitting its messages without distortion, to the extent that we are able to receive them.

However, I have observed that the use of art for purposes of transformation is largely enhanced if there is some preparation in terms of clearing up the unconscious. Without this preparation, the path to the soul remains too cluttered, and the results are neither consciously integrated nor as beneficial. Yet with adequate preparation, this approach makes it relatively easy to access the depths of the unconscious and the heights of the supraconscious. It is a very gentle approach that holds great potential for healing stemming from a direct connection with the wisdom and beauty of the soul.

> Art is liberating, for it is the breath of the soul

Some Other Possible Daily Activities

There are a number of other activities that are conducive to fostering a daily, simple contact with the soul and maintaining a high vibrational level. We know all that and yet, as we get caught in the vortex of daily turmoil, we forget how much these little things, which are so undervalued in our consumer society, are essential for the health of our soul, and our health in general: contacts with nature, listening to high vibrational music, reading inspiring books, exposure to beauty in all its forms…especially the beauty of flowers.

Flowers

Flowers, in fact, carry a very high rate of vibrational frequency, and if we can welcome them in our home and love them, they are a wonderful source of inspiration and healing. It is not for nothing that all over the world, no matter what the local culture may be, temples, churches or religious places are almost always graced with a profusion of flowers. This is not just a meaningless habit. There is spiritual significance embedded therein, though most people may not be aware of it. In our materialistic society, flowers have become consumer items just like everything else, and we have lost **the sense of sacredness of their presence.** Flowers do not thrust themselves upon us. We must know how to look at them with truly open eyes, and silently meditate in their presence, in order to receive what they have in store for us.

A practical suggestion: Always having a simple bouquet of flowers nearby, at home and at work, can help us remember the presence of our soul.

Silence

The disciple who seeks to enter within the Portals of Initiation cannot do so until he has learnt the power of speech and the power of silence.[4]

We live in a noisy society, and this noise dissipates our mental energy, consumes our nervous energy, undermines our concentration and makes people highly vulnerable. Practicing silence on a regular basis, taking the time to do it, is food for the soul. External silence fosters inner silence.

In particular, there is one form of silence that brings a great deal of peace and self-control—it is the silence created through **controlling one's speech.** When we speak, we consume energy. It is therefore essential to be aware of the purpose of this energy expenditure…does it serve the designs of our soul, or is our ego just feeding itself? Most of the words cast into this world are indeed the expression of our computer running out of control, the expression of an unconscious emotional energy needing an outlet. They are generally nothing more than the expression of the ego. We get together to talk, but what are we talking about really? We talk too much, way too much.

This silence, which is no less than the presence of our innermost being, where the noise/silence duality fades into the principle of wonder, into the dissolution of the self, into this love that no longer requires any object in order to burn, and which constitutes the state of grace.[5]

For some of us, a good exercise would be to try to spend a day without talking about our self or about our personal stuff. We realize then the extent to which we are far more focused on our self than on serving others. Beyond the rational meaning of words, the general flow of our speech is very revealing of our level of awareness. **Watching our words**, being aware of the true motivations behind them, **is a basic spiritual exercise** that helps us gain more understanding and control of the lower mind. Each time we are about to open our mouth, we can ask: What is my purpose in saying this? Is it useful? Or am I just activating my emotional word generator? What is the purpose motivating my speech?

He who guards his words, and who only speaks with altruistic purpose, in order to carry the energy of Love through the medium of the tongue, is one who is mastering rapidly the initial steps to be taken in preparation for initiation.[6]

Such good daily habits, and many others we might spontaneously make up, cost little in terms of energy and allow us to stay at a high level of vibration. *They are essential* in the world we live in, which is anything but supportive towards such inner states. Indeed, almost everything in our present society is designed to activate our emotional self, in some form or other, and tends to lower our vibrational level. It is important to know that staying in contact with the reality of the Self **requires effort and vigilance** at every moment. If our purpose is to move steadily ahead along our soul path, we need to make a conscious effort to rise above our collective state of hypnosis and consciously choose our activities, even if this means going against the grain in terms of the "usual" way of acting. It is up to each of us to choose suitable practical means to reinforce our inner state, and thus bring more and more light both inwardly and outwardly.

◆ ◆ ◆

We have acknowledged the positive outcomes of the manifestation of the Self on a personal level. We are heading towards the full expression of this manifestation. Yet the qualities of our soul, when they become manifest, do more than just illuminate our personal life: they in fact form the basis of a collective transformation. Humankind is now facing great challenges; how is our personal change in consciousness integrated in the reality of our present world?

---

[1] For some helpful clarifications, we recommend you read Chapter 116 of the book entitled *Think on These Things.* You will find it contains wise suggestions on the practice of meditation. Generally speaking, this book is a compilation of excerpts from the works of Alice Bailey. This is an enormous body of work that offers an interesting yet complex overview of scientific/esoteric knowledge. It takes years to study this work. This compilation, however, gives a first glimpse of the teachings of the Tibetan Master, which Alice Bailey channelled though her books.

[2] For those familiar with teachings concerning the seven rays, the decision to follow a spiritual path will obviously be conditioned by the rays in which a person dwells in any given incarnation. Very generally speaking, odd numbered rays will lean towards paths that develop the higher mind through left brain qualities, while even numbered rays will lean more towards right brain activity. But sooner or later, the two aspects will have to come together.

[3] In other times and other cultures, art was a natural part of daily living and spiritual practice.

[4] Alice Bailey, *Initiation, Human and Solar,* page 198.

[5] Christiane Singer, op. cit, page 132.

[6] Alice Bailey, *Initiation, Human and Solar,* page 74.

chapter 14

The Birth of a New World: Freedom for All Humanity

*I want neither kingdom, nor celestial bliss,
nor liberation from the cycle of incarnations.
All I want is the end of misery
for all humankind and all beings.*

—Bodhisattva prayer

If all humankind were to live at the level of awareness of the Self, or at least tried to attain this level with a minimum of good will, we would certainly have heaven on earth. However, for the time being, what is going on in this world is far from heavenly. There is much suffering and confusion, and we witness the coexistence of extremes:

- coexistence of tremendous power (space exploration, extremely sophisticated "scientific" experiments) and terrible powerlessness (famine, unemployment, epidemics);

- coexistence of great beauty (art, architecture, luxury products) and debilitating limitations (degrading living conditions, degenerating physical bodies);

- coexistence of the deepest compassion and outrageous brutality;

- coexistence of extreme wealth and extreme poverty;

- coexistence of a movement towards accelerated spiritual development and obtuse materialism.

Everyone is aware of this state of affairs through the media. In the past, each of us lived in his or her own little world, rich or poor, peaceful or violent, without knowing that life was different in other parts of the world. These days we know more, though we are still far from knowing everything. The have-nots of this world know that some people wallow in luxuries, while the more privileged among us know that others don't even have the most basic commodities. Those who are imprisoned, either physically or psychologically, know that others live in freedom, while those who are free know that others are not allowed even a fraction of their freedom. All of this is stirring world consciousness, and each of us responds in different ways, but we can no longer remain indifferent. All of this information certainly generates a state of confusion on a personal and collective level, yet this confusion could set the stage for major change.

Faced with this situation, what can we do? Is there, in fact, anything that we can do? As we have seen, there are two ways of reacting to the prevailing conditions all around us, of responding to "reality": either through our lower emotional mind, or through our higher mind.

In the face of so much pain and injustice, it is easy to be outraged, to feel aggressive and to fall into a pattern of blame, pessimism and powerlessness, or to revert to cynicism and unresponsiveness. None of this will do any good.

However, if we perceive this same reality through a broader scope of awareness, that is if we can better understand the process of transformation that is presently affecting humankind, we get a clearer picture of the actual causes underlying this state of affairs.

We have seen how the forces of involution, which tend to maintain us personally and collectively at a level where we are prisoners of matter and of ego mechanisms, must now make way for the forces of evolution, which will eventually allow everyone to live according to the dictates of their soul. All of us are now faced with this radical change in direction, and this is the source of all the powerful tensions and contrasts we presently see in our world. In the context of our personal life, this translates into crises, or a state of inner tension, an intense desire for change and a profound yearning for a better life. Similarly, at the global level, this translates into world crises, tensions, and an intense collective thrust to resolve major difficulties that for the time being appear to be getting more and more acute as time goes by. As we perceive the present reality in this context of confrontation between two opposing forces, we can better understand the dynamics involved, and thus find more effective ways of contributing to change.

The Source of the Present State of the World

Having observed our individual behaviour at two different levels of consciousness, we can easily understand what may be happening in our world at a collective level. Whether we look at the financial picture, politics, education, economics, health care or any other field of human activity, we find both aspects of consciousness being manifested: on the one hand we find that soul awareness is being manifested through generous, upright, competent, courageous people who are genuinely serving others in their respective fields of activity; on the other hand, we have all the manifestations of lower consciousness, including abuse of power, manipulation and exploitation for the sake of destructive materialistic pursuits. This lower level of consciousness is what feeds violence, fear, separativeness, and all the suffering and limitations we have described as being generated by the lower mind.

The difficulties, which presently confront all of humankind, do not stem from a lack of resources or from any kind of external cause. They are generated by the way people think and act, and by the choices they make. The present features of the human condition are not determined by external circumstances but by our limited level of consciousness.

> Our present difficulties stem from the level of con-
> sciousness prevailing among humankind.

Our present difficulties are just the expression of our level of consciousness. They stem from the fact that there is not enough soul energy to dispel the shadows that darken our world, and that the rule of ego is still all too pervasive. This means that in order for things to change, there has to be a change in the level of consciousness of humanity as a whole. Our behaviour naturally changes as our consciousness evolves, and a different world will naturally emerge as our behaviour reflects a higher level of consciousness and harmony.

> As wars are spawned in the spirit of man, it is in the spirit of man
> that the fortifications of peace must be built.
> **—Unesco Constitution**

This is a simple yet often forgotten fact. It is all too easy to see external factors as the source of all our troubles: economic conditions, government, capitalism, the bad guys. Yes, all of these factors exist, but where do they originate? They are generated by human beings and their lower level of consciousness. Economic conditions are created by human beings, and governments are just a reflection of the voters who elect them. Certainly the forces of involution, or materialistic forces, are still active in the world, holding our consciousness down to the lowest possible level. Yet this is the nature of things, and it is the test which humankind must pass in order to find freedom in a conscious, autonomous manner. For these forces have power only to the extent that the majority of human beings are subject to manipulation, to the extent that the majority of human beings live and think on an ego level. Once a large portion of humankind has chosen a higher level of consciousness, all the present manipulation techniques will become ineffective, and these forces of involution will lose their power.

• A Change in Consciousness—The Fundamental Basis for Effective Action

Being aware of the necessity for change, as well as inspired by new visions derived from a genuine, generous desire to contribute, we sometimes plunge into all kinds of humanitarian projects, with open hearts and all the good will in the world, yet without taking the time to check out what is happening inside.

Actions stemming from great ideas and visions of a better world, no matter how beautiful, may have very limited concrete outcomes, or may even be doomed to failure, if they are not founded on a clear state of consciousness. Many people of good will want to improve the present situation, yet they have not paid much attention to this aspect. They work very hard to reach an ideal, and are often disappointed by the poor results they

> When the collective level of consciousness changes, the world changes.

get. Many pacifist movements, ecological groups, etc.—being aware of the sorry state of the planet, and of all the injustice and suffering in different parts of the world—are fervently committed to changing things and are working courageously towards that end. Many visionaries are coming up with new economic, social and political systems, and several of these are full of wisdom and common sense. This is excellent news, yet for concrete changes to take effect, the average consciousness of individuals must be elevated, at least to some extent. What will change the world is not just a new system, no matter how brilliant or revolutionary it may be. **Only through a change in consciousness will it be possible to concretely establish a more just and balanced system in the world.** There is no shortage of good ideas, *but consciousness is what is lacking.* The practical task of building a new world will thus be dramatically facilitated if, as we initiate concrete actions (for one must obviously act), we also take care to *work directly on a change in consciousness.* As the present system is the product of our state of consciousness, it follows that if the latter changes, the system will also change.

Our state of consciousness is like the foundation of a house. If we want to rebuild the world, it is essential that we focus our attention on the foundation, otherwise the whole edifice may collapse at any moment, like a house of cards.

Since we know the cause of this situation, the next question is: Is there anything we can do to foster humanity's change in consciousness?

There are many factors to examine which may foster this transition to a new level of consciousness.

Means of World Transformation

Two types of action will facilitate this change. The first—being internal and discreet—is in fact the most fundamental since it lends power to the second type, which must also be undertaken, and that is external action.

Internal Action
Practising Soul Values in Everyday Life
Morphogenetic Fields of Information

◆ Collective Healing Through Personal Healing

Changing our own level of consciousness is already a challenge; changing the level of consciousness of several billion individuals seems a hopeless endeavour, given the present apparent level and the fact that there is so little time. Fear, violence, selfishness, ignorance, lust for power, and so on, seem too deeply entrenched in our collective unconscious for any transformation to occur any time soon. It seems a utopian fantasy to imagine this mass of people going from ego consciousness to soul consciousness in just a few years.

Yet this may indeed happen thanks to the now well-known phenomenon of morphogenetic fields of information. The principle goes as follows: if, within a given species (mineral, plant, animal or human), a large enough number of individuals learn a specific subject of knowledge, the rest of the species becomes more receptive to this knowledge, and can acquire it far more quickly if not spontaneously. This phenomenon is no mere theory: it has been tested, not just in the well-known hundredth monkey experiment, but in other scientific experiments as well, involving mineral, plant and human species.[1]

When applied to mankind's change in consciousness, this phenomenon means that it is not necessary for each of the billions of people who make up the world's population to go through an individual consciousness change in order to see our general level of consciousness rise. It is not even necessary for a majority of individuals to experience a consciousness change, since this would already involve several billion people. What is needed, however, is that a *certain number of individuals undergo such a change and create a so-called "critical mass"*. The moment this critical mass has been attained, a shift in consciousness for all humanity may occur within a few years or a few decades at the most. There lies our chance, our power.

This information transmission phenomenon has been known to the great Masters of wisdom since the dawn of time. They have long been teaching that all human beings are linked together, particularly through what we call the Universal Mind. For instance, each time an individual has a love-inspired thought or action, he or she feeds the love that is latent in every other human being. We know how much the power of love can heal. The same can be said of all states of consciousness, from the lowest to the highest. Each time we heal memories from the past, this healing resonates in the collective unconscious and fosters deliverance in others. Every time an individual gains a little more mastery of his lower mind and develops his higher mind, this level of mastery becomes available to the rest of humanity.

We can see how our personal transformation, to the extent that it is genuine and manifested in concrete ways in our everyday life, has a much greater impact than we might think. We are talking about the integration of soul values in everyday life, not spiritual theories or philosophies, however fine they may be. Many people who naturally manifest these values, such as extending oneself through love, service, and dedication, without necessarily referring to any particular spiritual system, are doing more for the liberation of humankind than those who know a great deal but are unable to control their ego in their daily life.

> An individual change in consciousness that is integrated in everyday life is a catalyst for a collective change in consciousness.

If enough people among us can have a positive impact within their circle of influence, our collective consciousness may change as a result of this dynamic of morphogenetic fields of information. Science and esoteric traditions converge on this point. By working on our own inner transformation, we naturally take part in building this critical mass, which has a leavening effect, acting as a catalyst for a rise in consciousness for the rest of humanity. And once our collective consciousness changes, the world will change.

Thus, by elevating our own consciousness, we contribute far more to the welfare of humankind than we might imagine. This is within everyone's reach, but it is, of course, far more demanding for our ego than spending our time blaming others or circumstances for the world's problems, especially since no one will congratulate us for the work we do in this respect, since no one will know about it except our soul. And yet it is the most radical means of contributing to the advent of a new world consciousness. So the arduous work we may be doing on our ego is not just for our own benefit. It is precisely what may help us eventually find a way out of the predicament we are now in.

External Action

Practical Actions that Foster Change

- **The Context**

Given the urgency of the situation, there are specific actions and concrete moves we can initiate in order to contribute to our collective change in consciousness, actions which will be concrete manifestations of this change in consciousness. But these actions will be effective only to the extent that their underlying motivation springs from the soul rather than the ego.

We must be very vigilant, even though our actions may seem most generous and courageous, and remember that the outcome of an action has less to do with the action per se than with the intention embedded within it. It is certainly essential to act in this world in transition, but we should avoid acting indiscriminately. Ego-inspired actions will sooner or later generate violence and suffering; on the other hand, **no matter what action we choose to take, if it is conceived in a spirit of love, service, detachment and other soul qualities, the results will always be beneficial, both for our self and for others.**

With this in mind, we can take action in a concrete sense in our daily life, even if we don't have a direct line to our soul to let us know whether what we are doing is "right". For we are obviously not expected to stay in our little cell, do nothing and wait for enlightenment, before we can act in a sane, effective manner. The process is one of successive approximations: we act as best we can with our present state of awareness, and the results of our actions will reveal where we are at in terms of consciousness, thus allowing us to improve our level of mastery. Only through

> The results of an action have less to do with the action per se than with the intention embedded within the action.

action will we be able to tell whether our spiritual realisation is real or artificial. Thus action is a crucible where we can refine our level of mastery. **Action, practised with vigilance, is spiritual training at its best,** for it is here that we are really confronted with our strengths and weaknesses.

Action is the fire that purifies our vision.
—*Carlos Castaneda*

As Roma's spiritual master taught (see Chapter 8), the real process of transformation of our consciousness does not take place out of this world, but through the very actions we take in our daily life. We learn from our mistakes and we strive to gain mastery through dealing with daily events. This is an attitude of constant acceptance of responsibility for the outcomes we produce, of ongoing questioning, of openness, of good will, of determination to manifest higher values in our daily actions. It is a conscious, intelligent attitude that leads us to take action for the greater benefit of all using whatever resources are available to us, while accepting our limitations and working to overcome them. This is all our soul requires of us.

Now that this context has been clarified, we can go over the main lines of concrete action that will enable us to make an active and effective contribution to change. There are presently two types of action available to us: one that leads us to withdraw from old institutions created as a result of lower consciousness, in order to take away some of their power (we are talking about withdrawal, not confrontation); and the other that leads us to build concrete new systems in our society, based on higher consciousness.

Withdrawal

First of all, it would be helpful to identify some of our present institutions and organisations, or some of their components, that are sustained by the mechanisms of lower consciousness at every level, be it political, economic, social, financial, educational, health-related, etc. We can actually recognise these parts of the system because they are based on fear, selfishness, competition, powerlessness, authority and ignorance—in other words on the manipulation of all the ego mechanisms we have described. They are maintained by the forces of involution: the forces of attraction to matter, also referred to as materialistic forces of darkness. They exist in order to keep us mired in our attachment to matter and in all our ego illusions. This is their purpose. This is neither good nor bad, just a rule of the great unfolding Cosmic Play. To the extent that we function within this part of the system, we feed these forces of involution, and the dependency, dissatisfaction and suffering they generate for our self and others.

We are so used to living in a system generated to a large extent by lower consciousness, and nurtured by our collective hypnosis, that we see it as normal and impossible to change. The forces of involution are dedicated to maintaining us in a mindset of powerlessness, by nurturing the thought that any beneficial change is impossible, utopian, or that it will at least require a very long time to achieve. We need to become aware of the extent to which we maintain inadequate systems, through a courageous, free and self-motivated act of consciousness.

It does indeed take courage to reassess all the habits of our daily life in the light of a broader, more generous consciousness. We thus find our self asking some very practical questions:

- Why do we work?
- Whom do we work for?
- How do we manage our finances?
- Who represents authority, as far as we are concerned?
- Where do we seek information? Are we sure we can trust our sources?
- What is the purpose behind our consumption of certain goods? Is it to meet essential needs, or is it to satisfy false ego needs?
- Do we make our choices freely, or do we follow consumer trends, like sheep?
- How do we spend our time and what do we spend our money on?
- What model for living do we offer our children? What educational system are we giving them?
- What do we feel is important in life?
- What are the values we consider important?

And, more generally speaking:

- To what extent do we allow our self to get caught up in ego mechanisms, and thus nurture the forces of darkness?
- To what extent do we nurture our soul qualities, thus supporting the forces of light?

> Each of our daily actions springs from a certain level of consciousness. What is the source of our choices and actions?

Yet, as we know, the lower mind has been bound for thousands of years in its fears and its narrow vision of life, and it clings to its habits, even when they are the source of a great deal of suffering.

For this reason, as we become aware of this reality, we also realise that the transition will not necessarily be easy. Our ego, first of all, will resist any attempt at letting go, and cling to its mechanisms. Furthermore, this resistance is fostered by materialistic forces whose purpose is to make sure all of us remain prisoners of matter, by feeding our lower consciousness through very sophisticated manipulative means. The media, especially most television programs, maintain people at the emotional level and are effective manipulation tools for the forces of involution. (But who would choose to watch these programs?) And there are many other sophisticated manipulative devices being used today. This creates a kind of collective hypnosis that generates a global pressure towards materialism, and it is not easy to liberate our self from this state of hypnosis and this pressure. People in general are largely unaware of all these mechanisms, and they reinforce them through pressure exerted at the social and family level.

This pressure is very strong at present, and any individual who wants to withdraw from this collective conditioning is likely to feel torn apart, both inwardly due to the pull of his ego, and outwardly due to social pressures steeped in materialism and fear. As we develop our consciousness, the strategies of these forces of darkness become more evident and it is easier to deflect them. But this takes courage, as well as the supportive light of our soul, since we need to struggle both against our own ego and against the influence of our social environment. This is part of the game. It is our great privilege as human beings to be able to choose our level of consciousness.

In concrete terms, if we are interested in seeing things change, we will have to get a good grasp of the operational mechanisms of the present system, and have the gumption to refuse to go on participating in some of them, so as to stop contributing to their maintenance. This takes backbone, along with a high level of awareness.

To this end, by the way, it is important not to work alone. The forces at work are too great, and the support of other people who share the same vision is essential in order to be able to cope with the various forms of inner and outer resistance that confront us when we attempt to go off the beaten path.

While it is a fact that the forces of involution are still active at present, and are doing all they can to maintain control, we must also note that these are the last convulsions of a dying order. On the other hand the forces of evolution that impel us towards a more complete manifestation of soul qualities such as love, right human relations and connectedness, are now powerfully active on this planet, and are beginning to generate a new type of environment through those who are attuned to them.

In fact, these positive forces have been active for thousands of years, helping humanity to develop knowledge and to better integrate the world. Since the start of the twentieth century, their influence has been felt even more acutely. Even though it may seem as if the world is now in very bad shape, we can see current events as a vast process of healing and transformation. The seriousness of the crises and problems will be such that we will be impelled to look for new solutions, and **humankind as a whole is ready** for this.

In her excellent book, *Children of Aquarius*, which has become a classic of its genre, Marilyn Ferguson describes in very clear terms the paradigms on which both worlds are based. As a professional journalist with a very keen and open mind, and without any particular spiritual allegiance, she has simply observed what is going on in today's world. And in effect, she has found two ways of functioning that are clearly evident in our present society. Slowly but surely, the light of the soul is gaining ground, a new world is naturally emerging, and we can make a conscious contribution to this emergence.

As far as the old system is concerned, we are talking about simple, quiet, yet firm withdrawal, not confrontation. Fighting to destroy the old order only wastes energy that would be better used to build the new one. War energies are related to lower consciousness; we cannot manifest higher consciousness using the means of lower consciousness. The end does not justify the means. Materialistic forces draw their power from the fact that people play by their rules. The best way to combat the forces of involution is to make them disappear from the planet by recognising them and consciously withdrawing from their influence. When no one is left to respond to their mirage, they will have lost all of their power without any need for us to combat them. We will then have a different world.

The end is reflected in the means, as the tree is in the seed.
—*Gandhi*

- **Willing or unwilling**

A new world? I can just hear the chuckles of the cynics, the world-weary, those who profit from this system (we all do to the extent that we live in a lower state of consciousness), or the wailing of the pessimists. Yet we no longer really have any other choice. At this moment, everywhere on Earth, we have an enormous quantity of nuclear arms, as well as other tools of destruction that are even more effective and refined, which can annihilate us collectively in a ruthless, radical manner. Pollution is destabilising our ecology in alarming ways. Injustice, poverty and violence are becoming unbearable. Entire nations are suffering. From our selfish viewpoint, this may be of little concern to us, as long as it does not happen to us personally; yet in a little while, if we continue along this track, will it be possible to even simply live on this planet? Through our selfishness, our love of power, our fear, we have been brought to the edge of the abyss. If we do not awaken in sufficient numbers to correct the situation by addressing the very roots of the problem, we run the risk of being faced with catastrophic situations. Is this what it will take for humanity to awaken and rediscover a sense of mutual support, respect, and connectedness?

Dream in order to awaken!
From dreamers, you will become the seeds of a new awakening!
—***Taken from a Jewish workshop in Budapest in 1944***

There are two ways of changing our consciousness: the "willing" way, through conscious and wilful choice, and the "unwilling" way, through suffering. We would like to favour the first, as light and beauty are part of the inherent makeup of every human being. Willingly or unwillingly, it would seem that humanity is now ready to take a forward leap, for an increasing number of people deeply aspire to change. It seems that the time has come, and nothing can stop the forces of light, the will to good, the expression of beauty and love, from spreading on this earth. It is worth our while to make the effort to transform our consciousness so that this change can take place as painlessly and peacefully as possible.

Creating a New World

These fools did not know that it was impossible
to do this thing, so they did it.
—Anonymous

Withdrawing from the old system does not in any way imply withdrawing from collective participation in life. On the contrary, we can participate even more actively in the development of a new collective operating system based on respect, sharing and responsibility, based on the dynamics related to the manifestation of the Self; a system in which there is no more room for power games and irresponsibility.

Utopias are merely premature truths.
—Lamartine

But for such a system to exist and last, once again, the people involved must be sufficiently free of their unconscious mechanisms and able to live, at least to some extent, on the basis of a higher level of consciousness. For this reason, this change will certainly not take place through some external "revolution". Humanity has had its fill of this type of change. If there is to be a revolution, it will be an inner revolution, and the change will occur through the power of our intelligence, good will, brotherhood and love, manifested in action.

• Practical aspects

We could elaborate more on the two aspects of concrete action: the refusal to participate in the lower, manipulative aspects of the present system, and the building of a new society. This would go beyond the scope of this book, as it is a vast and complex topic that is presently holding the attention of the best researchers in all fields of knowledge. Some excellent books and publications are now available that offer interesting food for thought and practical alternative solutions to various aspects of our decaying social system.[2]

Be realistic, demand the impossible!
—Graffiti, May 1968

Among other systems in need of a new approach, we would especially like to mention the field of education. Our children, who are the bearers of a new consciousness, want an environment that is more conducive to the development of all their qualities. The excessive development of left-brain skills, which has dominated the system until recently, will have to make way for a more holistic approach, which, in particular, will make art and creativity an important part of the curriculum. A rich and complete education will give everyone the power to be masters and creators of their life and to be free.

Many other major aspects of our society need to be renewed: our financial, economic, medical, political, and agricultural systems should all be recast in the light of higher consciousness. The strategy used by the forces of darkness is the same in all sectors: make sure people remain as separate, poor and powerless slaves to their emotions; and manipulate the lower mind by stimulating its automatic responses and thus create a more and more chaotic, painful and dangerous situation in order to remain in power. This is how we lose our freedom, not because the bad guys take it away from us but because as we function on an ego level, we automatically hand over more power to the forces of involution.

Slowly but surely, other systems are quietly being put in place.[3] In some cases, people choose a clearly alternative operating system; in other cases, they are not aware that they are taking part in a broad movement of fundamental social transformation. There is simply something inside of them that moves them to change some of their habits. In fact, this change in consciousness has been gaining momentum for quite some time. It is beginning to translate into concrete manifestations in numerous and sometimes quite unexpected ways.

For example, *Time Magazine* recently ran an article, over several pages, on the fact that many city dwellers are moving to the country. These are often professionals who refuse to continue living an increasingly artificial and stressful urban lifestyle. They want to go back to a more natural and wholesome pace of living for themselves and for their children. They are nothing like the hippies of the sixties. With today's sophisticated means of communication, they can continue their professional activities, while also pursuing all kinds of other activities, not just in relation to nature, but also social activities that have to do with the small community, town or village where they now live. This is the beginning of a transformation that will probably lead to a new way of structuring our life, one that is completely different from the one we have known up to now. There will be a decongestion of urban centres, which will become resource points for certain activities, while people will live in smaller centres on a much more human scale. People will be able to develop genuine relationships with their neighbours, take an active part in community life, and at the same time keep in touch with other communities through telecommunications media.

We are aware of many catastrophic scenarios that might result from misguided use of this communications technology, leading to an increasingly advanced state of mechanisation of human interactions, thus alienating us more and more from each other. It is true that state-of-the-art communications systems might be used in this manner. However, once again, it all has to do with the level of consciousness of the people using this technology. For it can also be used to sustain the small towns and villages of the new world and allow them to maintain links and exchange information while sustaining a rich community life on a more human level. This model is spontaneously spreading in concrete ways through free-thinking individuals without the need for any particular philosophy. Common sense and a truer awareness of things are leading a growing number of people to make different choices from what the old social model has offered until now.

This is all happening quietly, as is the development of many other networks focusing on information, communication, product distribution, agriculture, education, finance, and health. A new world is taking shape. We can choose to facilitate this emergence by consciously and calmly participating in this movement towards change.

◆ ◆ ◆

CONCLUSION

• Building right human relationships

The strength of the movement towards planetary renewal will depend on the quality of the relationships we are able to build, a quality that will naturally emerge when enough people will be living more in tune with their soul. This quality will generate the power to create an entirely new world. One of our great masters often mentions the importance of establishing right human relationships. Such relationships will lead to effective solutions for both the personal and collective problems we now face. This may appear quite simple, and yet it is the key that will open the door to freedom for all humanity.

This is not utopia, it is a necessity. There is a major struggle going on, as we are going through a decisive period in human history. The twenty-first century will be an era of reconstruction and new creation if we manage to awaken in time.

> *We know that this moment is a time of great opportunity for humanity, and that if men can overcome difficulties through the sheer strength of their soul, and triumph over present evils, then human evolution will be accelerated beyond anything believed possible. This liberation will be initiated and attained by man himself. It will have as much value in the life of humanity as it has in the life of an individual disciple. This chance, this opportunity must not be lost to man; the eternal spiritual values he acquires are of far greater importance than these temporary difficulties.*[4]

The transition to a new world will certainly require some time, as a change in consciousness will not happen overnight. Yet it can certainly occur quickly enough to produce concrete, and collectively very beneficial results very soon. The twenty-first century should be a time of liberation from all past tensions, a century that will see the building of a new world of peace and sharing. This is entirely possible if each one of us does his or her best to attain a higher level of consciousness and to live in the freedom and beauty of the soul.

We offer this book as a humble contribution to the building of strong inner foundations on which humanity can create this new world. The process of disengaging our self from ego mechanisms and developing our connection to our soul, which we strive to foster, form the essential basis from which all future actions can generate a world of peace, beauty and love, both personally and collectively speaking. It is also the key that will give each of us on this earth a chance to reclaim the power and freedom that are our birthright as human beings.

"To see a world in a grain of sand,
And a heaven in a wild flower,
To hold infinity in the palm of your hand,
And eternity in an hour."

—William Blake

---

[1] I have described this phenomenon in detail in a previous book entitled *Le défi de l'human-ité*, published by Éditions Universelles du Verseau. Another book by Rupert Sheldrake, a biologist with the International Crops Research Institute, entitled *A New Life Science*, contains a presentation of this phenomenon with all its dimensions and scientific implications.

[2] We especially recommend two books on this subject:
• *Spiritual Politics, Changing the World from the Inside Out,* by Corinne McLaughlin and Gordon Davidson, Ballantine New York: an in-depth, very well documented book that is both practical and profoundly inspired, suggesting that we apply the wisdom of the greatest spiritual traditions to find solutions to our present political predicaments. A remarkable breakthrough in how to approach the organization of our societies, making an exceptional contribution to the creation of an entirely new world order. The authors head an organization in Washington called "The Center for Visionary Leadership". To visit their site: www. visionarylead.org.
• *Planethood,* by Benjamin Ferencz, a specialist in international legislation, with a preface by Robert Muller, Under-Secretary General of the UN for thirty years. Written for a broad audience, this book offers a practical change in perspective with regard to our planetary organization, a change that concerns us all.
• Also for a beautiful, joyful message, we would like to mention the French film entitled *La belle verte,* by Coline Serreau, available on video.

[3] Even television is undergoing a transformation. For some time now, a television station in the Unites Sates offers a 24-hour a day channel dedicated to the development of consciousness ("A 24 hour channel devoted to mind, body and spirit"). It is called the Wisdom Channel (www.wisdomchannel.com). This is not an instant solution to the problems of humanity, but it is a sign of the times. Television can become an excellent medium for educating and elevating mass consciousness, depending on who is on its Board of Directors and who are the viewers.

[4] Alice Bailey, *Glamour, a World Problem.*

Bibliography

ANCELIN-SCHÜTZENBERGER, Anne, *The Ancestor Syndrome: Transgenerational Psychotherapy and the Hidden Links in the Family Tree*. Routledge, 1998

ASSAGIOLI, Roberto, *The Act of Will*. Psychosynthesis and Education Trust, 1999

BAILEY, Alice A., *Initiation Human and Solar – Education in the New Age – Discipleship in the New Age – The Externalisation of the Hierarchy – Problems of Humanity – Esoteric Psychology – Ponder on This – A Treatise on White Magic – Treatise on Cosmic Fire*. Lucis Trust Publishers, 1971 – 1987

BRENNAN, Barbara Ann, *Hands of Light: A Guide to Healing Through the Human Energy Field*. Bantam Books, 1988

CAPRA, Fridjof, *The Turning Point. Science, Society and the Rising Culture*. Bantam Books, 1984

DURKHEIM, Karfield Von, *The Two-Fold Origin of Mankind*. Crossroad Publishing Co., 1984

FERGUSON, Marilyn, *The Aquarian Conspiracy*. Tarcher Paper, 1998

FERRUCCI, Piero, *What We May Be*. Aquarian Press, 1995

FROMM, Erich, *To Have or to Be*. Continuum International Publishing Group, 1996

GENDLIN, Eugène T., *Focusing*. Aquarian Press, 1995

GIBRAN, Khalil, *The Prophet*. Alfred A. Knoff, 1982

GROF, Stanislav, *The Adventures of Self-Discovery*. Kösel Verlag GMBH and Co., 1987

HEINDEL, Max, *Rosicrucian Cosmo-Conception or Mystic Christianity*. Kessinger Publishing, 1998

JUNG, Carl Gustav, *Modern Man in Search of a Soul*. Harvest/HBJ Book, 1955

KEYES, Jr. Ken, *Handbook to Higher Consciousness*. Living Love Center, 1975

KRISHNAMURTI, *The First and the Last Freedom*. Harper San Francisco, 1975

LEBOYER, Frédéric, *Birth Without Violence*. Healing Arts Press, 2002

LINSSEN, Robert, *La Méditation Véritable*. Le Courrier du Livre, 2002

MACLAUGHLIN, Corinne and DAVIDSON, Gordon, *Builders of the Dawn; Community Lifestyles in a Changing World*. Book Publishing Company, 1990

MANDINO, Og, *The Greatest Salesman in the World*. Bantam Books, 1983

MARQUIER, Annie, *The Power of Free-Will* (working title). Findhorn Press, 2006

OUSPENSKY, *In Search of the Miraculous, Fragments of an Unknown Teaching*. Harvest Books, 1974

REDFIELD, James, *The Celestine Prophecy, An Adventure*. Warner Books, 1995

VERNY, Thomas, *The Secret Life of the Unborn Child*. Warner, 1988

WATTS, Alan W., *The Wisdom of Insecurity*. Vintage books USA, 1968

WILBER, Ken, *A Theory of Everything*. Gateway, 2001

WOOLGER, Roger J., *Other Lives, Other Selves*. Bantam New Age, 1988